THE PENGUIN POETS

THE PENGUIN BOOK
OF SOCIALIST VERSE

Alan Bold was born in Edinburgh in 1943. He was
educated at Edinburgh University and then worked on
the editorial staff of *The Times Educational Supplement*.
Since receiving a Scottish Arts Council bursary in 1967
he has worked as a full-time writer and occasional
journalist. His first book, *Society Inebrious*, was published
in 1965, and was followed by *The Voyage* (1966), *To Find
the New* (1967), and *A Perpetual Motion Machine* (1969). A
selection of his poems is included in *Penguin Modern
Poets 15*. His most recent book is the huge poem *The
State of the Nation*, which, in its scope, has 'set a new
standard for technical virtuosity' (*The Times*). He has
often read his work on television and throughout the
country, and has organized several large-scale readings
in Edinburgh. A painter as well as a poet, he is married
to an art teacher, Alice, and they live in Edinburgh with
their daughter, Valentina.

The Penguin Book of

SOCIALIST
VERSE

❋

EDITED WITH
AN INTRODUCTION BY
Alan Bold

PENGUIN BOOKS

Penguin Books Ltd, Harmondsworth, Middlesex, England
Penguin Books Inc., 7110 Ambassador Road, Baltimore, Maryland 21207, U.S.A.
Penguin Books Australia Ltd, Ringwood, Victoria, Australia

—

First published 1970
Copyright © Alan Bold, 1970

—

Made and printed in Great Britain by
C. Nicholls & Company Ltd
Set in Monotype Baskerville

CONTENTS

*Translators' names are given after each
poem. The description after the names of translated
poets refers to language not nationality
(for which see biographical notes).*

5

CONTENTS

6

CONTENTS

CONTENTS

CONTENTS

CONTENTS

CONTENTS

CONTENTS

CONTENTS

13

CONTENTS

CONTENTS

CONTENTS

CONTENTS

CONTENTS

CONTENTS

CONTENTS

1. The translators have suppressed the name of this poet 'for various reasons'.

ACKNOWLEDGEMENTS

For permission to reprint poems in copyright, thanks are due to the following:

AI'CHING: to the translators, Jerome Ch'en and Michael Bullock.

RAFAEL ALBERTI: from *Selected Poems* (1966), reprinted by permission of the Regents of the University of California.

MARUF AL-RUSAFI: from *Arabic Poetry*, edited by A. J. Arberry (1965), to the author and Cambridge University Press.

YEHUDA AMICHAI: from *Selected Poems of Yehuda Amichai*, translated by Assia Gutmann, to Cape Goliard Press, and from *Poems*, by Yehuda Amichai, translated from the Hebrew by Assia Gutmann. Copyright © 1968 by Yehuda Amichai. English translation copyright © 1968, 1969 by Assia Gutmann. Reprinted by permission of Harper & Row, Publishers, Inc.

MARCOS ANA: from *From Burgos Jail* (1964), to The Appeal for Amnesty in Spain.

LOUIS ARAGON: to Éditions Gallimard and the author.

W. H. AUDEN: 'The shield of Achilles', copyright 1952 by W. H. Auden, and 'Musée des Beaux Arts', copyright 1940 and renewed 1968 by W. H. Auden, reprinted from *Collected Shorter Poems 1927–1957*, by W. H. Auden, by permission of Random House Inc. and Faber & Faber Ltd.

DAVID AVIDAN: from *An Anthology of Modern Hebrew Poetry*, edited by Abraham Birman (1968), to Abelard-Schuman Ltd.

LÁSZLÓ BENJÁMIN: from *The Plough and the Pen*, edited by Ilona Duczyńska and Karl Polyani (1963), published by Peter Owen, to Peter Owen Ltd and the author.

HAYYIM NAHMAN BIALIK: an extract from 'The city of slaughter', from *An Anthology of Modern Hebrew Poetry*, edited by Abraham Birman (1968), to Abelard-Schuman Ltd.

MIRON BIALOSZEWSKI: to the author.

ALEXANDER BLOK: to the translators, Jon Stallworthy and Max Hayward.

JOHANNES BOBROWSKI: from *Shadow Land* (1966), to Rapp & Whiting Ltd.

ACKNOWLEDGEMENTS

ALAN BOLD: 'Cause and effect' from *To Find the New* (1967), and an extract from *The State of the Nation* (1969), both published by Chatto & Windus, to Chatto & Windus Ltd.

MATEJ BOR: from *Slovene Poets of Today* (1965), to the Slovene Writers' Association.

BERTOLT BRECHT: from *Selected Poems of Bertolt Brecht*, translated by H. R. Hays, copyright 1947 by Bertolt Brecht and H. R. Hays. Reprinted by permission of Harcourt, Brace & World Inc., Methuen & Co. Ltd, who will be publishing *The Selected Poems of Bertolt Brecht* in 1971, and Ann Elmo Agency Inc. For 'The Solution', to the translator, Michael Hamburger.

IAN CAMPBELL: to Essex Music Ltd.

REMCO CAMPERT: from *In the Year of the Strike* (1968), to Rapp & Whiting Ltd and the author.

C. P. CAVAFY: from *Six Poets of Modern Greece* (1960), edited by Edmund Keeley and Philip Sherrard. Copyright © 1960 by Edmund Keeley and Philip Sherrard, reprinted by permission of Alfred A. Knopf, Inc.

FERNANDO GORDILLO CERVANTES: from *Our Word* (1968), translated by Edward Dorn and Gordon Brotherston, to Cape Goliard Press. *Our Word* is distributed in America by Grossman Publishers Inc.

AIMÉ CÉSAIRE: This extract, translated by John Berger and Anna Bostock, is taken from *Cahier d'un retour au pays natal*, published by Présence Africaine, Paris (1956). *Return to My Native Land* published in English by Penguin Books (1969).

CHAIRIL ANWAR: from *Modern Indonesian Poetry* (1964), reprinted by permission of the Regents of the University of California.

RENÉ CHAR: from *Poèmes et prose choisis* by René Char, to Éditions Gallimard. Copyright © Éditions Gallimard, 1957.

JOHN CORNFORD: from *John Cornford: a Memoir*, edited by Pat Sloan (1938), to Jonathan Cape Ltd and the Executors of the John Cornford Estate.

JOE CORRIE: from *Rebel Poems* (1932), to the Independent Labour Party.

RUBÉN DARÍO: from *Selected Poems of Rubén Darío* (1965), to the University of Texas Press.

C. DAY LEWIS: two extracts from 'The Magnetic Mountain' taken from *Collected Poems* (1954), to the author and the

Hogarth Press. Copyright © C. Day Lewis. Reprinted by permission of Harold Matson Company Inc.

DAVID DIOP: 'Listen Comrades' ('Écoutez Camarades'), 'Africa' ('Afrique') and 'The Vultures' ('Les Vautours') were first published in David Diop's *Coups de pilon* by Présence Africaine, Paris (1956).

GUNNAR EKELÖF: from *Late Arrival on Earth* (1967), to Rapp & Whiting Ltd.

PAUL ÉLUARD: from *Le dur désir de durer*, to the Trianon Press, Paris; and from *Selected Writings* (1952), translated by Lloyd Alexander. All Rights Reserved. Reprinted by permission of New Directions Publishing Corporation, New York.

ODYSSEUS ELYTIS: from *Modern Poetry in Translation 4*, translated by Paul Merchant (1968), to Odysseus Elytis and Paul Merchant.

HANS MAGNUS ENZENSBERGER: 'middle class blues' and 'karl heinrich marx' translated by Michael Hamburger, and 'vending machine' translated by Enzensberger, from *Selected Poems* (1966), to Martin Secker & Warburg Ltd, Atheneum Publishers Inc., New York, and the author.

ALDO DO ESPIRITO SANTO: from *Modern Poetry from Africa* (Penguin Books, 1963) to Pierre-Jean Oswald.

FAIZ AHMAD FAIZ: from *The Poems of Faiz*, translated by V. G. Kiernan (not yet published), to George Allen & Unwin Ltd.

PABLO ARMANDO FERNÁNDEZ: 'July 26, 1959', translated by J. M. Cohen, and an extract from 'Barracks and nets', translated by Margaret Randall, from *Writers in the New Cuba* (Penguin Books, 1967), to the author, Margaret Randall and J. M. Cohen. 'Barracks and nets' was first published in *TriQuarterly* magazine.

FRANCO FORTINI: from *Contemporary Italian Poetry* by G. Singh (1968), to the *London Magazine*.

FERDINAND FREILIGRATH: to the translator, Miss E. Louise Mally.

ERICH FRIED: from *On Pain of Seeing* (1969), to Rapp & Whiting Ltd and the author.

GÁBOR GARAI: 'A man is beaten up', which first appeared in English in *The New Hungarian Quarterly*, to the author.

ALEKSEI GASTEV: from *Modern Russian Poetry* edited by Vladimir Markov and Merrill Sparks (1966), to MacGibbon & Kee Ltd.

ACKNOWLEDGEMENTS

GIOVANNI GIUDICI: from *Contemporary Italian Poetry* by G. Singh (1968), to the *London Magazine*.

LEAH GOLDBERG: from *An Anthology of Modern Hebrew Poetry*, edited by Abraham Birman (1968), to Abelard-Schuman Ltd.

GÜNTER GRASS: 'In the egg', reprinted by permission of Harcourt, Brace & World Inc, from *Selected Poems* by Günter Grass, translated by Michael Hamburger, copyright © 1960 by Hermann Luchterhand Verlag GmbH; English translation copyright © 1966 by Martin Secker & Warburg Ltd. Originally published in *Gleisdreieck* by Hermann Luchterhand Verlag GmbH. 'Powerless, with a guitar' reprinted by permission of Harcourt, Brace & World Inc., from *New Poems* by Günter Grass, translated by Michael Hamburger, copyright © 1967 by Hermann Luchterhand Verlag GmbH; English translation © 1968 by Harcourt, Brace & World Inc. Originally published in Germany by Hermann Luchterhand Verlag GmbH under the title *Ausgefragt*.

ERNESTO CHE GUEVARA: from *Our Word*, translated by Edward Dorn and Gordon Brotherston (1968), to Cape Goliard Press. *Our Word* is distributed in America by Grossman Publishers Inc.

PAAVO HAAVIKO: from *Selected Poems of Paavo Haaviko*, translated by Anselm Hollo (1968), to Cape Goliard Press and to the author. The book is distributed in America by Grossman Publishers Inc.

HEINRICH HEINE: 'The weavers' from *Heine* (1966), a book in the series *Studies in Modern European Literature and Thought*, published by Bowes & Bowes Ltd, to the author and Bowes & Bowes Ltd. Seven poems from *Heinrich Heine: Paradox and Poet*, translated by Louis Untermeyer, copyright 1937 by Harcourt, Brace & World Inc.; renewed 1965 by Louis Untermeyer. Reprinted by permission of the publisher.

JAVIER HERAUD: from *Our Word*, translated by Edward Dorn and Gordon Brotherston (1968), to Cape Goliard Press. *Our Word* is distributed in America by Grossman Publishers Inc.

ZBIGNIEW HERBERT: from *Zbigniew Herbert: Selected Poems* (Penguin Books, 1968), to the translator, Peter Dale Scott.

MIGUEL HERNÁNDEZ: from *Poems for Spain* (1939), to the Hogarth Press and the author.

GEORG HERWEGH: to the translator, Miss E. Louise Mally.

ACKNOWLEDGEMENTS

NAZIM HIKMET: from *Selected Poems* (1967). Nazim Hikmet's poems are translated by Taner Baybars and published by Jonathan Cape Ltd. The book is distributed in America by Grossman Publishers Inc.

HO CHI-MINH: from *Prison Diary*, to The Foreign Languages Publishing House, Hanoi.

MIROSLAV HOLUB: from *Miroslav Holub: Selected Poems* (Penguin Books, 1967) to the translators, Ian Milner and George Theiner. 'Planning' first appeared in the Australian journal *Overland*.

LANGSTON HUGHES: 'I, too, sing America', 'Dream variation', 'The Weary Blues', 'Mother to son', 'The Negro speaks of rivers', 'Cross', copyright 1926 by Alfred A. Knopf, Inc. and renewed 1954 by Langston Hughes, and 'Song for a dark girl', copyright 1927 by Alfred A. Knopf, Inc. and renewed 1955 by Langston Hughes, reprinted from *Selected Poems*, by Langston Hughes, by permission of the publisher. 'Merry-go-round', copyright 1942 by Langston Hughes, reprinted from *The Panther and the Lash*, by Langston Hughes, by permission of Alfred A. Knopf, Inc.

VERA INBER: from *Modern Russian Poetry*, edited by Vladimir Markov and Merrill Sparks (1966), to MacGibbon & Kee Ltd.

MUHAMMAD IQBAL: from *Poems of Iqbal*, translated by V. G. Kiernan (1955), a book in the series *Wisdom of the East*, to John Murray (Publishers) Ltd.

ISHIKAWA TAKUBOKO: from *Modern Japanese Poetry*, to Kenkyusha Ltd.

JAROSLAV IWASZKIEWICZ: from *Introduction to Modern Polish Literature* (1963), to Twayne Publishers Inc. and the author.

FAYAD JAMIS: to the author and the translator, J. M. Cohen.

LEROI JONES: from *The dead Lecturer* (1964). Copyright © by LeRoi Jones. Reprinted by permission of The Sterling Lord Agency.

ATTILA JÓZSEF: to the translator.

FERENC JUHÁSZ: to the author.

JURE KAŠTELAN: from *An Anthology of Modern Jugoslav Poetry* (1963), to Calder & Boyars Ltd.

EDVARD KOCBEK: from *Slovene Poets of Today* (1965), to the Slovene Writers' Association.

KAJETAN KOVIČ: from *Slovene Poets of Today* (1965), to the Slovene Writers' Association.

PETER KUCZKA: from *The Plough and the Pen* (1963), edited by

27

ACKNOWLEDGEMENTS

Ilona Duczyńska and Karl Polyani, published by Peter Owen, to Peter Owen Ltd and the author.

KUO MO-JO: from *Modern Chinese Poetry* (1936), to the translators, H. Acton and Ch'en Shih Hsiang, Duckworth & Co. Ltd and Curtis Brown Ltd.

HUDDIE LEDBETTER: from *The Leadbelly Songbook*, to Kensington Music Ltd and Folkways Music Publishers Inc.

CHRISTOPHER LOGUE: to the author.

LUHSÜN: to the translators, Jerome Ch'en and Michael Bullock.

HUGH MACDIARMID: Reprinted by permission of The Macmillan Company, from *Collected Poems* by Hugh MacDiarmid. Copyright © Christopher Murray Grieve, 1948, 1962.

ANTONIO MACHADO: from *Castilian Ilexes*, translated by Charles Tomlinson and Henry Gifford (1963), to Oxford University Press.

GIANCARLO MAJORINO: from *Contemporary Italian Poetry* by G. Singh (1968) to the *London Magazine*.

OSIP MANDELSTAMM: from *Modern Russian Poetry*, edited by Vladimir Markov and Merrill Sparks (1966), to MacGibbon & Kee Ltd.

MAO TSE-TUNG: from *Mao and the Chinese Revolution*, translated by Jerome Ch'en (1965), to Oxford University Press.

SAMUEL MARSHAK: from *Modern Russian Poetry*, edited by Vladimir Markov and Merrill Sparks (1966), to MacGibbon & Kee Ltd.

VLADIMIR MAYAKOVSKY: '6 nuns' and 'Past one o'clock' from *Modern Russian Poetry*, edited by Vladimir Markov and Merrill Sparks (1966), to MacGibbon & Kee Ltd; 'Lenin' first published in *Sputnik*; 'The cloud in trousers', 'Order no. 2 to the army of the arts', 'My university', 'Back home!', 'At the top of my voice' reprinted by permission of the World Publishing Company from *The Bedbug and Selected Poetry* by Vladimir Mayakovsky. Copyright © 1960 by the World Publishing Company.

THOMAS MCGRATH: 'Letter to an Imaginary Friend', to *Chelsea* Magazine, the original publishers of the poem, and to the author.

MIGJENI: from *Selected Works of Migjeni* to Naim Frasheri.

ADRIAN MITCHELL: from *Poems* (1964) to Jonathan Cape Ltd and from *Out Loud* (1968) to Cape Goliard Press, and to the author. *Out Loud* is distributed in America by Grossman Publishers Inc.

ACKNOWLEDGEMENTS

NAKANO SHIGEHARU: to the author and the translators, Anthony Thwaite and Geoffrey Bownas.

PABLO NERUDA: Reprinted from *Twenty Poems of Pablo Neruda*, translated by James Wright and Robert Bly, The Sixties Press, Madison, Minnesota, 1967. Copyright © 1967 by The Sixties Press, reprinted by permission of Robert Bly. *Twenty Poems* published in the United Kingdom (1968) by Rapp & Whiting Ltd.

VIDAL DE NICOLAS: from *From Burgos Jail* (1964), to The Appeal for Amnesty in Spain.

OKAMOTO JUN: from *Modern Japanese Poetry*, to Kenkyusha Ltd.

WILFRED OWEN: from *Collected Poems*, to Mr Harold Owen and Chatto & Windus Ltd. Copyright Chatto & Windus Ltd, 1946, © 1963. Reprinted by permission of New Directions Publishing Corporation.

LEZ OZEROV: from *Modern Russian Poetry*, edited by Vladimir Markov and Merrill Sparks (1966), to MacGibbon & Kee Ltd.

NICANOR PARRA: from *Poems and Antipoems* (1968), to Jonathan Cape Ltd and the author.

PIER PAOLO PASOLINI: from *Contemporary Italian Poetry* by G. Singh (1968), to the *London Magazine*.

VASKO POPA: from *An Anthology of Modern Jugoslav Poetry* (1963), to Calder & Boyars Ltd.

MIKLÓS RADNÓTI: to the translators, Stevan Polgar, Stephen Berg, and S. J. Marks.

YANNIS RITSOS: 'Romiosyne', first published in English by the *Running Man* magazine, to the author and the translator, Eleftherios K. Parianos.

DAVID ROKEAH: from *Eyes in the Rock* (1968), to Rapp & Whiting Ltd and the author.

HENRIETTE ROLAND HOLST: 'Little Winding Paths' and 'Holland' from *Poetry of the Netherlands in its European Context 1170–1930*, translated by Theodoor Weevers, to the Athlone Press of the University of London.

TADEUSZ RÓŻEWICZ: from *Faces of Anxiety*, translated by Adam Czerniawski (1969), to Rapp & Whiting Ltd and the author.

ROBERT ROZHDESTVENSKY: from *Modern Russian Poetry*, edited by Vladimir Markov and Merrill Sparks (1966), to MacGibbon & Kee Ltd.

PENTTI SAARIKOSKI: from *Helsinki* (1967), to Rapp & Whiting Ltd and the author.

ACKNOWLEDGEMENTS

NELLY SACHS: from *Selected Poems* (1968), to Jonathan Cape Ltd, the author, and the translators, Michael Hamburger and Ruth and Matthew Mead.

CARL SANDBURG: an extract from *The People, Yes*, by Carl Sandburg, copyright 1936 by Harcourt, Brace & World Inc.; renewed 1964 by Carl Sandburg. Reprinted by permission of the publishers. 'The hammer', from *Complete Poems*, copyright 1950 by Carl Sandburg. Reprinted by permission of Harcourt, Brace & World Inc.

ILYA SELVINSKY: from *Modern Russian Poetry*, edited by Vladimir Markov and Merrill Sparks (1966), to MacGibbon & Kee Ltd.

LÉOPOLD SÉDAR SENGHOR: from *Chants d'ombres*, translated by Gerald Moore and Ulli Beier, published in *Black Orpheus*, to Longmans of Nigeria Ltd.

VITTORIO SERENI: from *Contemporary Italian Poetry* by G. Singh (1968), to the *London Magazine*.

AVRAHAM SHLONSKY: from *An Anthology of Modern Hebrew Poetry*, edited by Abraham Birman (1968), to Abelard-Schuman Ltd.

ANTONI SLONIMSKI: to the author.

BORIS SLUTSKY: from *Modern Russian Poetry*, edited by Vladimir Markov and Merrill Sparks (1966), to MacGibbon & Kee Ltd.

WILLIAM SOUTAR: from *The Expectant Silence* (1944), to the Trustees of the National Library of Scotland.

WOLE SOYINKA: from *Idandre and Other Poems* by Wole Soyinka, copyright © Wole Soyinka, 1967. Reprinted by permission of Hill & Wang Inc. and Methuen and Co. Ltd.

LAJOS TAMÁSI: to the author.

DYLAN THOMAS: from *Collected Poems*. Copyright 1939 by New Directions Publishing Corporation. Reprinted by permission of New Directions Publishing Corporation, New York, J. M. Dent & Sons Ltd and the Trustees for the Copyrights of the late Dylan Thomas.

T'IEN CHIEN: to the translators, Jerome Ch'en and Michael Bullock.

TO HUU: to the British-Vietnam Committee.

ERNST TOLLER: to the translator, Miss E. Louise Mally.

TSANG K'E-CHIA: to the translators, Jerome Ch'en and Michael Bullock.

TSOU TI-FAN: to the translators, Jerome Ch'en and Michael Bullock.

ACKNOWLEDGEMENTS

NANOS VALAORITIS: to the author and to the translator, Kimon Friar.

CÉSAR VALLEJO: from *Poemas humanos*, translated by Clayton Eshelman, to the estate of Cesar Vallejo and Jonathan Cape Ltd. Reprinted by permission of Grove Press Inc. Copyright © 1968 by Grove Press Inc.

YEVGENY VINOKUROV: from *Modern Russian Poetry*, edited by Vladimir Markov and Merrill Sparks (1966), to MacGibbon & Kee Ltd.

ANDREI VOZNESENSKY: from *Antiworlds* by Andrei Voznesensky, edited by P. Blake and M. Hayward (1968), to Oxford University Press.

GEORG WEERTH: to the translator, Miss E. Louise Mally.

ERICH WEINERT: to the translator, Miss E. Louise Mally.

YEVGENY YEVTUSHENKO: 'I journeyed through Russia' from *The Bratsk Station and Other Poems*, translated by Tina Tupikina-Glaessner, Geoffrey Dutton, and Igor Mezhakoff-Koriakin, to Rupert Hart-Davis Ltd. Copyright © 1966 by Sun Books Pty Ltd. Reprinted by permission of Double-day and Company Inc. 'Conversation with an American writer' from *Modern Russian Poetry*, edited by Vladimir Markov and Merrill Sparks (1966), to MacGibbon & Kee Ltd.

YI KWANG-SU: from *Voices of Dawn*, translated by Peter Hyun (1960), a book in the series *Wisdom of the East*, to John Murray (Publishers) Ltd.

YI YUK-SA: from *Voices of Dawn* translated by Peter Hyun (1960), a book in the series *Wisdom of the East*, to John Murray (Publishers) Ltd.

DANE ZAJC: from *Slovene Poets of Today* (1965), to the Slovene Writers' Association.

ZOLTÁN ZELK: from *The Plough and the Pen*, edited by Ilona Duczyńska and Karl Polyani (1963), published by Peter Owen, to Peter Owen Ltd and the author.

Every effort has been made to trace copyright holders, but in a few cases this has proved impossible. The publishers would be interested to hear from any copyright holders not here acknowledged.

INTRODUCTION

SOCIALISM, as a potential political practice and as a philosophical programme, has almost as many definitions as it has adherents. If a British monarch could say 'We are all socialists nowadays' in 1895, the common assumption of a collectively experienced and affirmative response to enlightened opinion is even more general today. For socialism has won the battle of linguistic usage, if nothing else. The word connotes progress, equality, protection from corruption, human mastery over initially hostile surroundings. Its various claims to have history on its side have won wide acceptance, and opponents of this view – from Sir Karl Popper in *The Open Society* and *The Poverty of Historicism* to contemporary conservative politicians – have, often unfairly, been dismissed as academic anachronisms or vicious reactionaries. Though few confessed socialists claim that their ideals have been strictly attained in any one country, most would approve of the proposition contained in Ezra Pound's Canto LXXVII:

> WOT IZZA COMIN'?
> 'I'll tell you wot izza comin'
> Sochy-lism is a-comin'

Permanent revolution or Fabian gradualism, Lenin's party élitism (*What Is To Be Done?*) or social democracy, the dictatorship of the proletariat or the populism of the Narodniki, Proudhon's decentralized society of property-owners or Fourier's phalansteries, Werner Sombart's German Spirit or Norman Douglas's radicalism: what is socialism? It is capable of so many interpretations that at times ideological struggles lacerate the labour movement. So much emphasis is put on arcane points of revolutionary methodology that at times it appears that

33

capitalism is being left to determine its own inevitable atrophy. Yet the opposition to capitalism – on an ethical and economic basis – is what socialism is about. It insists that the rationale of capitalism is the cynical exploitation of the broad mass of people by a self-perpetuating minority who control the means of production in their own interests and for their own profit. According to socialist theory, when the means of production, distribution and exchange are commonly owned and administered, mankind will be emancipated from the restrictions of an imposed social order and be in a position to realize the heights hitherto stunted by the selfish manipulation of privately owned economic machinery.

The end of socialism, then, is the liberation of man. Marx, who insisted he had put socialism on a scientific basis, expressed this succinctly in terms of his own phraseology:

Communism is the *positive* abolition of *private property*, of *human self-alienation*, and thus, the real *appropriation* of *human* nature, through and for man. It is therefore the return of man himself as a *social*, that is, really human, being, a complete and conscious return which assimilates all the wealth of previous development. Communism as a complete naturalism is humanism, and as a complete humanism is naturalism. It is the *definitive* resolution of the antagonism between man and Nature, and between man and man. It is the true solution of the conflict between existence and essence, between objectification and self-affirmation, between freedom and necessity, between individual and species. It is the solution of the riddle of history and knows itself to be this solution.[1]

If many of Marx's predictions about the inexorable unfolding of historical laws have been refuted by subsequent events, nevertheless his finality and confidence are common to socialist prognostications. It is not surprising, thus, that such a philosophy will have a unique attraction for artists, who are notoriously unreconciled to the state of the world at any given time, and

1. Karl Marx, *Selected Writings in Sociology and Social Philosophy*, Penguin, 1963, p. 250.

who urge on society the satisfying perfection of the greatest works of art. Of course this quest for a systematic method of solving social problems is not peculiar to socialist artists; Yeats, Pound, and Gottfried Benn were only the most gifted artists sympathetic to fascism.

In part, this attraction to ideology is a result of the political impotence an artist experiences. He is, or should be, the master of a medium that allows him to make comments on the very nature of life, and yet the executive control of the social structure proceeds as if immune to moral injunctions. Ernst Neizvestny, the Soviet sculptor, confronted by the paternal philistinism of Nikita Khrushchev, shouted at him: 'You may be Premier and Chairman but not here in front of my works. Here I am Premier and we shall discuss as equals.'[2] However courageous this may seem, there is definitely a desperate note of wishful thinking to it. The politician's power is implemented, not asserted; the artist's is experienced, and, if he is successful, communicated. But it is the cold official order conceived in expedient political terms that is the causal agent in crises, not the finely wrought phrases of the creative writer.

Despite this, writers continue to assume a universal audience, or the artists who are politically orientated do, even though they know their books may be distributed in tiny editions. Rilke's order, 'You must change your life' ('Torso of an archaic Apollo') is a message to all mankind. It may be unspecific but it tacitly claims an infinite wisdom that is to pass from the poet to the reader. Though the artist has to rely on a subjective reaction to events, he speaks as a saviour of humanity if only humanity will listen. If the message he brings is totally ignored the resulting feeling of isolation and frustration can lead to self-inflicted violence (Mayakovsky, Hart Crane, Attila József) as the sacrifice to a recalcitrant public unable to meet the artist as a matter

2. John Berger, *Art and Revolution*, Weidenfeld & Nicolson/ Penguin, 1969, p. 83.

of course. The pattern of such a crisis is vividly illustrated in a passage moving from confidence to depression in Ishikawa Takuboku's remarkable *Romanji Diary*:

One may cross the world by two paths and only two. *All or Nothing!* The one is to fight against everything. To win or else to die. The other is to fight against nothing . . . . But even though I have these opinions they don't cheer me or give me the slightest strength.

My character is an unhappy character.

I am a weakling with a marvellous sword inferior to none.

I can't stand it unless I fight, and yet I'm unable to win. That means that death is the only possible course for me. But I dislike the thought of death. I don't want to die! Then, how am I to live?[3]

Here is the dilemma of personal guilt in the face of powerlessness against social exigencies. In speaking for all mankind the artist accepts responsibility for all mankind. But when it comes to alleviating the plight of the dispossessed the frightening knowledge that his activity is, usually, confined to the lonely pursuit of a minority interest is often overwhelming. At the same time this makes nonsense of the claim that an interest in politics precludes sensitivity towards personal themes. Rather, the political context can make the treatment of these themes more intense and more authentic. Erich Fried's poem, 'My girlfriends', is a good example of this, so is Remco Campert's 'It was in the year of the strike'. Or, as Pasternak's Zhivago put it:

> But the plan of action is determined,
> And the end irrevocably sealed.
> I am alone; all round me drowns in falsehood:
> Life is not a walk across a field.[4]

And yet the strength of politically inspired art, whether it be the apocalyptic resonance of Yeats's *Michael Robartes and the Dancer*, or the satirical savagery of Brecht's *The Resistible Rise of Arturo Ui*, cannot be tamed by the re-

3. Donald Keene, *Modern Japanese Literature*, Grove Press, 1956, p. 218.

4. 'Hamlet', translated by Lydia Pasternak Slater.

cognition that personal feelings of inadequacy, as well as altruism, play a part in artistic conception. It has often been admitted by socialists that man's greatness lies in *what he's not*. In other words, culture – in the broadest sense of the word – is man's construction of the wholeness he lacked in his primitive state. Eyes alone were useful for observing the immediate environment, but the extension of vision through the telescope was a development crucial to progress. Similarly, works of art can expand human consciousness, advancing that insubstantial quality we quantify as 'humanity'. The artist intuitively knows this and is rightly outraged that his contribution to this evolution of humanity is crudely rejected by the use of the weapons of death, the abuse of technology. Of course, for the artist unable to accept this conflict, there is an alternative, a retreat into the arbitrary images of introspection.

Narcissism in the arts, which takes the artist's every aberration to be universally significant, is not blessed with nobility because of its pious declarations of innocence, is not morally superior merely because it considers itself to be so. The purely private manipulation of artistic forms, however sensuous, however exciting, will be no more interesting than the totality of the artist's ignorance of external events. And surely individuality can be better expressed by first discovering what people share. Political and social references, far from making art only topical, tend to make it universal, as the work of Chaucer or Dante or Shakespeare shows. Though it is important to stress that intentions alone are not enough. It is possible for someone to care honestly about war and misery and yet to parody grotesquely his feelings through lack of art. The difficulty of absorbing political material into art is not confined to the occasional poets who explode with moral indignation with the impact of each distant bomb. Sympathy with the sufferings and aspirations of other people is simply not enough; one must do justice to artistic problems, and not expect art to acquiesce when approached by political material. In a poem 'In praise of communism' Brecht defined his political philosophy as 'the simple thing/So difficult to achieve'. In the arts the extent of these difficulties is magnified. As MacDiarmid formulated it in his 'Second hymn to Lenin', 'politics is bairns' play/To what this maun be!'

Two celebrated examples of artistic defeat at the hands of promising political subjects come to mind. One is by an innovator, one by a formally conservative artist, so the point may be valid for the whole gamut of styles. On 26 April 1937, a small town in Basque was destroyed by bombers acting on German orders.[5] Picasso, vibrant with anger and grief, preserved his feelings in *Guernica*, often called his masterpiece. But, while the sketches for the picture do convey pain and mutilation, the compositional limitations of *Guernica* undermine the work's thematic intentions. The painting has a symbolic power, it is true, but by relying on a feeble pictorial formula Picasso, it seems to me, oversimplified his emotions to the point of superficiality. Provoked by historical information about this war crime, the spectator may unconsciously charge the work with a profundity it doesn't justify in itself. And for socialists there is enormous prestige in having a man of Picasso's stature on their side. Bereft of such assistance, the painting surely stands revealed as a massive failure.

An equally famous piece, Shostakovich's seventh symphony, took, as its subtitle 'Leningrad' implies, one of the most heroic episodes of World War II as its inspiration. Shostakovich's sincerity is not in doubt, but it may be that the loaded programmatic extra-musical burden the work carries intimidated the composer from the start. Certainly, the pedestrian rhythms of the opening movement – a travesty of Mahler's epic style – place the symphony a long way behind Shostakovich's first

5. For a description of the bombing of Guernica, see Hugh Thomas, *The Spanish Civil War*, Penguin, 1965, Chapter 52.

cello concerto, written ostensibly to do no more than exploit the technique of a great virtuoso, Mstislav Rostropovich. External emotions have overlaid *Guernica* and the 'Leningrad' symphony with overtones of greatness, but as autonomous works of art they are less than masterpieces. They lack sufficient power *in themselves* and depend on given data. No work of art is autonomous in the sense of dispensing with an interaction between art and life (indeed it is when we pretend to separate the two that we introduce the solecism). But art *is* required to speak for itself, in that it needs no apology and no extrinsic narrative. It is not necessary to know in detail the iconography of Max Beckmann's triptych *Departure* (1932–3) to succumb to its visual energy, nor is it essential to know that Berg's violin concerto was dedicated to the memory of a young woman who died tragically or that it was the composer's last work. On a political level, Mayakovsky's poems do not need to be read with the help of a history of the Russian revolution, but contain in themselves the information they explore.

I say this to anticipate the antagonism of people who consider all attempts to classify art by political affiliation factitious. It is important for them to concede the complex formulations of those who advocate an art that utilizes political experience. I personally, for example, do not believe that a socialist will automatically produce a greater work of art than a politically apathetic artist. Though a socialist poem which fulfils poetic criteria is likely to be more powerful, more lasting, than an entirely internal poem. I would be dubious about the level of a mind that remained totally closed to politics. Cynicism, in this field, is generally the aggressive face of ignorance. I do not believe that we should promote a public that will despise the work of an artist who finds any commitment odious; but an empirically-minded public, suspicious of pretension, is desirable. Finally, I do not believe that socialists can claim a monopoly of morality. In this connexion perhaps the worst excess of socialism has been to approach the mental attitude that can say, 'The definition of the individual was: a multitude of one million divided by one million.'[6] I can even see the point of T. S. Eliot's statement that 'A political association may help to give poetry immediate attention: it is in spite of this association that the poetry will be read, if it is read, tomorrow.'[7] Because unless the political matter is humanized and transformed into poetry, it deserves to be forgotten.

What I do believe is that the contemporary poetry that gets most attention, in Britain at least, is technically inadequate, thematically limited, and socially soporific. At its best it is pleasant, at its worst pathetic. It may be that it is able to hog the spotlight because our leading critical sensibilities have so much irony in their souls they recoil from a direct and explicit admission of concern for other people. It may be that in order to consolidate the rather trivial work they have championed they refuse to discuss art that would jeopardize this. This operation is not confined to the weekend critics. There is a rather perverse abdication of the critical faculty in Dr Leavis's *Retrospect* of 1950 when he finds 'the history of English poetry since then (1932) ... depressing in the extreme'[8] although his own standards informed the poetry. Or it may be that, far from forming any conspiracy against politically orientated art, our critics are simply ignorant of its power. In any case it is wrong and an act of artistic cowardice to imagine that the currently fashionable or approved constitutes the work of permanent importance. I hope this anthology will demonstrate the existence of an internationally significant body of relevant poetry capable of appealing to large audiences because it is, in the final instance, addressed to them. And by *them* I do not wish to invoke a

6. Arthur Koestler, *Darkness at Noon*, Penguin, 1964, p. 204.

7. T. S. Eliot, *A Choice of Kipling's Verse*, Faber, 1963, p. 7.

8. F. R. Leavis, *New Bearings in English Poetry*, Penguin, 1963, p. 181.

vision of toiling masses who can read a poem, analyse a painting, take in a piece of music as easily as they swing a hammer. Such people don't exist. I mean anyone at all who is aware of the plight of the majority on this planet and who is convinced that the suffering on it is not a consequence of so-called human nature, but something that can be overcome. If such people are not in a majority now, socialist poetry postulates a day when they will be. Thus the range of socialist poetry is justified, a range that has no resemblance to a solipsistic delusion of grandeur.

Many of those who are professionally engaged in reducing poetry to a useful space-filler in periodicals take the view that, however extravagant and ambitious poetry is outside Britain, in these islands it is essentially quiet. After all, the argument goes, we as a nation reject the metaphysical absurdities of continental thought and stick by a rather cautious brand of empiricism which we sometimes dignify politically as 'pragmatism'. So why should we accept something so fundamentally un-English as political poetry? Poetry has no essential epithet, least of all 'political' or 'socialist'. So the argument goes. Yet poetry needs no such protection from the nastiness of the outside world; at least there was a time in Britain when it didn't. If we take the greatest English poets we will find in their work a line packed with power and passion, a political emphasis because it teaches us how to govern man's aspirations:

> Avenge, O Lord thy slaughter'd Saints, whose bones
> Lie scatter'd on the Alpine mountains cold,
> Ev'n them who kept thy truth so pure of old
> When all our Fathers worship't Stocks and Stones,
> Forget not: in thy book record their groanes . . .
> (Milton, 'On the late Massacher in Piemont')

> I will not cease from Mental Fight,
> Nor shall my Sword sleep in my hand
> Till we have built Jerusalem
> In England's green & pleasant Land.
> (Blake, Preface to 'Milton')

An old mad, blind, despised, and dying king –
Princes, the dregs of their dull race, who flow
Through public scorn, – mud from a muddy spring, –
Rulers who neither see, nor feel, nor know,
But leech-like to their fainting country cling,
Till they drop, blind in blood, without a blow, –
A people starved and stabbed in the untilled field . . .
                    (Shelley, 'Sonnet: England in 1819')

These poems extend the reader's consciousness by urging him to active dissent. Milton is asking his contemporaries to *be* God, and to confidently carry out his wishes. To act out desirable reform. Unfortunately the greatness of Milton has never been less apparent. Eliot's attack of 1936 ('The most important fact about Milton ... is his blindness ... he may still be considered as having done damage to the English language from which it has not wholly recovered.') and his 1947 retraction in the Henriette Hertz lecture only make sense if we believe with Eliot that poets coming after Milton had only Miltonic language to build on. In fact they had his example of linguistically recreating reality in exalted terms, and had no need to imitate when they could emulate his achievement. Ezra Pound went further: 'Milton is the worst sort of poison. He is a thoroughgoing decadent in the worst sense of the term . . . he is the worst possible food for a growing poet.'[9] Again the notion that poets parasitically depend on poetry alone. This would be bad enough, but the calumny is given the stature of fact when a serious historian can say that 'Milton's uniquely elevated and dignified style, perfect for his high purposes, established the deplorable "poetic diction" of the eighteenth-century poetasters.'[10] The fault lies with the poets who followed Milton in thinking they could take the shell of his work without going over the substance. Even now one can obtain a more profound perception of the conflict in the world from

9. Ezra Pound, *Literary Essays*, Faber, 1954, p. 216.
10. Christopher Hill, *The Century of Revolution*, Nelson, 1961, p. 252.

Milton than from many of our British contemporaries.

These misguided attempts to explain poetic penury by accusing Milton of the original sin contain the fallacy that poetry grows, and ought to grow, only from other poetry. That literature develops only within a literary matrix. Milton's greatness lies in his ability to grasp the living traditions of his time in his poetry. Shelley and Blake have been more fairly treated, perhaps because they were so popular in organized labour movements. Shelley has had to contend with Arnold's description of him as 'a beautiful and ineffectual angel, beating in the void his luminous wings in vain'. However, two scientifically trained readers have seen in these poets what the literary critics missed. Typical of Dr J. Bronowski's approach is the observation that 'the greatest of social critics, Karl Marx, believed that the society for which he fought was shaped by the needs of history itself, to put an end to the waste of the wellbeing of men. This is no less a myth than Blake's Jerusalem, and no less noble.'[11] And the mathematician Desmond King-Hele has eloquently examined Shelley's 'lifelong aversion to cruelty, tyranny, authority, institutional religion, custom and the formal shams of respectable society'.[12] There is no vicarious claim by this type of critic to express the truths of poetry more knowingly than the poet himself. Consequently no wedge is driven between the poet and his public.

Milton, Blake, Shelley: great English poets whose efforts to speak to people rather than other poets have been frustrated by futile critics claiming to be the custodians of culture. Trust the poet, not the exegesis.

There is something reprehensible in claiming for our poetry a purity and virginity that will resist all attempts at political penetration: reprehensible because untrue,

11. J. Bronowski, *A Man Without a Mask*, Secker & Warburg, 1943, p. 142.

12. Desmond King-Hele, *Shelley: His Thought and Work*, Macmillan, 1960, p. 367.

and because it ignores these precedents. The idea of socialist poetry in English is not foreign. Though, we have to place British poetry in the context of world-literature. In one thing I can see the reluctance of some to accept the interpenetration of political thought and poetic insight. The example of British poetry in the 1930s is not, on the whole, a happy one. One could have misgivings about poetry during this period if one isolated the British contribution from the work of Vallejo, Alberti, Hernández, Machado. As Robin Skelton has pointed out in an anthology of the period (which inexplicably omits MacDiarmid), the British poets of the 1930s were 'almost to a man, members of the bourgeoisie'.[13] True, Auden went to Spain as a stretcher-bearer and Spender attempted to run a broadcasting station. But their gestures towards activism were a consequence of the stand they had taken in their poetry, and as such were appendages to their stance as political poets. In the case of Auden his poetry is never at home with what were probably temperamentally alien political beliefs. His accommodation of political thought was done very much as a literary innovation (which it no doubt was to Oxbridge). So his work has a strained quality to it. Some poems are vitiated by a superfluity of epithet and abstraction, and the accent on idiosyncratic euphony often deprives the poem of any meaning beyond the poet's self-indulgent free-association:

> Into this neutral air
> Where blind skyscrapers use
> Their full height to proclaim
> The strength of Collective Man,
> Each language pours its vain
> Competitive excuse
>
> ('September 1, 1939')

Another feature of Auden's work imitated by would-be political poets – again in the belief that poetry springs only from poetry, not from life – is the stereotyped verbal

13. Robin Skelton, ed., *Poetry of the Thirties*, Penguin, 1964, p. 18.

pattern, as in 'fashionable madmen' ('Lullaby') or 'conscious unbelievers' ('Friday's child'). As the most skilful wordsmith of the 1930s group, and as something of a self-styled *guru*, Auden has passed on his stylistic affectations: Day Lewis's 'Down dropsy avenues he cries/A novel great affair' ('From feathers to iron') is unmistakably an Auden cadence.

It would be a mistake to try to fuse poetry and politics in order to be an Auden. To take the politics from his poetry would be to place the reader at a second remove from reality. The function of politics in poetry is to show the reader how events external to his inviolability as an individual continually impinge on his behaviour. Auden's aim was more one of telling the reader which faction to vote for.

There *were* fine poems by the 1930s poets, but it is arguable that the revulsion from the idea of political poetry is based on the limitations of the poems then widely circulated. C. Day Lewis, remembering his flirtation with political commitment in 'An Italian Visit' (1953) wrote:

> We who 'flowered' in the Thirties
> Were an odd lot; sceptical yet susceptible, –
> Dour though enthusiastic, horizon addicts
> And future-fans, terribly apt to ask what
> Our all-very-fine sensations were in aid of.

This confession of a certain frivolity corroborates my suspicion that much of the poetry of the period displayed its political imagery like a trophy brought back from another country. For its impact it depended on the middle-class capacity to absorb shock. It charmed the class it pretended to eliminate. Perhaps the realization of this inspired MacDiarmid's bitter epitaph 'British leftish poetry, 1930–1940':

> Auden, MacNeice, Day Lewis, I have read them all,
> Hoping against hope to hear the authentic call . . .
> And know the explanation I must pass is this
> – You cannot light a match on a crumbling wall.

and his description in 'Third hymn to Lenin' of

> Michael Roberts and All Angels! Auden, Spender, those bhoyos,
> All yellow twicers: not one of them
> With a tithe of Carlile's courage and integrity.
> Unlike these pseudos I am *of* – not *for* – the working class.

Because of his working-class origins MacDiarmid could be entirely serious about politics and eschew the fashion of aiming a *frisson* across the bows of the bourgeoisie. His work is informed with an honesty and integrity lacking in Auden and the other. Their privileged despair usurped their good intention.

C. Day Lewis's strictures, for example, concentrate on imaginary opponents. There is nothing of the power through precision we find in Mayakovsky's poem '6 nuns'. Even in his most impressive poem, 'The magnetic mountain', Day Lewis shows an enervating predilection for personification:

> Lipcurl, Swiveleye, Bluster, Crock and Queer,
> Mister I'll-think-it-over, Miss Not-to-day,
> Young Who-the-hell-cares and old Let-us-pray,
> Sir Apres-moi-le-déluge.

This lack of half-tone, this knocking down of crude caricatures, has come to be thought of as the *sine qua non* of political poetry. It is nothing of the kind, and to persist in believing that it is only confirms the scandalous indifference to non-English poetry that exists in Britain. Blok could delineate character in 'The twelve', but then he did not see the making of history as an invasion of his poetry. Despite the examples of Blok, of Mayakovsky, of Brecht, of Ritsos, of MacDiarmid, too many British poets have confined their study of poetry and politics to the British poets of the 1930s. Compare Day Lewis's reluctant British public

> We'd like to fight but we fear defeat,
> We'd like to work but we're feeling too weak,
> We'd like to be sick but we'd get the sack,

We'd like to behave, we'd like to believe,
We'd like to love, but we've lost the knack.
   ('The magnetic mountain', 33)

with Adrian Mitchell's belligerent U.S. soldiers:

Want to be humane, but we're only human.
Off with the old skin, on with the new.
We maim by night.
We heal by day.
Just the same as you.
   ('Make and break')

Both these poets have, of course, written better passages, but in taking models for his poetry the young poet is more likely to reproduce the easy effects of his chosen mentor rather than the masterwork. By making his targets ridiculous the political poet at this level underestimates them. At the back of the display of passion there is a schematic straitjacket that reduces his expression of it to a mediocre precedent. It has to be said that political poetry is the most difficult thing to do well. It requires a Baudelairean plunge 'to the bottom of the Unknown to find the *New*'.

In his essay, 'The cartoonist's armoury', E. H. Gombrich has pointed out that by seeing abstract concepts (democracy, the nation, freedom) as recognizable objects, the cartoonist can either brilliantly condense complexity in one image, or he can, like the Nazi cartoonists, dangerously suggest a reality for a myth. Whereas the Greeks had their gods to personify the abstract we have the cartoonist to help us make 'an easy and effortless transition from abstract noun to an imagined reality'. Exactly the same thing obtains in poetry. Gombrich says that 'when perplexed and frustrated, we all like to fall back on a primitive physiognomic picture of events which ignores the realities of human existence and conceives the world in terms of impersonal forces'.[14] So, it is the task of poets, if they

14. E. H. Gombrich, *Meditations on a Hobby Horse*, Phaidon, 1963, p. 140.

aspire to more than the reification of the cartoonist's armoury, to go to the concrete reality that lies behind the abstraction. It is foolish to bring poetic gifts to a lyric and then think that a political poem can be dashed off.

By way of contrast we may take Neruda's 'The heights of Macchu Picchu',[15] which, in my opinion, is one of the very greatest poems written this century and which has been brilliantly translated into English by Nathaniel Tarn. It is a subtle and sustained meditation on the meaning of human effort. Neruda does not just state, but shows us how life for many is a meaningless and repetitive ritual of drudgery:

the drover, the son of harbours, the dark captain of ploughs,
the rodent wanderer through dense streets:
all of them weakened waiting for their death, their brief
  and daily death

and despises this because 'I wished to swim in the most ample lives'. Through the tragedy of human wastage he is 'dying of my own death'. Then Neruda is challenged by the towering magnificence of Macchu Picchu, 'Tall city of stepped stone'. If men die and are forgotten, this 'permanence of stone' survives. But is it really more desirable than modern urban squalor, really more magnificent, or was it created out of the destruction of lives?

> Macchu Picchu did you lift
> stone above stone on a groundwork of rags?
> coal upon coal and, at the bottom, tears?

If constructions can be achieved only through human misery then man himself must take priority over ostentation:

> Let me have back the slave you buried here!
> Wrench from these lands the stale bread
> of the poor . . .

Neruda believes that man must exercise his wonderful

15. Pablo Neruda, *The Heights of Macchu Picchu*, Cape, 1966.

inventive powers, but *for* man, not through exploitation of man.

Today let me forget this happiness, wider than all the sea,
because man is wider than all the sea and her necklace of islands

Neruda desires a social structure in which great things can be built up for the benefit of all men. By speaking for those who suffered building Macchu Picchu for the privileged

> Arise to birth with me, my brother

the poet is championing the wretched of the earth described in Section II of the poem. Poetry will speak for the poor, for the illiterate so that the labour taken from them will be used for them:

> Come quickly to my veins and to my mouth.
> Speak through my speech, and through my blood.

Sharing language with all men, the poet will not use his great gift in the service of his private cogitations, but will give voice to the wishes of the hitherto suppressed. The massive formal unity of Neruda's poem, the interplay of private and public images, the juxtaposition of despair and militancy, make this poem greater than any English poem (with the possible exception of the best of Eliot and Yeats) written this century. Edmund Wilson, considering whether prose fiction, in the hands of a Flaubert or a Joyce, had taken over the role traditionally held by poetry, asked, 'Is verse a dying technique?'[16] Neruda's poem answers with a resounding No!

In an interview with Robert Bly, Neruda gave a reason for his fully developed style:

I come from a country which is very political. Those who fight have great support from the masses. Practically all the writers of Chile are out to the left – there are almost no exceptions. We

16. Edmund Wilson, *The Triple Thinkers*, Penguin, 1962, pp. 22–40.

feel supported and understood by our own people. . . . As poets we are really in touch with the people. . . . I read my poems everywhere in my country – every village, every town – for years and years, and I feel it is my duty to do it.[17]

This is why I am encouraged by the great increase in public performances of poetry in recent years. It is more difficult to let the obscure masquerade as the profound before a critical audience. And it is significant that the concept of public readings has been consistently attacked in the weekly journals who consider these readings undignified, and who wish to preserve the tradition of a poet containing himself in the orderly cycle of school/ university/reviewer/academic/literary editor. Increasingly, poetry is being written with an audience in mind. Increasingly, the young people who go to these readings are becoming politically conscious. So even if many of the poems are aimed at the erotic giggle or the would-be profound nod, we can expect the demands of the audiences for quality to grow, and with a new politically educated audience the standards of poetry to increase.

At the moment there is much to be done, and it would be premature to be optimistic about British poetry. A desire to approximate to the current received opinion disarms the poet. He chooses, all too often, the easy way of obsequious careerism. In Britain, too many wilt before the grandeur of 'the rule of law', 'tradition', 'the mother of Parliaments' and other such supposed equations of democracy. A kind of dichotomy syndrome arises where there are two sides to a problem, and two only, the British and the non-British approach. British becomes a synonym for wise. Certainly in times of war this leads to unity, but it also promotes a shared insularity that passes for normality. Governments can be criticized but they are all honourable men. New states can do their best, but their best is only worthy of the great British sneer. Statesmanship is admirable in an Englishman, deplorable in anyone else. Churchill is a

17. Pablo Neruda, *Twenty Poems*, Rapp & Whiting, 1967.

great leader of his people, Mao Tse-tung is a barbarian. And so the colonial mentality persists. In accepting this the population endorses Pope's definition of conservatism in *An Essay on Man*: 'One truth is clear, Whatever is, is right.' A poet snarling with all the spent passion of a member of Her Majesty's Opposition is legitimate; but for a writer to advance revolutionary views is un-British, unpatriotic. Hence the appalling neglect of MacDiarmid. Hence the resistance to non-English poets. So though 'We are all socialists nowadays' the royal plural can shrink to a self-appointed omniscient few when the vulgarity of political action breaks through the progressive surface. The reluctance of governments to accept extra-parliamentary militancy may be the real face of power, or it may be the strength of civilization. It is an open question and socialist poets by no means agree on the answer. But they all share a distrust of the claims of governments and believe that suffering is intolerable no matter what the political coloration of those who inflict it. The key images of the sixties – Vietnamese women and children mutilated by napalm, and the hideous clatter of Soviet tanks in the streets of Prague – ensure this. Politics are not only too important to be left to the politicians, but much too dangerous. It is the poet who is uniquely positioned to rescue politics from the arrogance of those who claim to understand society exclusively. For that reason, the political poet needs courage as well as talent, and must be prepared to counter violent opposition to his work.

Outside Britain politics have been more extreme than here, and the question of political involvement presents itself in a direct rather than an academic fashion. As David Craig has said, 'Brecht was forced to a deadly point of responsibility and a pitch of urgency by the most savage of all reactionary antagonists – German fascism. The duties of a communist poet could hardly have been clearer than in such a society.'[18] Similarly

18. *Hugh MacDiarmid: A Festschrift*, Duval, 1962, p. 99.

René Char fought the Nazi occupation; Machado, Hernández and Alberti resisted Spanish fascism; Chinese poets fought against successive attempts to destroy the popular movement they supported (and one Chinese poet led his forces to victory). Compared to these poets, British writers have had a limited experience. Not because of the relatively undramatic political development of modern Britain: if poetry was at its best in a violent society then the hope of every socialist would be for the conditions that throttle poetry. But because poets have been, in this country, cut off from industrial conflict. Though financially allied to the working class, they have had middle-class pretensions. It is not true that a certain level of affluence absolves us from the problems of world poverty. Investments in countries run by dictatorships, diplomatic support for racist governments: these things thrust responsibility on us. It is the triumph of the news media to have vividly confirmed Lenin's thesis in *Imperialism*: *The Last Stage of Capitalism* that exploitation is a truly international affair. Evidence for the truth of this is delivered to our doors daily in newsprint and invades our homes on the television screen.

Given all this, we have seen that politically admirable thoughts do not magically metamorphose into poetry. It is necessary for the socialist poet to have more impressive technical equipment than his apolitical contemporaries because his task is that much more important. Indeed, this is the case with the greatest socialist poets. Neruda is unsurpassed for the majestic development of complex themes, Brecht for diversity in brevity, MacDiarmid for controlled fury. This triumvirate, probably supreme in twentieth-century poetry, upholds skill. But because their work refers to reality, not myth, to the essential, not the peripheral, the inevitability that permeates their finished products is often derided as being obvious, as if the accusers were capable of going over politics on that level. The reason why technical eccentricities – arbitrary typographical arrangements, syntactical extremity, etc. – do not decorate their work is that these things are incidental felicities only necessary as a substitute for the movement of the intellect through speech. Mayakovsky's individual use of typography *is* justified because it reinforces the urgency of his metaphors. But to use type as a visual instrument alone is to deny the function of language. It is apposite to recall Trotsky's statement, made originally with regard to the breathless literary schools that followed the revolution, that 'technique is noticed most markedly in the case of those who have not mastered it'.[19] The rhythmical fluency and verbal vivacity of the greatest socialist poetry does not draw attention to itself, because it is a projection of natural speech to a consummate aesthetic level.

Art is a research into life, and life is contained in societies, and societies are governed by political institutions. This makes a political choice imperative for thinking individuals. The choice may be to opt out of politics (as far as this is possible) but it will still be a choice. Or it may be to accept that 'whatever is, is right'. Or it may be dissent. These choices and the implications involved in them are part of the research into life that is art. To present the reader, spectator, or listener with the clumsy mechanics of expression is not art at all, but the dull thud of failure. Such clumsy failures should not be elevated to 'experiments' that claim to be above criticism. An experiment is the exploration of a possibility, not the means by which we set up the experiment. Scientific experiments come after a creative conjecture and must fit into the discipline imposed by this hypothesis. So-called artistic 'experiments' are unrelated to creativity or conclusion. To see this in its better manifestations the example of Mondrian, Malevich and Kandinsky can be cited. They thought, in their various ways, that in making the pictorial

19. Leon Trotsky, *Literature and Revolution*, Ann Arbor, 1960, p. 204.

innovations that led to abstract art and emancipating form and colour from figurative restrictions, they would instigate an art capable of conveying definite ideas. Kandinsky's *Concerning the Spiritual in Art* is the classic statement of this. But has an abstract pictorial language been evolved to make art more profound? I think not. It seems that E. H. Gombrich was correct in postulating that painting needs the dimension of subject-matter as much as music needs time.[20] By repudiating the intellectual and emotional achievements of representational painting, artists committed themselves, certainly, but to the view that they could dispense with meaningful metaphors. In the same way it is ludicrous to imagine that the careful little 'experiments' of contemporary poets who ignore the positive aspects of man can amount to important contributions to artistic edifices. Rather I think posterity may find it incredible that in an age of revolutionary importance some writers – traditionally responsive to injustice and the possibility of change – built up artefacts with no relation to the events around them. With political poetry we go to the heart of the matter and can dispense with both the neo-Georgian domesticity of 'traditional' poets, and the graffiti of 'experimental' poets. Taking up Gombrich's analogy, poetry exists in a philosophical context. However delightful its sound, language remains a method of classifying the world. In poetry this language is as tentative, as dynamic, as reality itself. It bends with the change of the world. As in science the testing of hypotheses comes after the creative impulse, the poet deploys information to test his ideas. Scientific language, as used by scientists, is rarely memorable in the way poetry is, as so often the human considerations are left out. Poetry considers the impact of events on mankind.

It *is* possible to create an art of social importance without a definite espousal of an identifiable political belief. Let us be clear about that. Poetry, the com-

20. E. H. Gombrich, op. cit., pp. 143–51.

munication of important insights in a memorable way, is flexible enough to encompass all the varieties of human thought. Political poetry need not be affirmative, offering visionary vistas for immediate edification. Allen Ginsberg's 'Howl' shows how cosmic disgust and denunciation can be a valid second way:

I saw the best minds of my generation destroyed by madness,
  starving hysterical naked,
dragging themselves through the negro streets at dawn looking
  for an angry fix,
angelheaded hipsters burning for the ancient heavenly con-
  nection to the starry dynamo in the machinery of night,
who poverty and tatters and hollow-eyed and high sat up
  smoking in the supernatural darkness of cold-water flats
  floating across the tops of cities contemplating jazz, . . .

Here man is perceived as a creature trying to liberate himself from repression (the Freudian reading of behaviour is important here) which is thrust on man. This art of violent dissent is too often ignored, at least by British critics, and it has taken the Austrian Marxist, Ernst Fischer, to say that 'to provoke dreams of terror in the slumber of prosperity has become the moral duty of literature'.[21]

A more rigid Marxist than Fischer, Georg Lukács, has claimed – with considerable justification – that modernism is based on an untenable ontological dogma (man's isolation) and expresses the values of modern capitalism (nihilism) often unconsciously. By refusing to take cognizance of socialism, the modernist condemns himself to sterile and regressive technical experimentation, and accumulates naturalistic details without regard to a hierarchy of values. The Ginsbergs, Becketts, are superb artists who expose the vicious depths beneath the calm surface of society, but they stop short of an acceptance of socialism as the economic argument for democracy. As Lukács puts it:

21. Ernst Fischer, *Art Against Ideology*, Allen Lane The Penguin Press, 1969, p. 24.

Not everyone who looks for a solution to the social and ideo-
logical crisis of bourgeois society – and this is necessarily the
subject-matter of contemporary bourgeois literature – will be a
professed socialist. It is enough that a writer takes socialism
into account and does not reject it out of hand. But if he rejects
socialism – and this is the point I want to make – he closes his
eyes to the future, gives up any chance of assessing the present
correctly, and loses the ability to create other than purely static
works of art.[22]

And let no one attempt to discredit socialism by equating
it with Stalinism or institutional communism. They will
find no backing for the accusation in the work of socialist
poets. Instead they will find a deeper critique of totali-
tarianism than will ever come from the bourgeoisie
who, in times of crisis, are all too anxious to support the
anti-democratic leader. It is encouraging to note here
though that the novels of the great Alexander Solzhenit-
syn, which try to find the values of socialism after the
Stalinist nightmare, are being widely read and appre-
ciated in the West.

But poetry? Surely that, of all literary forms, is
unsuited to political utterance? To believe this is to
believe that politics is as crude and insensitive as those
who make a career out of it. At its most extreme the case
against poetry was made by Sartre: 'poets are men who
refuse to "utilize" language .... In fact the poet has
withdrawn from language-instrument in a single
movement. Once and for all he has chosen the poetic
attitude which considers words as things and not signs.'[23]
This is true of some poets, but hardly a prescription for
poetry. Poetry, as the use of language at its most precise
and most memorable, could hardly be unsuited to
political thought *in principle*. It is worth remembering
that there is never any objection to poets expressing
cranky hunches in their work. It is political sharpness
that offends. Yeats is allowed his gyres, Graves his White

22. Georg Lukács, *Realism in Our Time*, Harper & Row, 1964, p. 60.
23. J. P. Sartre, *What Is Literature?*, Methuen, 1950, p. 5.

Moon Goddess. But not Mayakovsky his revolution. In an age that pays lip-service to the genius of Wittgenstein, it is paradoxical to accept as poetic what is most illogical. But poetry is not light relief from the problems of living. It is the discussion of what is of permanent value in endurable language.

If the poet refuses to concern himself with non-poetic people, then these people are justified in reciprocating his indifference. This has happened in Britain. Neruda and Yevtushenko can reach mass audiences, whereas British poets are content with the handful of readers they feel happy in addressing. If this anthology were only to convince English poets that they are fundamentally mistaken in their interpretation of what poetry is it would have served a purpose. But it goes beyond that to the public who have not yet come to poetry, and shows *them* that poetry is not peculiar or 'effeminate' or any of the things they have been conditioned to believe. The poets represented here insist and *prove* that poetry has important truths to communicate, that poets should be equipped to understand the complexities of the modern world, that critics should judge modern work by the rigorous standards their predecessors applied to the art of the past, and that there is nothing intrinsically private about poetry. And now poetry can regain its importance and lose the status of a poor illiterate relative to fiction. There is talent today, but the bigger it is the less the pundits have to say about it. This will not matter if the poet can go straight to his reader without worrying about the recommendations of critics he probably finds repugnant anyway. It is perhaps not surprising, after all that has happened this century, that some poetic progeny are unsightly mutations. But a sick world does not mean a sick art, despite the reflective theory of art, and a healthy poetry does contribute to a healthy society. By showing the world where its future must lie, it is possible to create a better world for our poetry and through our poetry, trying not only to preserve an art form, but, with it, a better, more open, more integrated world. To those who say that poetry is not equal to this, I say that failure is only a consequence of diffidence. It is up to the poets in the following pages to convince *you* that a society without poetry is even more arid and pointless than a poetry without society.

Edinburgh, 1969   ALAN BOLD

EDITOR'S NOTE

As will be apparent, the poems in this anthology fall
into two main categories: (1) poems written by socialist
poets aimed at extending the reader's consciousness of
socialism; (2) poems not necessarily by socialists, but
likely to appeal to socialists and to reinforce the assump-
tions of socialism because they examine events so radically.
Mayakovsky's poems are obviously included under the
first, Cavafy's 'Waiting for the barbarians' under the
second category. I have adopted no theory of translation
in selecting non-English poems, but just as the English
poems have to fulfil poetic criteria, so do the translations
have to work as English poems. Some nineteenth-century
translations were crippled by archaisms and inversions
and unlikely to appeal to a modern reader. Today we
are better served by translators, whether they give
literal or imaginative versions of non-English poems.
Peter Levi, introducing Yevtushenko's *Bratsk Station*, said
that 'a translated poem is like a ruined building'. It is
to be hoped that the reader can make of that ruined
building what Neruda made of Macchu Picchu.

Because an anthology of this sort has to begin some-
where it was accepted that Marx's lifetime saw the transi-
tion of socialism from a desirable ideal to a realizable
necessity. Hence the book begins with Marx's contem-
porary and friend, Heine. Naturally, there was a case
for including Blake and Shelley, expecially as poems
like 'Men of England' gained great currency in the
labour movement. However, I think then I would have
been obliged to redefine the anthology as a collection of
radical, rather than socialist verse. The adumbrations of
socialism are there, in Shelley and others, but their work
is basically pre-industrial in detail.

It was Schoenberg who said, in a letter to Rudolf

Kolisch, dated 27 July 1932: 'I can't say it often enough: my works are twelve-tone *compositions*, not *twelve-tone* compositions.' In the same way my emphasis has been on creativity rather than ideology, and this makes for great variety in a given unity.

The selection is obviously personal in some respects, but I have tried to be representative. Poets who are omitted are those whose poetic flavour did not satisfy me as much as their label.

Copyright difficulties prevented the inclusion of poems by Robert Lowell and Bob Dylan, and decimated the number of poems I had originally selected by Brecht. I also wished to include W. H. Auden's 'Spain', but Mr Auden wrote to say: 'As you know, I disapprove of my poem "Spain", in particular of the last two lines which assert the immoral doctrine (it may be marxist, but it certainly isn't socialist) that whoever succeeds historically is just.'

I would like to thank Nikos Stangos of Penguin Books for his exemplary courtesy and his intelligent support while I was editing the book. I am also grateful to John Berger and David Craig for perceptive comments on my introduction, and to Barry Cole for reading the book in proof. I had thought of dedicating this anthology to an individual, but it seemed presumptuous to so treat the work of other poets. So this book is dedicated, sincerely, to whoever approaches it with a desire to learn.

HEINRICH HEINE
1797–1856

✳

Absolutely!

When the Spring comes in and the sun is bright
Then every small blossom beckons and blows.
When the moon on her shining journey goes
Then stars swim after her through the night.
When the singer looks into two clear eyes
Then something is stirred and lyrics arise ...
But flowers and stars and songs just begun,
And moonbeams and eyes and the light of the sun,
No matter how much such stuff may please,
One can't keep living on things like these.   ✓

A promise

Freedom, stumbling through the stews
    Barefoot, spat upon, and shocking.
Cheer up! Some day you'll have shoes,
    And perhaps (who knows) a stocking.

Freedom, some day you will wear
    A warm cap with ear-laps showing;
Then you will not have to care
    In the path of all winds blowing.

Men will nod to you, no less;
    They may even house and feed you;
They may love you to excess,
    But, of course, they will not heed you.

You, however, must, you see,
    Listen to your lords and heed 'em.
Hold your tongue and bend your knee,
    And you'll have a future, Freedom.

The weavers

Their eyes are dry, for tears are blinding,
They sit at the loom and their teeth are grinding.
'We weave thy shroud, O Germany,
We weave a triple curse for thee,
We're weaving and weaving!

'A curse to the God to whom we were crying
In the winter's cold and from hunger dying,
We hoped and prayed and implored him in vain,
He fooled us, he teased us, he mocked our pain.
We're weaving and weaving!

'A curse to the king who's a rich man's lord,
Who with poor men's misery is merely bored,
Who collects his taxes from hovels and bogs,
And has us shot down in the streets like dogs.
We're weaving and weaving!

'A curse to the fatherland which we thought ours,
Where only the vilest corruption flowers,
Where blossoms are scattered before their day,
Where the worm grows fat on rot and decay.
We're weaving and weaving!

'The shuttle flies in the creaking loom.
All day and all night we weave thy doom,
We weave thy shroud, Old Germany,
We weave a triple curse for thee.
We're weaving and weaving!'

Only wait!

What! Think you that my flashes show me
    Only in lightnings to excel?
Believe me, friends, you do not know me,
    For I can thunder quite as well.

In sorrow you shall learn your error;
    My voice shall grow, and in amaze
Your eyes and ears shall feel the terror,
    The thundering word, the stormy blaze.

Oaks shall be rent; the word shall shatter.
    Yea, on that fiery day, the crown,
Even the palace-walls shall totter,
    And domes and spires come crashing down!

Remembering Krähwinkel's reign of terror

We, the senate and the Mayor,
After intensive thought and prayer
For all the various creeds and classes,
Enjoin these laws upon the masses:

'Beware of aliens, for they sow
Seeds of revolt where'er they go;
Rebellious souls and other vermin
Are scarcely ever (praise God) German.

'Obedience to their ruler's due
From Christian and (much more) from Jew;
And Jew and Christian, every one,
Must close their shops when day is done.

'No one shall walk abroad at night
Unless accompanied by a light.
If three shall walk in any street
They shall disperse – before they meet.

'Discard your weapons, bring them all
Hastily to the City Hall;
Retain no sort of ammunition
Unless you long for quick perdition.

'Who holds another point of view,
He shall be shot without ado;
And argument by gestures is
Even more dangerous than this.

'Honour your Mayor; it is he
Who guards the State and zealously
Decides what's best for old and young.
So listen well – and hold your tongue.'

King David

Tyrants when they come to die
Laugh and look death in the eye,
For they know one thing is sure:
Tyranny will still endure.

There they go, the common folk,
Cattle bowing to the yoke;
Never daring to complain,
Docile to the bit and rein.

To the stalwart Solomon
David, dying, said: 'My son,
Apropos of Joab, too,
There is this for you to do:

'This proud general has been
A rankling thorn beneath my skin;
Yet for all my hatred, none
Has done the thing I should have done.

'You, my son, the one I love,
You are good and strong enough;
So remembering all I've said,
Kill this Joab when I am dead.'

The one method

You are inspired to hardihood –
Ah, that is good!
Yet inspiration's not sufficient;
Remember, evil is omniscient.

The foe, I grant you, does not fight
For light or right.
But he is armed whatever happens;
His always are the heavier weapons.

So arm yourself, steady your hand,
And take your stand.
Aim well; and if the shot should carry,
Rejoice and let your heart make merry.

THOMAS HOOD
1799–1845

❋

The song of the shirt

With fingers weary and worn,
    With eyelids heavy and red,
A woman sat, in unwomanly rags,
    Plying her needle and thread –
        Stitch! stitch! stitch!
In poverty, hunger, and dirt,
    And still with a voice of dolorous pitch
She sang the 'Song of the Shirt'.

    'Work! work! work!
While the cock is crowing aloof!
    And work – work – work,
Till the stars shine through the roof!
    It's Oh! to be a slave
    Along with the barbarous Turk,
Where woman has never a soul to save,
    If this is Christian work!

    'Work – work – work
Till the brain begins to swim;
    Work – work – work
Till the eyes are heavy and dim!
Seam, and gusset, and band,
    Band, and gusset, and seam,
Till over the buttons I fall asleep,
    And sew them on in a dream!

'Oh, Men with Sisters dear!
  Oh, men, with Mothers and Wives!
It is not linen you're wearing out,
  But human creatures' lives!
    Stitch – stitch – stitch,
  In poverty, hunger and dirt,
Sewing at once, with a double thread,
  A Shroud as well as a Shirt.

'But why do I talk of Death?
  That Phantom of grisly bone,
I hardly fear its terrible shape,
  It seems so like my own –
  It seems so like my own,
  Because of the fasts I keep;
Oh, God! that bread should be so dear,
  And flesh and blood so cheap!

'Work – work – work!
  My labour never flags;
And what are its wages? A bed of straw,
  A crust of bread – and rags.
That shatter'd roof – and this naked floor –
  A table – a broken chair –
And a wall so blank, my shadow I thank
  For sometimes falling there!

'Work – work – work!
From weary chime to chime,
  Work – work – work –
As prisoners work for crime!
    Band, and gusset, and seam,
    Seam, and gusset, and band,
  Till the heart is sick, and the brain benumb'd,
    As well as the weary hand.

'Work – work – work,
In the dull December light,

67

And work – work – work,
When the weather is warm and bright –
While underneath the eaves
  The brooding swallows cling
As if to show me their sunny backs
  And twit me with the spring.

'Oh! but to breathe the breath
Of the cowslip and primrose sweet –
  With the sky above my head,
And the grass beneath my feet,
For only one short hour
  To feel as I used to feel,
Before I knew the woes of want
  And the walk that costs a meal!

'Oh! but for one short hour!
  A respite however brief!
No blessed leisure for Love or Hope,
  But only time for Grief!
A little weeping would ease my heart,
  But in their briny bed
My tears must stop, for every drop
  Hinders needle and thread!'

With fingers weary and worn,
  With eyelids heavy and red,
A woman sat in unwomanly rags,
  Plying her needle and thread –
    Stitch! stitch! stitch!
  In poverty, hunger, and dirt,
And still with a voice of dolorous pitch, –
Would that its tone could reach the Rich! –
She sang this 'Song of the Shirt'!

FERDINAND FREILIGRATH
1810–76

✳

The revolution

And if that noble savage ye with servile hangmen have
    entrapped,
And if beneath your fortress-wall she goes, by martial
    law's decree,
And if ye long have heaped her mound, where on its
    green at morning red,
The peasant maiden lays her wreath – I say to you, she
    is not dead.

And if from off her lofty brow the lock of tossing hair
    you crop,
And if for comrades ye decree that murderer and thief
    she know,
And if she prison stripes must wear, her hunger sate
    with pulse and peas,
And if she hemp and woollen spins – I tell you plainly,
    she is free!

And if ye hunt her from her home and harry her from
    land to land,
And if she seeks out alien hearths, and dumb in dust and
    ashes sits,
And if, in watercourses far, her feet she bathes in misery,
Yet nevermore her harp will she hang upon Babel's
    willow tree.

Oh, no! she lifts it up in strength, defiantly you to defy,
Laughing, she mocks at banishment as she mocked at the
    scaffold's height!

She sings a song that in dismay will drive ye from your
    seats of pride,
That makes your traitor hearts to beat in your false
    bodies, terrified.

No song of woe, no song of tears, no song of any hero,
    lost,
And even less a song that mocks at this depravèd
    Interlude,
This Beggar's Opera, whose gross scenes full prompt ye
    act, full well ye know:
How moth-eaten those ermine robes, how filthy does
    that purple show!

Oh, no, what she sings to the streams is not her sorrow,
    not disgrace,
But hymns of victory, triumph songs, songs of the future's
    gleaming grace!
The future far away no more! She speaks in daring
    prophecy,
Veraciously, as once your God: I was, I am, and I will be.

Yea, I will be, and in my turn before the people I will
    stride.
Upon your necks, upon your heads, upon your regal
    crowns I'll stamp!
Deliverer, I vengeful wait, and judge, I wait with naked
    sword.
My mighty arm I will stretch out; that arm will liberate
    the world.

Ye see me only in my chains, ye see me only in a grave,
Ye see me only wandering upon the exile's thorny
    ground –
Ye imbeciles! Do I not dwell there where your powers
    ended be?
Behind each forehead, in each heart, is not my place
    prepared for me?

In every head that dares to think? that high, unbowed
    and bold goes forth?
Is my asylum not each breast where fervour dwells,
    where anger strikes?
Not every shop where hammers beat? not every hut
    where misery sighs?
Am I not mankind's ardent breath that endless thirsts for
    liberty?

Hence I will be, and in my hour before the people I will
    stride.
Upon your necks, upon your heads, upon your regal
    crowns I'll stamp!
For this is history's iron law! conceit it is not, threats
    are none.
The day grows hot – how cool your shade, oh willow
    leaves of Babylon.

Honour to labour

He who swings a mighty hammer,
He who reaps a field of corn,
He who breaks the marshy meadow
To provide for wife, for children,
He who rows against the current,
He who weary at the loom
Weaves with wool and tow and flax
That his fair-haired young may flourish,

Honour that man, praise that worker!
Honour every callous hand!
Honour every drop of sweat
That is shed in mill and foundry!
Honour every dripping forehead
At the plough. And let that man
Who with mind and spirit's labour
Hungering ploughs be not forgotten.

EUGÈNE POTTIER
1816–87

✻

The International

TO CITIZEN GUSTAVE LEFRANÇAIS,
MEMBER OF THE COMMUNE
(*To the march tune of Pierre Deygeter*)

Rise up, the curs'd of every nation,
In all your hunger-gaols arise!
The lava-roar of liberation
Erupts at last to storm the skies.
Wipe out the past of want and sorrow;
The house of slavery shall fall,
And we will build a great tomorrow;
We who are nothing shall be all!

There is no saviour high above us,
No judge, no emperor, no God.
We, workers, know the way they love us,
And only we can will our good.
We'll make the robbers yield their plunder
And free the soul of man from gaol.
Our breath shall fan the furnace under
A forge of might that will prevail.

All States and statutes but deceive us.
Their tribute grinds us to the ground.
No duty makes the rich relieve us;
Law for the poor is empty sound.
The voice of Justice ends our anguish:

'No rights where duties none' says she;
'No rightless dues shall have you languish
In endless inequality.'

Obscene in their self-consecration,
The kings of mine and rail and soil
Can find no better occupation
Than living on our blood and toil.
By us their surplus was created,
And we decree it be restored,
Not in their strongrooms dissipated
By bandits of the workshop and the sword.

The kings' foul perfume drugs our senses;
But, Soldiers! Bring the tyrants down!
Break ranks! Surrender their defences
To us and make our cause your own!
If still they reckon to devour us,
Together we'll soon let them know
That their own arsenals empower us
To lay each king and captain low.

We are the party of all labour.
The whole earth shall be ours to share
And every race and craft our neighbour.
No idle class shall linger there
Like vultures on the wealth we render
From field and factory, mill and mine.
Tomorrow's sun will rise in splendour
And light us till the end of time.

    So march, march, the fury
    Of the final fight to find!
    The International's glory
    Belongs to all mankind.

GEORG HERWEGH
1817–75

✳

Up!

Can you break the chains of love
Who the others do not break?
Can you speak to hate in love,
Judge your love for justice's sake?
Must the heart be overthrown
If the will's to rise again?
Heaven, heaven, to right our wrong
Break, break first those ancient chains!
Up! Up!

Heart and love are burst asunder,
Hate and hands, they still are whole!
Lead your sweetheart out in dancing,
Swing your heart, when singing's done.
Prouder will the waves leap, bolder –
Let them dash against hard stone.
Heart, but break, and grow in breaking!
Freedom needs full many a soldier!
Up! Up!

Song of unity for the General Federation of German Trade Unions

'You are many, they are few.'

Prayer and labour, cries the world,
Pray in haste, for time is gold.
Poverty thumps at your door –
Swift your praying, time is bread.

And you weave, and you spin,
And you plough and sow the grain,
And you hammer, and you saw –
Well now, tell me what you gain!

Night and day you serve the loom,
You sweat in coal and iron mine,
You fill *their* horn of plenty high –
It overflows with corn and wine.

And where is your table laid?
And where is your Sunday suit?
Tell me, where's your fireside's warmth?
Say, where is your sword's sharp tooth?

All that's made's your making! Speak!
All, but not a thing for you?
Of the iron that you forge
Are the chains alone your due?

Human bees, has nature only
Given you honey, given you wings?
Those are drones that flock about you!
Has she given you no stings?

Men of labour, rouse you up!
Know the power of your will!
If you raise your mighty arm
Every wheel shall stand still.

Your oppressors' cheeks will pale
When you, weary of the weight,
Lean your plough against the wall,
Cry, 'Enough. The time is late.'

Break and end your double yoke:
Down with slavery of need!
Down with grief of slavery!
Bread is freedom, freedom bread!

WALT WHITMAN
1819–92

*

Europe

The 72d and 73d years of these states[1]

Suddenly out of its stale and drowsy lair, the lair of
    slaves,
Like lightning it le'pt forth half startled at itself,
Its feet upon the ashes and the rags, its hand tight to the
    throats of kings.

O hope and faith!
O aching close of exiled patriots' lives!
O many a sicken'd heart!
Turn back unto this day and make yourselves afresh.
And you, paid to defile the People – you liars, mark!
Not for numberless agonies, murders, lusts,
For court thieving in its manifold mean forms, worming
    from his simplicity the poor man's wages,
For many a promise sworn by royal lips and broken and
    laugh'd at in the breaking.
Then in their power not for all these did the blows strike
    revenge, or the heads of the nobles fall;
The People scorn'd the ferocity of kings.

But the sweetness of mercy brew'd bitter destruction,
    and the frighten'd monarchs come back,
Each comes in state with his train, hangman, priest,
    tax-gatherer,
Soldier, lawyer, lord, jailer, and sycophant.

1. 1848–9, years of revolution in Europe.

Yet behind all lowering stealing, lo, a shape,
Vague as the night, draped interminably, head, front
and form, in scarlet folds,
Whose face and eyes none may see,
Out of its robes only this, the red robes lifted by the arm,
One finger crook'd pointed high over the top, like the
head of a snake appears.

Meanwhile corpses lie in new-made graves, bloody
corpses of young men,
The rope of the gibbet hangs heavily, the bullets of
princes are flying, the creatures of power laugh aloud,
And all these things bear fruits, and they are good.

Those corpses of young men,
Those martyrs that hang from the gibbets, those hearts
pierc'd by the gray lead,
Cold and motionless as they seem live elsewhere with
unslaughter'd vitality.

They live in other young men O kings!
They live in brothers again ready to defy you,
They were purified by death, they were taught and
exalted.

Not a grave of the murder'd for freedom but grows seed
for freedom, in its turn to bear seed,
Which the winds carry afar and re-sow, and the rains
and the snows nourish.

Not a disembodied spirit can the weapons of tyrants let
loose,
But it stalks invisibly over the earth, whispering,
counseling, cautioning.
Liberty, let others despair of you – I never despair of you.
Is the house shut? is the master away?
Nevertheless, be ready, be not weary of watching,
He will soon return, his messengers come anon.

To a foil'd European revolutionaire

Courage yet, my brother or my sister!
Keep on – Liberty is to be subserv'd whatever occurs;
That is nothing that is quell'd by one or two failures,
    or any number of failures,
Or by the indifference or ingratitude of the people, or
    by any unfaithfulness,
Or the show of the tushes of power, soldiers, cannon,
    penal statutes.

What we believe in waits latent forever through all the
    continents,
Invites no one, promises nothing, sits in calmness and
    light, is positive and composed, knows no discourage-
    ment,
Waiting patiently, waiting its time.

(Not songs of loyalty alone are these,
But songs of insurrection also,
For I am the sworn poet of every dauntless rebel the
    world over,
And he going with me leaves peace and routine behind
    him,
And stakes his life to be lost at any moment.)

The battle rages with many a loud alarm and frequent
    advance and retreat,
The infidel triumphs, or supposes he triumphs,
The prison, scaffold, garrote, handcuffs, iron necklace
    and lead-balls do their work,
The named and unnamed heroes pass to other spheres,
The great speakers and writers are exiled, they lie sick in
    distant lands,
The cause is asleep, the strongest throats are choked with
    their own blood,

The young men droop their eyelashes toward the ground
  when they meet;
But for all this Liberty has not gone out of the place, nor
  the infidel enter'd into full possession.
When Liberty goes out of a place it is not the first to go,
  nor the second or third to go,
It waits for all the rest to go, it is the last.

When there are no more memories of heroes and martyrs,
And when all life and all the souls of men and women are
  discharged from any part of the earth,
Then only shall liberty or the idea of liberty be discharged
  from that part of the earth,
And the infidel come into full possession.

Then courage European revolter, revoltress!
For till all ceases neither must you cease.

I do not know what you are for, (I do not know what I am
  for myself, nor what any thing is for,)
But I will search carefully for it even in being foil'd,
In defeat, poverty, misconception, imprisonment – for
  they too are great.

Did we think victory great?
So it is – but now it seems to me, when it cannot be help'd,
  that defeat is great,
And that death and dismay are great.

ERNEST JONES
1819–69

❋

The song of the low

We're low – we're low – we're very, very low,
    As low as low can be;
The rich are high – for we make them so –
    And a miserable lot are we!
    And a miserable lot are we! are we!
    A miserable lot are we!

We plough and sow – we're so very, very low,
    That we delve in the dirty clay,
Till we bless the plain with the golden grain,
    And the vale with the fragrant hay.
Our place we know – we're so very low,
    'Tis down at the landlord's feet:
We're not too low – the bread to grow
    But too low the bread to eat.

We're low – we're low – we're very, very low,
    As low as low can be;
The rich are high – for we make them so –
    And a miserable lot are we!
    And a miserable lot are we! are we!
    A miserable lot are we!

Down, down we go – we're so very, very low
    To the hell of the deep sunk mines.
But we gather the proudest gems that glow,
    When the crown of a despot shines;

And whenever he lacks – upon our backs
    Fresh loads he deigns to lay,
We're far too low to vote the tax
    But we're not too low to pay.

We're low – we're low – we're very, very low,
    As low as low can be;
The rich are high – for we make them so –
    And a miserable lot are we!
    And a miserable lot are we! are we!
    A miserable lot are we!

We're low, we're low – mere rabble, we know,
    But at our plastic power,
The mould at the lordling's feet will grow
    Into palace and church and tower –
Then prostrate fall – in the rich man's hall,
    And cringe at the rich man's door,
We're not too low to build the wall,
    But too low to tread the floor.

We're low – we're low – we're very, very low,
    As low as low can be;
The rich are high – for we make them so –
    And a miserable lot are we!
    And a miserable lot are we! are we!
    A miserable lot are we!

We're low, we're low – we're very, very low,
    Yet from our fingers glide
The silken flow – and the robes that glow,
    Round the limbs of the sons of pride.
And what we get – and what we give,
    We know – and we know our share.
We're not too low the cloth to weave –
    But too low the cloth to wear.

We're low – we're low – we're very, very low,
    As low as low can be;
The rich are high – for we make them so –
    And a miserable lot are we!
    And a miserable lot are we! are we!
    A miserable lot are we!

We're low, we're low – we're very, very low,
    And yet when the trumpets ring,
The thrust of a poor man's arm will go
    Through the heart of the proudest king!
We're low, we're low – our place we know,
    We're only the rank and file,
We're not too low – to kill the foe,
    But too low to touch the spoil.

We're low – we're low – we're very, very low,
    As low as low can be;
The rich are high – for we make them so –
    And a miserable lot are we!
    And a miserable lot are we! are we!
    A miserable lot are we!

GEORG WEERTH
1822–56

✳

The hundred men of Haswell

The hundred men of Haswell,
They died on the selfsame day,
They died upon the selfsame hour,
They died in the selfsame way.

And as they were quietly buried,
A hundred women trudged down,
A hundred women of Haswell wept
For the dead of Haswell town.

They came with their young children,
With sons and daughters also.
'You wealthy master of Haswell town,
Pay us the debt you owe!'

The rich mine-owner of Haswell,
He did not dally long,
He counted out the weekly wage
Of every murdered man.

And when the wage was counted out
He shut his coffer once more.
The bolt of iron clanged and rang;
The women wept full sore.

The cannon moulder

The dew lay heavy on the hills,
The larks there sang in joy,
And there a poor young woman bore
And suckled a poor boy.

Now when he came to sixteen years
The youth grew strong and tall,
And soon he came to work at a forge
With apron and hammer and all.

He rammed the oven in the gut
With heavy iron rods,
And gleaming from the smoke and slag
Sprang forth the metal gods.

It was cannon he cast there – many a one !
They roared on every ocean,
They brought misfortune to the French
And the Indies to subjection.

They hurled hot balls, right heavy, too,
At many a Chinese port,
Exulting in Great Britain's fame
With iron lips and throat.

And ever the lusty hero cast
The thundering weapons of war
Till old age finally tripped him up –
His hands were skilled no more.

Now when his hands refused their task
There was no mercy shown –
They pushed him out into the street
Along with the crippled and poor.

He went – but in such fury he
You'd think in his bosom roared
The thunder of every mortar and gun
That he had ever poured.

Yet he spoke low, 'Not far's the time,
Ye cursed master founders,
When we shall cast for our own sport
The four-and-twenty pounders.'

WILLIAM MORRIS
1834–96

✻

All for the cause

Hear a word, a word in season, for the day is drawing
nigh,
When the Cause shall call upon us, some to live, and
some to die!

He that dies shall not die lonely, many an one hath gone
before;
He that lives shall bear no burden heavier than the life
they bore.

Nothing ancient is their story, e'en but yesterday they
bled.
Youngest they of earth's beloved, last of all the valiant
dead.

E'en the tidings we are telling was the tale they had to
tell,
E'en the hope that our hearts cherish, was the hope for
which they fell.

In the grave where tyrants thrust them, lies their labour
and their pain,
But undying from their sorrow springeth up the hope
again.

Mourn not therefore, nor lament it, that the world
outlives their life;
Voice and vision yet they give us, making strong our
hands for strife.

Some had name, and fame, and honour, learn'd they
    were, and wise and strong;
Some were nameless, poor, unlettered, weak in all but
    grief and wrong.

Named and nameless all live in us; one and all they
    lead us yet
Every pain to count for nothing, every sorrow to forget.

Hearken how they cry, 'O happy, happy ye that ye
    were born
In the sad slow night's departing, in the rising of the
    morn.

'Fair the crown the Cause hath for you, well to die or
    well to live
Through the battle, through the tangle, peace to gain
    or peace to give.'

Ah, it may be! Oft meseemeth, in the days that yet
    shall be,
When no slave of gold abideth 'twixt the breadth of
    sea to sea.

Oft, when men and maids are merry, ere the sunlight
    leaves the earth,
And they bless the day beloved, all too short for all their
    mirth,

Some shall pause awhile and ponder on the bitter days
    of old,
Ere the toil of strife and battle overthrew the curse of
    gold;

Then 'twixt lips of loved and lover solemn thoughts of
    us shall rise;
We who once were fools and dreamers, then shall be the
    brave and wise.

There amidst the world new-builded shall our earthly
  deeds abide,
Though our names be all forgotten, and the tale of
  how we died.

Life or death then, who shall heed it, what we gain or
  what we lose?
Fair flies life amid the struggle, and the Cause for each
  shall choose.

Hear a word, a word in season, for the day is drawing
  nigh,
When the Cause shall call upon us, some to live, and
  some to die!

A death song

What cometh here from west to east awending?
And who are these, the marchers stern and slow?
We bear the message that the rich are sending
Aback to those who bade them wake and know.
Not one, not one, nor thousands must they slay,
But one and all if they would dusk the day.

We asked them for a life of toilsome earning,
They bade us bide their leisure for our bread;
We craved to speak to tell our woeful learning:
We come back speechless, bearing back our dead.
Not one, not one, nor thousands must they slay,
But one and all if they would dusk the day.

They will not learn; they have no ears to hearken.
They turn their faces from the eyes of fate;
Their gay-lit halls shut out the skies that darken.
But, lo! this dead man knocking at the gate.
Not one, not one, nor thousands must they slay,
But one and all if they would dusk the day.

Here lies the sign that we shall break our prison;
Amidst the storm he won a prisoner's rest;
But in the cloudy dawn the sun arisen
Brings us our day of work to win the best.
Not one, not one, nor thousands must they slay,
But one and all if they would dusk the day.

ARTHUR RIMBAUD
1854–91

✳

The hands of Jeanne-Marie

Jeanne-Marie's hands are powerful,
In the summer they get tanned,
They are, like dead hands, pale.
– Is this a lady's hand?

Do they draw their dusky cream tones
From the seas of sensuality?
Are they drenched in moons
In the pools of serenity?

Have they drunk in the atmosphere
While they rested unafraid
On pretty knees? Rolled a cigar
Or dabbled in the diamond trade?

At the zealous feet of Madonnas
Have they flung golden flowers?
Is it the black blood of belladonnas
In their palms that sleeps and glowers?

Do they guide the diptera
Struggling through the bluish dawn
Towards the nectar?
Do they help the poison down?

O what dream has gripped them
In pandiculation?
An unprecedented dream
Of Asia, Khenghavar or Zion?

– These hands have not sold fruit
Or been scorched at the feet of gods:
They have never washed out
The garments of babies with closed eyelids.

These hands don't belong to a cousin, or
To working women with big brows
Burnt with a sun drunk on tar,
Rising from forests stinking of factories.

These are the moulders of the spine,
Hands that never put a finger wrong,
More inexorable than the machine.
As for the horse: twice as strong!

Smouldering like furnaces,
Dismissing all their fears,
Their flesh chants the Marseillaise
But no religious scores.

They will wring your necks, you evil
Women! Noblewomen, their might
Will smash your hands we still
Relate to carmine and to white.

The radiance of these hands of love
Turns the heads of the sheep;
On their sweet divisions the sun above
Places a ruby to sleep.

A mark on the people makes
Them brown like yesterday's breasts;
And it is there on their backs
That every rebel's kiss rests.

Beautifully they whitened once
The sunshine of revolt warmed
The metal of machine-guns
Through Paris as the people armed.

Ah, there are times you sacred fist
When chains of shining links
Weep on your wrist
As our lips drip with drinks.

And, angelic hands, there is a strange new
Impulse in us when they try
To strip the sun from you
And make your fingers bleed and cry.

ÉMILE VERHAEREN
1855–1916

*

The peasants

These men of the soil, those Greuze romanticized
In the pale colours of the rustic scene,
So sprucely dressed and ruddy, we're not surprised
They make a pretty pattern among the saccharine
Of a Louis-Quinze pastel-pampered salon, yet
They are dull, coarse, brutal – all of that.

They stick together as if the village were a pen.
The people in adjacent market-towns are feared
As aliens, intruders, sworn enemies, men
Fit to be cheated, fooled, devoured.
Their country? Come off it! Which one respects the state
That arms their children to defend its lands?
They see nothing of their mother earth in that,
The earth they fertilize with their hands.
Their country? Deep in their fields they remain
Indifferent to it. What attracts these folk
Is a vague image of a man of gold, say Charlemagne,
Sitting in the fringed velvet of his cloak.
All the pomp of swords and crowns hanging
Escutcheoned on the panelled palace wall,
Guarded by soldiers – tasselled sabres clanging –
This is their idea of power. And that's all.
Otherwise their wits, dull on finer points,
Would clump in clogs through duty, right,
Justice, liberty – instinct slows their joints,
A squalid almanac gives them intellectual light.

94

And if they faintly hear the roar
Of revolution spreading from the town
They remain slaves in human conflict for fear
If they rebelled they would be brutally put down.

Towards the future

Mankind, determined on a golden destiny,
Have you questioned what formidable force
Has disturbed your colossal powers
Suddenly, in a century?

The impulse to extend knowledge, to find new ways,
Penetrates the massive forest of being like a novice,
And despite some feet struggling through the bushes
Man masters the limitations of his laws.

In entropy, atoms, and dust
Spectacular life is summoned and appears.
Everything is trapped in the infinity of snares
That immortal matter has expanded or reduced.

Hero, guru, artist, apostle, adventurer,
Each in his turn goes through the black wall of the
    unknown,
Yet thanks to this solitary or collective brain
The new being becomes universally aware.

And it is you, you the cities,
There
At long intervals, from one end to the other
Of plains and estates,
Who contain in you enough humanity
Enough scarlet strength and new clarity
To inspire with fertile rage and fury
The patient or violent minds
Of those

Who remake the rules and impose
Them on the world.

The rural spirit was the spirit of God;
It shrunk from research and revolution,
It failed; and now dies in the shade
Of axle-trees and the fiery harvest of a new solution.

Ruin settles and blows to the four corners
Where winds persist, on the empty plains,
While far away the city extracts as hers
The passion from the agony that remains.

The red factory glitters where once only fields shone;
The floods of black smoke sweep over church tops;
The spirit of man advances and the setting sun
Is no longer the golden host come to bless the crops.

Will the fields exorcised of their errors,
Their blunders, their horrors, some day create
Gardens to reward effort and labours,
And be cups full of health and pure light?

Will they remake, with the necessary sun,
With the wind, the animals and the rain,
At the hours of wakening and beginning, one
World saved at last from the grasp of the town?

Or will they become the last paradise
Rid of gods and their ominous grip,
Where at dawn or noon, before evening clears, the wise
Ones will come and dream before they take their sleep?

Meanwhile, life is complete and strong,
A human unrestrained creation;
And rights? And duties? The arbitrary dreams the
    young
Evolve before the newest aspiration!

J. BRUCE GLASIER
1859–1920

❈

We'll turn things upside down

O, the world is overburdened
With the idle and the rich !
They bask up in the sunshine
While we plod in the ditch ;
But, zounds ! we'll put some mettle
In their fingers and their thumbs,
For we'll turn things upside down, my lads,
When the Revolution comes !

Oh, we'll turn things upside down,
Oh, we'll turn things upside down,
They will wonder what has happened
When we turn things upside down.

Plain living may be wholesome,
And wondrous virtues may
Abound beneath ribs scant of flesh
And pockets scant of pay.
It may be poverty is best
If rightly understood ;
But we'll turn things upside down, my lads !
We don't want all the good !

Oh, we'll turn things upside down,
Oh, we'll turn things upside down,
May they thrive on their philosophy
When we turn things upside down.

They're never done extolling
The nobility of work;
But, the knaves! They always take good care
Their share of toil to shirk,
Do they send their sons and daughters
To the workshop or the mill?
Oh, we'll turn things upside down, my lads,
It will change their tune, it will!

Oh, we'll turn things upside down,
Oh, we'll turn things upside down,
They can practise all their precepts
When we turn things upside down!

They live in splendid mansions,
And we in hovels vile;
Their lives are spent in pleasure,
And ours in cheerless toil;
They jaunt about the world, while we
Are pinned down to one spot;
But we'll turn things upside down, we will!
It's time, lads, is it not?

Oh, we'll turn things upside down,
Oh, we'll turn things upside down,
Life then may be worth living,
When we've turned things upside down!

Then let us, lads, right lustily
Support the glorious cause,
To overturn the whole vile lot
With their lying and their laws.
And let us all together
Put our shoulder to the wheel,
That will turn things upside down, hurrah!
All for the Commonweal.

Oh, we'll turn things upside down,
Oh, we'll turn things upside down,
The world will be far better
When we turn things upside down.

C. P. CAVAFY
1863–1933

❈

Waiting for the barbarians

What are we waiting for, gathered in the market-place?

 The barbarians are to arrive today.

Why so little activity in the Senate?
Why do the Senators sit there without legislating?

 Because the barbarians will arrive today.
 Why should the Senators bother with laws now?
 The barbarians, when they come, will do the legislating.

Why has our emperor risen so early,
and why does he sit at the largest gate of the city
on the throne, in state, wearing the crown?

 Because the barbarians will arrive today.
 And the emperor is waiting to receive
 their leader. He has even prepared
 a parchment for him. There
 he has given him many titles and names.

Why did our two consuls and our praetors go out
today in the scarlet, the embroidered, togas?
Why did they wear bracelets with so many amethysts,
and rings with brilliant sparkling emeralds?
Why today do they carry precious staves
splendidly inlaid with silver and gold?

Because the barbarians will arrive today;
and such things dazzle barbarians.

And why don't the worthy orators come as always
to make their speeches, say what they have to say?

Because the barbarians will arrive today;
and they are bored by eloquence and public speaking.

What does this sudden uneasiness mean,
and this confusion? (How grave the faces have become!)
Why are the streets and squares rapidly emptying,
and why is everyone going back home so lost in thought?

Because it is night and the barbarians have not come,
And some men have arrived from the frontiers
and they say that there are no barbarians any longer.

And now, what will become of us without barbarians? ¿
They were a kind of solution.

RUBÉN DARÍO
1867–1916

❉

To Roosevelt

The voice that would reach you, Hunter, must speak
in Biblical tones, or in the poetry of Walt Whitman.
You are primitive and modern, simple and complex;
you are one part George Washington and one part
  Nimrod.
    You are the United States,
future invader of our native America
with its Indian blood, an America
that still prays to Christ and still speaks Spanish.

You are a strong, proud model of your race;
you are cultured and able; you oppose Tolstoy.
You are an Alexander-Nebuchadnezzar,
breaking horses and murdering tigers.
(You are a Professor of Energy,
as the current lunatics say).

You think that life is a fire,
that progress is an irruption,
that the future is wherever
your bullet strikes.

                    No.

The United States is grand and powerful.
Whenever it trembles, a profound shudder
runs down the enormous backbone of the Andes.
If it shouts, the sound is like the roar of a lion.
And Hugo said to Grant: 'The stars are yours.'

(The dawning sun of the Argentine barely shines;
the star of Chile is rising. . .) A wealthy country,
joining the cult of Mammon to the cult of Hercules;
while Liberty, lighting the path
to easy conquest, raises her torch in New York.

But our own America, which has had poets
since the ancient times of Nezahualcóyotl;
which preserved the footprints of great Bacchus,
and learned the Panic alphabet once,
and consulted the stars; which also knew Atlantis
(whose name comes ringing down to us in Plato)
and has lived, since the earliest moments of its life,
in light, in fire, in fragrance, and in love –
the America of Montezuma and Atahualpa,
the aromatic America of Columbus,
Catholic America, Spanish America,
the America where noble Cuauhtémoc said:
'I am not on a bed of roses' – our America,
trembling with hurricanes, trembling with Love:
O men with Saxon eyes and barbarous souls,
our America lives. And dreams. And loves.
And it is the daughter of the Sun. Be careful.
Long live Spanish America!
A thousand cubs of the Spanish lion are roaming free.
Roosevelt, you must become, by God's own will,
the deadly Rifleman and the dreadful Hunter
before you can clutch us in your iron claws.

And though you have everything, you are lacking one
    thing: God!

HENRIETTE ROLAND HOLST
1869–1952

❋

'Little winding paths . . .'

Little winding paths lead over the moor
and mark the way to the huts of the needy:
theirs is the only token of pity
for those who in loneliness bear their care.

On the moorland wander the hungry sheep;
they look out bleating for another track
towards sweeter herbs and gently rippling beck;
shepherds and dogs are weary and asleep.

In the huts are the people who dumbly yearn
like sheep that know not where to find a meadow;
their thoughts go roaming over the heather,
but find no passage and always return.

The dwellings and the paths stretch far away,
beyond this moorland lies another moor,
people yield up the joyless life of care,
others assume it and all these things stay.

Moorlands fade into the sea; the sea
fades into the sky; and into the whole
endless domain of human pain and toil
fades this despondent haunt of poverty.

Holland

1

Holland, you have cloud trains stately and fleeting
from far fields of the heavens hither flying,
you have horizons in faint circles lying
from eastern sky to western never meeting

a crossing line; and sweeps widely extending
of beaches and of seas around them, surging
onwards to where the heavens with them merging
enhance the illusion of space unending.

The lines of your land, your tidal streams and meres
waken in us unfathomable thoughts,
they lengthen into infinite desiring.
Our eyes sense what is great, we feel a force
that lends a greatness to our minds' aspiring
and hence we are at home in boundless spheres.

2

But when we strive to build what we designed,
where is the wide expanse of endless distance?
In tiny fields by narrow bounds confined
each of us finds his plot, his little existence.

All things impinge on one another here,
our feet lack space in which to wander,
and tremendous shocks experienced yonder
but faintly sway the barges on our mere.

Life to environment conforms in stature:
it here grows dwarfed like plants on barren soil
and no longer knows of its pristine nature.
Gone is the greatness which in dream we find
when once we bear our share of human toil:
Holland, you give no space but to the mind.

MUHAMMAD IQBAL
1873–1938

✳

Lenin before God

All space and all that breathes bear witness; truth
It is indeed; Thou art, and dost remain.
How could I know that God was or was not,
Where Reason's reckonings shifted hour by hour?
The peerer at planets, the counter-up of plants,
Heard nothing there of Nature's infinite music;
Today I witnessing acknowledge realms
That I once thought the mummery of the Church.
We, manacled in the chains of day and night!
Thou, moulder of all time's atoms, builder of aeons!
Let me have leave to ask this question, one
Not answered by the subtleties of the schools,
That while I lived under the sky-tent's roof
Like a thorn rankled in my heart, and made
Such chaos in my soul of all its thoughts
I could not keep my tumbling words in bounds.
Oh, of what mortal race art Thou the God?
Those creatures formed of dust beneath these heavens?
Europe's pale cheeks are Asia's pantheon,
And Europe's pantheon her glittering metals.
A blaze of art and science lights the West
With darkness that no Fountain of Life dispels;
In high-reared grace, in glory and in grandeur,
The towering Bank out-tops the cathedral roof;
What they call commerce is a game of dice:
For one, profit, for millions swooping death.
There science, philosophy, scholarship, government,

Preach man's equality and drink men's blood;
Naked debauch, and want, and unemployment –
Are these mean triumphs of the Frankish arts!
Denied celestial grace a nation goes
No further than electricity or steam;
Death to the heart, machines stand sovereign,
Engines that crush all sense of human kindness.
– Yet signs are counted here and there that Fate,
The chessplayer, has check-mated all their cunning.
The Tavern shakes, its warped foundations crack,
The Old Men of Europe sit there numb with fear;
What twilight flush is left those faces now
Is paint and powder, or lent by flask and cup.
Omnipotent, righteous, Thou; but bitter the hours,
Bitter the labourer's chained hours in Thy world!
When shall this galley of gold's dominion founder?
Thy world Thy day of wrath, Lord, stands and waits.

The voice of Karl Marx

Your chessmatch of research and erudition –
Your comedy of debate and disputation! –
The world has no more patience left to watch
This comedy of threadbare speculation.
What after all, sapient economists,
Is to be found in your biblification?
A comedy of nicely-flowing curves,
A sort of Barmecidal invitation.
In the idolatrous shrines of the Occident,
Its pulpits and its seats of education,
Greed and its murderous crimes are masked under
Your knavish comedy of cerebration.

HAYYIM NAHMAN BIALIK
1873–1934

*

From '*The city of slaughter*'

Leave now this place at twilight to return
And to behold these creatures who arose
In terror at dawn, at dusk now, drowsing, worn
With weeping, broken in spirit, in darkness shut.
Their lips still move with words unspoken.
Their hearts are broken.
No lustre in the eye, no hoping in the mind,
They grope to seek support they shall not find:
Thus when the oil is gone the wick still sends its smoke;
Thus does an old beast of burden still bear its yoke.
Would that misfortune had left them some small solace
Sustaining the soul, consoling their grey hairs!
Behold, the fast is ended; the final prayers are said.
But why do they tarry now, these mournful
    congregations?
Shall it be also read,
The Book of Lamentations?
It is a preacher mounts the pulpit now.
He opens his mouth, he stutters, stammers. Hark
The empty verses from his speaking flow.
And not a single mighty word is heard
To kindle in the hearts a single spark.
The old attend his doctrine, and they nod.
The young ones hearken to his speech; they yawn.
The mark of death is on their brows; their God
Has utterly forsaken every one.

And thou, too, pity them not, nor touch their wound;
Within their cup no further measure pour.
Wherever thou wilt touch, a bruise is found.
Their flesh is wholly sore.
For since they have met pain with resignation
And have made peace with shame,
What shall avail thy consolation?
They are too wretched to evoke thy scorn.
They are too lost thy pity to evoke.
So let them go, then, men to sorrow born,
Mournful and slinking, crushed beneath their yoke.
Go to their homes, and to their hearth depart –
Rot in the bones, corruption in the heart.
And when thou shalt rise upon the morrow
And go upon the highway,
Thou shalt then meet these men destroyed by sorrow,
Sighing and groaning, at the doors of the wealthy,
Proclaiming their sores like so much peddler's wares,
The one his battered head, the other his limbs unhealthy,
One shows a wounded arm, and one a fracture bares.
And all have eyes that are the eyes of slaves,
Slaves flogged before their masters;
And each one begs, and each one craves:
Reward me, Master, for that my skull is broken,
Reward me for my father who was martyred!
The rich ones, all compassion, for the pleas so bartered
Extend them staff and bandage, say 'good riddance' and
The tale is told:
The paupers are consoled.

Away, you beggars, to the charnel-house!
The bones of your father disinter!
Cram them into your knapsacks, bear
Them on your shoulders, and go forth
To do your business with these precious wares
At all the country fairs!
Stop on the highway, near some populous city,
And spread on your filthy rags

Those martyred bones that issue from your bags,
And sing, with raucous voice, your pauper's ditty.
So will you conjure up the pity of the nations,
And so *their* sympathy implore.
For you are now as you have been of yore
And as you stretched your hand so you will stretch it,
And as you have been wretched so are you wretched.

What is thy business here, O son of man?
Rise, to the desert flee!
The cup of affliction thither bear with thee!
Take thou thy soul, rend it in many a shred,
With impotent rage, thy heart deform,
Thy tear upon the barren boulders shed,
And send thy bitter cry into the storm!

ANTONIO MACHADO
1875–1939

❋

The ephemeral past

Habitué of a small-town club, this man
who saw Carancha poised one day
to take the bull,
has a withered skin, hair going grey,
eyes dim with disenchantment, and beneath
the grey moustache, lips bent
in nausea and a look
that's sad – yet sadness it is not
but something more, and less: the void
of the world in the hollow of his head. He still
sports a jacket coloured currant-red
in a three pile velvet, breeches
booted at their extremities and a caramel
Córdoba hat, turned and furbished well.
Three times he inherited, then lost the lot
three times at cards and twice
was widowed. An illegal round of chance
alone will make him brighten
sprawled at the green baize table;
once more the blood begins to flow
as he recollects a gambler's luck
or the afternoon of some torero,
drinks in an episode from the life
of a daring bandit of the road
or the bloody prowess of a knife.
He satirizes with a yawn the government's
reactionary politics and then

predicts the liberals will come to power
again, just as the stork returns to the bell-tower.
Something of a farmer still, he eyes
the heavens, fears them and at times will sigh
thinking of his olives and, disconsolate,
watches for weather-signs when rain is late.
For the rest, boredom. Taciturn, hypochondriac,
shut in the Arcadia of the present,
and to his brow
only the movement of the smoke gives now
its look of thought. This man is neither
of yesterday nor tomorrow
but of never. Hispanic stock, he's not
the fruit that grew to ripen or to rot,
but shadow-fruit
from a Spain that did not come to be,
that passed away, yet, dead,
persists to haunt us with a greying head.

MARUF AL-RUSAFI
1875–1945

*

'Comrade, affairs are in a ferment . . .'

Comrade, affairs are in a ferment; what calamities will
   night and day bring upon us?
Glory be to the Lord of men! Every day He is engaged
   in some almighty enterprise;
The Creator of being, the Glorious, is Pre-Eternal, One –
   in His sight the centuries are but seconds.
All that His Kingdom enfolds is Words by Him spoken,
   and to Him finally reverts every Meaning.
We have today a bubbling of events like the bubbling of
   cooking-pots on stoves.
Surely I perceive the harbingers of a dawn diffusing
   itself over the shadows of desires;
That blood shed in the war is merely a twilight of its
   crimson radiance.
Surely I descry a revolution of the changes of time
   embracing every place,
Whereby the near will appear far, and the far will
   appear near,
And the revered will be other than revered, and the
   despised will be other than despised,
And the weak will become respected as to his right, and
   the tyrant will end in utter loss.
The Pleiades will mount up in security from the
   aggression of Capella and Aldebaran,
And the Milky Way will show forth as a she-camel
   cleaving to her young, the twin stars of Ursa Minor
   drawing near to her Taurus.

The Lord of the heavens and earth will reveal Himself
  to us in His justice and compassion,
And the colonialists will acknowledge defeat, and the
  lands will shine forth in prosperity.
Company of Arabs! Where will you stand amongst the
  people, when Time's revolution is complete?
Asleep, whilst Destiny opens amongst you the two eyes
  of a waker, its day and night?
The people have broken compact with you before this,
  and have made light of keeping it in the taverns;
They have held in contempt their promise and gone back
  on it, and they have exploited the buried treasures of
  the homelands,
And they have established there air-bases to muster arms
  and aircraft.
Then they disseminated spies therein, working mischief
  and corruption in its courtyards and ed ces.
Then they proceeded to rule the country like a ship in
  which they held the rudder.
All this, whilst you are independent – so they allege – by
  grace of themselves.
They have fettered you with treaties for their benefit,
  treaties speaking ostensibly of your interest;
Thereby they have fastened you firmly in bondage, and
  said,
'This is nothing but a kindness to you.'
Those treaties, O people, are simply like treaties of wolves
  with lambs.
Do you not remember how your ancestors were scornful
  when they were treated with misprision?
The day when they rode out, glory accompanying their
  ranks, armed with the ridged Indian sword,
And their banners fluttered on high, in armies to which
  East and West submitted.
So arise today, seeking to renew a glory such as that which
  surpassed the sun and the moon.
Glory has a lofty place in earnest strivings, not to be
  attained by the laggard.

Tell him who seeks to split and divide us, 'You are like
    a goat butting against rocks!
Out upon you! Islam has united us in a unity like the unity
    of the All-Merciful,
And we have laid hold of it by a firm cord, the cord of
    brotherhood and faith.'
The meaning of our unitarian belief in God, our religion,
    is none other than our unification as an entity.
For this, yea, for this, for this we believe in the Unity of
    the Supreme Judge –
A unity not impaired by the successive vicissitudes of ages
    and times,
A unity regarding which there came to us from God a
    Messenger with the Book and the Discrimination,
A unity whereby a God Pre-Eternal, One, has guided us,
    in Whose sight the centuries are as but seconds.
We do not consider that any creature has authority over
    us, only the authority of the Creator of beings.

CARL SANDBURG
1878–1967

❋

The people, yes: 29

The people, yes –
Born with bones and heart fused in deep and violent
    secrets
Mixed from a bowl of sky blue dreams and sea slime
    facts –
A seething of saints and sinners, toilers, loafers, oxen, apes
In a womb of superstition, faith, genius, crime, sacrifice –
The one and only source of armies, navies, work gangs,
The living flowing breath of the history of nations,
Of the little Family of Man hugging the little ball of
    Earth,
And a long hall of mirrors, straight, convex and concave,
Moving and endless with scrolls of the living,
Shimmering with phantoms flung from the past,
Shot over with lights of babies to come, not yet here.

    The honorable orators, the gazettes of thunder,
    The tycoons, big shots and dictators,
    Flicker in the mirrors a few moments
    And fade through the glass of death
    For discussion in an autocracy of worms
While the rootholds of the earth nourish the majestic
    people
And the new generations with names never heard of
Plough deep in broken drums and shoot craps for old
    crowns,

Shouting unimagined shibboleths and slogans,
Tracing their heels in moth-eaten insignia of bawdy
    leaders –
Piling revolt on revolt across night valleys,
Letting loose insurrections, uprisings, strikes,
Marches, mass-meetings, banners, declared resolves,
Plodding in a somnambulism of fog and rain
Till a given moment exploded by long-prepared events –
    Then again the overthrow of an old order
    And the trials of another new authority
    And death and taxes, crops and droughts,
    Chinch bugs, grasshoppers, corn borers, boll weevils,
    Top soil farms blown away in a dust and wind,
    Inexorable rains carrying off rich loam,
    And mortgages, house rent, groceries,
    Jobs, pay cuts, layoffs, relief
    And passion and poverty and crime
    And the paradoxes not yet resolved
    Of the shrewd and elusive proverbs,
    The have-you-heard yarns,
    The listen-to-this anecdote
    Made by the people out of the roots of the earth,
    Out of dirt, barns, workshops, timetables,
    Out of lumberjack payday jamborees,
    Out of joybells and headaches the day after,
    Out of births, weddings, accidents,
    Out of wars, laws, promises, betrayals,
    Out of mists of the lost and anonymous,
    Out of plain living, early rising and spare belongings:

The hammer

I have seen
The old gods go
And the new gods come.

Day by day
And year by year
The idols fall
And the idols rise.

Today
I worship the hammer.

ALEXANDER BLOK
1880–1921

✳

The twelve

I

Darkness – and white
snow hurled
by the wind. The wind!
You cannot stand upright
for the wind: the wind
scouring God's world.

The wind ruffles
the white snow, pulls
that treacherous
wool over the wicked ice.
Everyone out walking
slips. Look – poor thing!

From building to building over
the street a rope skips nimbly,
a banner on the rope – ALL POWER
TO THE CONSTITUENT ASSEMBLY.
This old weeping woman is worried to death,
she doesn't know what it's all about:
that banner – for God's sake –
so many yards of cloth!
How many children's leggings it would make –
and they without shirts – without boots – without . . .

The old girl like a puffed hen picks
her way between drifts of snow.

'Mother of God, these Bolsheviks
will be the death of us, I know!'

Will the frost never lose its grip
or the wind lay its whips aside?
The bourgeois where the roads divide
stands chin on chest, his collar up.

But who's this with the mane
of hair, saying in a
whisper: 'They've sold us down
the river. Russia's down and out.'?
A pen-pusher, no doubt,
a word-spinner . . .

There's someone in a long coat, sidling
over there where the snow's less thick.
'What's happened to your joyful tidings,
Comrade cleric?'

Do you remember the old days:
waddling belly-first to prayer,
when the cross on your belly would blaze
on the faithful there?

A lady in a fur
is turning to a friend:
'We cried our eyes out, dear . . .'
She slips up –
smack! – on her beam end.

Heave ho
and up she rises – so!

The wind rejoices,
mischievous and spry,
ballooning dresses
and skittling passers-by.

It buffets with a shower
of snow the banner-cloth: ALL POWER
TO THE CONSTITUENT ASSEMBLY
and carries voices.

. . . Us girls had a session . . .
. . . in there on the right . . .
. . . had a discussion . . .
. . . carried a motion:
ten for a time, twenty-five for the night . . .
and not a rouble less
from anybody . . . coming up . . . ?

Evening ebbs out.
The crowds decamp.
Only a tramp
potters about.
And the wind screams . . .

Hey you! Hey
chum,
going my way . . . ?

A crust!
What will become
of us? Get lost!

Black sky grows blacker.

Anger, sorrowful anger
seethes in the breast . . .
Black anger, holy anger . . .

Friend!
Keep your eyes skinned!

2

The wind plays up: snow flutters down.
Twelve men are marching through the town.

Their rifle-butts on black slings sway . . .
Lights left, right, left, wink all the way . . .

Cap tilted, fag drooping, every one
looks like a jailbird on the run.

Freedom, freedom,
down with the cross!

Rat-a-tat-tat!

It's cold, boys, and I'm numb!

Johnny and Kate are living it up . . .
She's banknotes in her stocking-top.

John's in the money, too, and how!
He *was* one of us; he's gone over now!

Well, mister John, you son of a whore,
just you kiss my girl once more!

Freedom, freedom,
down with the cross!
Johnny right now is busy with Kate.
What do you think they're busy at?

Rat-a-tat-tat!

Lights left, right, left, lights all the way . . .
Rifles on their shoulders sway . . .

Keep A Revolutionary Step!
The Relentless Enemy Will Not Stop!

Grip your gun like a man, brother!
Let's have a crack at Holy Russia,
Mother
Russia with her big, fat arse!
Freedom, freedom! Down with the cross!

3

The lads have all gone to the wars
to serve in the Red Guard –
to serve in the Red Guard –
and risk their hot heads for the cause.

Hell and damnation,
life is such fun
with a ragged greatcoat
and a Jerry gun!

To smoke the nobs out of their holes
we'll light a fire through all the world,
a bloody fire through all the world –
Lord, bless our souls!

4

The blizzard whirls; a cabby shouts;
away fly Johnny and Kate
with a 'lectric lamp
between the shafts . . .
Hey there, look out!

He's in an Army overcoat,
a silly grin upon his snout.
He's twirling a moustachio,
twirling it about,
joking as they go . . .

Young Johnny's a mighty lover
with a gift of the gab that charms!

He takes her in his arms,
he's talking her over . . .

She throws her head back as they hug
and her teeth are white as pearl . . .
Ah, Kate, my Katey girl,
with your little round mug!

5

Across your collar-bone, my Kate,
a knife has scarred the flesh;
and there below your bosom, Kate,
that little scratch is fresh!

Honey, honey, hey there, what
a pair of legs you've got!

You carried on in lace and furs –
carry on, dear, while you can!
You frisked about with officers –
frisk about, **dear**, while you can!

Honey, honey, swing your skirt!
My heart is knocking at my shirt!

Do you remember that officer –
the knife put an end to him . . .
Do you remember that, you whore,
or does your memory dim?

Honey, honey, let him be!
You've got room in bed for me!

Once upon a time you wore grey spats,
scoffed chocolates in gold foil,
went out with officer-cadets –
now it's the rank and file!

Honey, honey, don't be cruel!
Roll with me to ease your soul!

6

Carriage again and cabby's shout
come storming past: 'Look out! Look out!'

Stop, you, stop! Help, Andy – here!
Cut them off, Peter, from the rear!

Crack – crack – reload – crack – crack – reload!
The snow whirls skyward off the road.

Young Johnny and the cabman run
like the wind. Take aim. Give them one

for the road. Crack – crack! Now learn
. . . .
to leave another man's girl alone!

Running away, you bastard? Do.
Tomorrow I'll settle accounts with you!

But where is Kate? She's dead! She's dead!
A bullet hole clean through her head!

Kate, are you satisfied? Lost your tongue?
Lie in the snow-drift then, like dung!

Keep A Revolutionary Step!
The Relentless Enemy Will Not Stop!

7

Onward the twelve advance,
their butts swinging together,
but the poor killer looks
at the end of his tether.

Fast, faster, he steps out.
Knotting a handkerchief
clumsily round his throat
his hand shakes like a leaf.

What's eating you, my friend?
Why so downhearted, mate?
Come, Pete, what's on your mind?
Still sorry for Kate?

Oh, brother, brother, brother,
I loved that girl . . .
such nights we had together,
me and that girl . . .
For the wicked come-hither
her eyes would shoot at me,
and for the crimson mole
in the crook of her arm,
I shot her in my fury –
like the fool I am . . .

Hey, Peter, shut your trap!
Are you a woman or
are you a man, to pour
your heart out like a tap?
Hold your head up
and take a grip!

This isn't the time now
for me to be your nurse!
Brother, tomorrow
will be ten times worse!

And shortening his stride,
slowing his step,
Peter lifts his head
and brightens up . . .

What the hell!
It's not a sin to have some fun!

Put your shutters up, I say –
There'll be broken locks today!

Open your cellars: quick, run down . . . !
The scum of the earth are hitting the town!

8

My God, what a life!
I've had enough!
I'm bored.

I'll scratch my head
and dream a dream . . .

I'll chew my quid
to pass the time . . .

I'll swig enough
to kill my drought . .

I'll get my knife
and slit your throat!

Fly away, mister, like a starling,
before I drink your blue veins dry
for the sake of my poor darling
with her dark and roving eye . . .

Blessed are the dead which die in the Lord . . .

I'm bored!

9

Out of the city spills no noise,
the prison tower reigns in peace.

'We've got no booze but cheer up, boys,
we've seen the last of the police!'

The bourgeois where the roads divide,
stands chin on chest, his collar up:
mangy and flea-bitten at his side
shivers a coarse-haired mongrel pup.

The bourgeois with a hangdog air
stands speechless, like a question mark,
and the old world behind him there
stands with its tail down in the dark.

10

Still the storm rages gust upon gust.
What weather! What a storm!
At arm's length you can only just
make out your neighbour's form.

Snow twists into a funnel,
a towering tunnel.

'Oh, what a blizzard! . . . Jesus Christ!'
Watch it, Pete, cut out that rot!
What did Christ and his bloody cross
ever do for the likes of us?
Look at your hands. Aren't they still hot
with the blood of the girl you shot?

Keep A Revolutionary Step!
The Enemy Is Near And Won't Let Up!

Forward, and forward again
the working men!

11

Abusing God's name as they go,
all twelve march onward into snow . . .
prepared for anything,
regretting nothing . . .

Their rifles at the ready
for the unseen enemy
in back streets, side roads
where only snow explodes
its shrapnel, and through quag-
mire drifts where the boots drag . . .

before their eyes
throbs a red flag.

Left, right,
the echo replies.

Keep your eyes skinned
lest the enemy strike!

Into their faces day and night
bellows the wind
without a break . . .

Forward, and forward again
the working men!

12

On they march with sovereign tread . . .
Who else goes there? Come out! I said
come out! It is the wind and the red
flag plunging gaily at their head.

The frozen snow-drift looms in front . . .
Who's in the drift? Come out! Come here!

There's only the homeless mongrel runt
limping wretchedly in the rear.

You mangy beast, out of the way
before you taste my bayonet.
Old mongrel world, clear off I say!
I'll have your hide to sole my boot!

The shivering cur, the mongrel cur
bares his teeth like a hungry wolf,
droops his tail, but does not stir.
Hey, answer, you there, show yourself.

Who's that waving the red flag?
Try and see! It's as dark as the tomb!
Who's that moving at a jog
trot, keeping to the back-street gloom?

Don't you worry – I'll catch you yet;
better surrender to me alive!
Come out, comrade, or you'll regret
it – we'll fire when I've counted five!

Crack – crack – crack! But only the echo
answers from among the eaves . . .
The blizzard splits his seams, the snow
laughs wildly up the whirlwind's sleeve.

Crack – crack – crack!
Crack – crack – crack!

. . . So they march with sovereign tread . . .
Behind them limps the hungry dog,
and wrapped in wild snow at their head
carrying a blood-red flag –
soft-footed where the blizzard swirls,
invulnerable where bullets crossed –
crowned with a crown of snowflake pearls,
a flowery diadem of frost,
ahead of them goes Jesus Christ.

LU HSÜN
1881–1936

✳

For a forgotten memory

A habit now – to spend spring in this eternal night,
In exile, with wife, child and greying temples.
In dreams, I dimly see my mother's tears,
On battlements, ever-changing, lords' banners.
With sorrow, I watch friends become new ghosts;
In anger, I look for ballads among bushes of bayonets.
Then I lower my eyes and find nowhere to write
Save, on my black robe, in bright moonlight.

Autumn 1935

Startled by the awe of autumn that reigns over the earth,
Dare I instil the warmth of spring into the tip of my pen?
In this vast sea of dust a hundred feelings have sunk;
In the rustling wind a thousand officials have fled.
In old age, I return to the lake, only to find no reeds on
    which to rest;
On vacant clouds, my dreams fall; a chill numbs hair
    and teeth.
My longings for cockcrow in the wilderness encounter
    only silence.
I rise to watch the setting constellations.

ALEKSEI GASTEV
1882–1941

✻

We grow out of iron

Look! Here I stand: among lathes, hammers, furnaces and forges – among hundreds of comrades.

There are iron-forged spaces above me.

Girders and angle-bars on the sides,

Rising seventy-five feet,

Bending right and left.

They are tied to the cupola rafters, and like a giant's shoulders, support the whole, iron frame.

They are impetuous, sweeping, strong.

They require a still greater strength.

I look at them and I stand straighter.

New iron blood pours into my veins.

And I'm growing taller.

Steel shoulders and immeasurably strong arms grow out from me. I merge with the building's iron.

Then I stretch myself.

With my shoulders I push out the rafters, the highest girders and the roof.

My feet are still on the ground, but my head is above the building.

I'm out of breath from this superhuman effort, but I'm already shouting:

'I ask for the floor, Comrades! For the floor!'

The iron echo has drowned my words; the whole structure is trembling with impatience. And I've risen still higher, I'm even with the smokestacks.

And I'm going to shout – not a story, not a speech, but one single iron phrase:

'The victory will be ours!'

ISHIKAWA TAKUBOKU
1885–1912

❀

A clenched fist

Pitied by a friend richer than I,
or ridiculed by a friend stronger than I,
I swing up my clenched fist – only
to find an angerless heart
squatting in a corner of the angry heart
quietly like a criminal
blinking its eyes –
and that helplessness!

O that helplessness!

Whom are you going to strike
with that fist of yours
which you do not know what to do with? –
your friend, or yourself,
or a blameless pillar beside you?

After an endless discussion

The way we read, the way we discuss,
And the way our eyes shine
Match the young in Russia fifty years ago.
We discuss what we should do.
But, there is no one who with a clenched fist bangs on
    the table
And declares: 'VNARÓD'[1]

> 1. The Russian slogan, 'To the people'.

We know what we are seeking after;
We know what the people are seeking after;
And we know what we should do.
We know more than the young in Russia fifty years ago.
But, there is no one who with a clenched fist bangs on
the table
And declares: 'V NARÓD'

They are the young who gather here;
They are the young who always give the world what is
new.
We all knew that the old would die soon, and victory
would be ours.
Behold, how our eyes are shining and how hot is our
discussion!
But there is no one who with a clenched fist bangs on the
table
And declares: 'V NARÓD'

Ah, though the candles were already replaced three
times,
And the bodies of small bird-lice float in the tea-cups,
And young ladies are as eager as they ever were,
There is tiredness in their eyes after a long discussion.
And yet, there is no one who with a clenched fist bangs
on the table,
And declares: 'V NARÓD'

SAMUEL MARSHAK
1887–1964

＊

A minister of the disarmament conference

Peace-loving Stassen who appears so pious
Is most inflammable and could well fry us.
He wears an olive branch in his lapel,
But sits on bombs like some hen doing well
In her present condition. Still he can
Consider any disarmament plan.

HUDDIE LEDBETTER
1889–1949

✻

Bourgeois blues

Look a here people, Listen to me,
Don't try to find no home down in Washington D.C.

  Lord it's a bourgeois town
  Ooh, it's a bourgeois town
  I got the Bourgeois Blues
  I'm gonna spread the news all around.

Me and Martha was standin' upstairs,
I heard a white man say, 'Don't want no coloured up
    there.'

  Lord it's a bourgeois town
  Ooh, it's a bourgeois town
  I got the Bourgeois Blues
  I'm gonna spread the news all around.

Home of the brave, land of the free –
I don't want to be mistreated by no bourgeoisie.

  Lord it's a bourgeois town
  Ooh, it's a bourgeois town
  I got the Bourgeois Blues
  I'm gonna spread the news all around.

White folks in Washington, they know how,
Throw a coloured man a nickel to see him bow.

136

Lord it's a bourgeois town
Ooh, it's a bourgeois town
I got the Bourgeois Blues
I'm gonna spread the news all around.

Tell all the coloured folks to listen to me,
Don't try to find a home in Washington D.C.

Lord it's a bourgeois town
Ooh, it's a bourgeois town
I got the Bourgeois Blues
I'm gonna spread the news all around.

VERA INBER
b. 1890

❉

It will come to pass

Inevitably, years will pass by, filing –
A long, long row.
Into one orchard city, asphalt beehive,
All cities will grow.

Beautiful roses planted on glass roof-tops
Will flourish, too.
But we – alas ! – will neither see nor hear it ;
Not I, nor you.

Despite all this, it's easy to imagine
This city and
Its greenery, framed in sunlight's brilliance,
In all men's land.

There'll be a statue centred in a certain
Square's octagon,
Constructed so the sunset's gold spills, streaming
Onto the jacket's bronze.

All kinds of little children go there, happy,
Mindless of care.
Glowing, they send their smiles into the rich sunset
To him who towers there.

A mother lifts her baby to the stone steps
And watching sunbeams piled
Above them utters softly, 'This is Lenin,
My child.'

ERICH WEINERT
1890–1953

✼

Song of the paving stones

Full hundred thousand years we slept
As granite, cold as ice,
Then we were roused by dynamite
And turned into merchandise.

In the quarry, the labourer moaned aloud,
His chisel spurted fire,
The labourer's blood and sweat have we
Drunk down into our core.

We were pounded down in an avenue,
The labourer pounded us down.
His sweat dropped down. His sweat dried up,
But the salt is in the stone.

Then over us rolled all things that roll,
Carts, trucks and limousines,
And yet we felt in our breasts of stone
The heart of the working man.

One day a thousand tramping feet
Roared up in demonstration –
The workers sang, and oh, we clanged –
Our stony foreheads kindled.

Then shots banged into our pitted heads
And dirt and fire rained –
The blood and brains of the workingman –
We drank down the blood that drained.

They tore us up out of the road –
Then were we barricades!
We heard the worker load his gun
And the clamour of his rage.

And once again dirt rained and fire;
We guarded our brothers – with back's
And stony body's strength
We beat down the attack.

The blood of the workers pounds in stone,
It flows in our hearts; aye, brave
We'll stand, the trophy of victory
Upon our comrade's graves!

NELLY SACHS
b. 1891

✳

To you that build the new house

' There are stones like souls.' Rabbi Nachman

When you come to put up your walls anew –
Your stove, your bedstead, table and chair –
Do not hang your tears for those who departed,
Who will not live with you then,
On to the stone.
Nor on the timber –
Else weeping will pierce the sleep,
The brief sleep you have yet to take.

Do not sigh when you bed your sheets,
Else your dreams will mingle
With the sweat of the dead.

Oh, the walls and household utensils
Are responsive as Aeolian harps
Or like a field in which your sorrow grows,
And they sense your kinship with dust.

Build, when the hourglass trickles,
But do not weep away the minutes
Together with the dust
That obscures the light.

You onlookers

Whose eyes watched the killing.
As one feels a stare at one's back
You feel on your bodies
The glances of the dead.

How many dying eyes will look at you
When you pluck a violet from its hiding place?
How many hands be raised in supplication
In the twisted martyr-like branches
Of old oaks?
How much memory grows in the blood
Of the evening sun?

O the unsung cradlesongs
In the night cry of the turtledove –
Many a one might have plucked stars from the sky,
Now the old well must do it for them!

You onlookers,
You who raised no hand in murder,
But who did not shake the dust
From your longing,
You who halted there, where dust is changed
To light.

If I only knew

If I only knew
On what your last look rested.
Was it a stone that had drunk
So many last looks that they fell
Blindly upon its blindness?

Or was it earth,
Enough to fill a shoe,
And black already
With so much parting
And with so much killing?

Or was it your last road
That brought you a farewell from all the roads
You had walked?

A puddle, a bit of shining metal,
Perhaps the buckle of your enemy's belt,
Or some other small augury
Of heaven?

Or did this earth,
Which lets no one depart unloved,
Send you a bird-sign through the air,
Reminding your soul that it quivered
In the torment of its burnt body?

OSIP MANDELSTAMM
1891–1938

※

Notre Dame

Where Roman judges tried an alien people
A basilica stands. Being first and joyful
(As Adam was once), stretching out its nerve-endings,
The vault, shaped like a cross, plays with its muscles.

Outside, the secret plan betrays its purpose:
For here the tightening arches' strength took measures
So walls would not be crushed by heavy masses,
So that the bold vault's rams would be more static.

A primal labyrinth, an unknown forest,
A reasoned chasm of the Gothic Spirit,
Egyptian power with a Christian shyness,
Next to oaks, reeds – and the plumb, the king always.

And so the more attentively I studied
Your monstrous ribs, O Notre Dame, O fortress,
The more often I thought: I, too, from ugly
Harsh heaviness shall build a shining Beauty.

'Nature equates with Rome. . .'

Nature equates with Rome – and is reflected in it.
We see its images of civic power revealed
In the transparent air as in blue Colosseums,
In columnades of groves, in the forum of a field.

Nature equates with Rome and it would seem to follow
We have no reason now to bother gods: from spilled
Entrails of sacrifices there is war predicted,
There are slaves to be silent – and stones from which to
  build!

'Brothers, let's glorify the twilight of freedom'

Brothers, let's glorify the twilight of freedom,
The great crepuscular year.
A heavy forest of nets has been dropped
Into the seething waters of the night.
You are rising during gloomy years,
O sun and judge, O people.

Let's glorify the destined burden
Which the people's leader tearfully assumes.
Let's glorify the sombre burden of power,
Its unbearable yoke.
He who has a heart, O time,
Must hear your ship sinking to the depths.

We have bound swallows
Into fighting legions, and now
We cannot see the sun; this entire element
Is chirping, stirring, living;
Through the mesh, the thick twilight,
We cannot see the sun and the land floats away.

Well then, let's try: an enormous, clumsy,
Creaking turn of the rudder.
The land floats away. Courage, men.
Cleaving the ocean as with a plough,
We shall remember even in Lethe's cold
That Earth cost us as much as ten heavens.

My age

My age, my beast, who will be able
To look into the pupils of your eyes –
And with his own blood cement
The vertebrae of two centuries?
Blood that builds gushes through the throat
Of things upon the earth;
Only a parasite trembles
On the threshold of new days.

A creature, as long as it has enough
Life left, must carry its backbone;
And any wave plays
With an invisible spine.
This age of the infant earth
Is like a baby's tender cartilage,
And once again the cranium of life
Has been sacrified like a lamb.

In order to tear life out of captivity
And start a new world,
One must tie the knotty elbows
Of days together with a flute.
It is the age that rocks
The wave with human anguish,
And a viper in the grass
Breathes in gold measures of the age.

The buds will swell again,
And the sprouts will burst.
But your spine has been shattered,
My beautiful, pitiful age.
And you look back, cruel and weak,
With a senseless smile,
Like a beast that was once supple,
At the tracks of your own paws.

'We exist in a country grown unreal and strange'[1]

We exist in a country grown unreal and strange;
No one ten steps away hears the talk we exchange.
But when chances for half-conversations appear,
We will never omit the Kremlin mountaineer.

Each thick finger, a fattened worm, gesticulates,
And his words strike you like they were many-pound
   weights.
His full cockroach moustache hints a laughter benigning,
And the shafts of his boots: always spotlessly shining.

And the gang of thick-skinned leaders near him obeys;
Semi-humans are at his disposal always.
Decree after decree he incessantly coins
Which hit people on foreheads, eyebrows, eyes and groins.

He possesses the broad chest, a Georgian perfection,
And each new death for him is a berry confection.

1. Mandelstamm's satire of Stalin which led to his arrest and exile
to a concentration camp.

YI KWANG-SU

b. 1892

*

A wind-flower

The ruined grave by the barley field
Must be the tomb of a farmer
Who once lived in that hut.

A wind-flower is there,
With neck bent down.

O the field he once lived in!
O the barley he once loved!
Green and yellow,
Many a spring must have passed.

This spring too
The barley is green,
The wind-flower is in bloom.
The vegetable-knives
In his children's hands
Are spattered with mud.

O the perpetual spring in country villages!
O the life that flows on and on!

HO CHI-MINH
1892–1969

*

The leg-irons

1

With hungry mouth open like a wicked monster,
Each night the irons devour the legs of people:
The jaws grip the right leg of every prisoner:
Only the left is free to bend and stretch.

2

Yet there is one thing stranger in this world:
People rush in to place their legs in irons.
Once they are shackled, they can sleep in peace.
Otherwise they would have no place to lay their heads.

Advice to oneself

Without the cold and desolation of winter
There could not be the warmth and splendour of spring.
Calamity has tempered and hardened me,
And turned my mind into steel.

Restrictions

To live without freedom is a truly wretched state.
Even the calls of nature are governed by restrictions!

When the door is opened, the belly is not ready to ease
   itself.
When the call of nature is pressing, the door remains
   shut.

On reading 'Anthology of a Thousand Poets'

The ancients used to like to sing about natural beauty:
Snows and flowers, moon and wind, mists, mountains,
   and rivers.
Today we should make poems including iron and steel,
And the poet also should know how to lead an attack.

CÉSAR VALLEJO
1892–1938

✳

'*The anger that breaks man into children . . .*'

The anger that breaks man into children,
that breaks child into equal birds,
and bird, after, into little eggs;
the anger of the poor
has one oil against two vinegars.

The anger that breaks tree into leaves,
leaf into unequal buds
and bud into telescopic grooves;
the anger of the poor
has two rivers against many seas.

The anger that breaks good into doubts,
doubt into three similar arcs
and arc, then, into unforeseeable tombs;
the anger of the poor
has one steel against two daggers.

The anger that breaks soul into bodies,
body into dissimilar organs
and organ into thought eights;
the anger of the poor
has a central fire against two craters.

The nine monsters

And, unfortunately,
pain grows in the world every moment,
grows thirty minutes a second, step by step,
and the nature of the pain is the pain twice
and the condition of the voracious carnivorous
    martyrdom
the pain, twice
and the function of the very pure grass, the pain twice
and the good of being, to bend us double.

Never, human men,
was there so múch pain in the chest, in the lapel, in
    the wallet,
in the glass, in the butcher's, in arithmetic!
Never so múch painful tenderness,
never did what is far rush so close,
never did the fire ever
play better its role of dead cold!
Never, mister minister of health, was health
more mortal,
did the migraine extract so múch forehead from the
    forehead!
did furniture have in its drawer, pain,
the heart in its drawer, pain,
the newt in its drawer, pain.

The wretchedness grows, man brothers,
sooner than the machine, than ten machines, and it grows
with the cattle-head of Rousseau, with our beards;
evil grows for reasons we know not
and is a flood with its own liquids,
its own clay, its own solid cloud!
Suffering inverts positions, stages shows
in which the watery humour is vertical
to the pavement,

the eye is seen and this ear heard,
and this ear strikes nine times at the hour
of lightning, nine funhouse roars
at the hour of wheat, nine female sounds
at the hour of weeping, nine canticles
at the hour of hunger, nine thunders
nine whips, minus a cry.

The pain grabs us, man brothers,
from behind, in profile,
and drives us crazy in the movies,
nails us up on the gramophones,
pries us loose in bed, falls perpendicularly
to our tickets, to our letters;
and it is very serious to suffer, one can pray ...
So because
of the pain there are some
who get born, others grow, others die,
and others that get born and don't die and others
who without having been born die and others
who neither get born nor die (The majority).
And likewise because
of the suffering I'm sad
to my head and sadder to my ankle
seeing bread crucified, the turnip
bloodsmeared,
weeping, the onion,
cereal, in general, flour,
salt turned dust, water fleeing,
wine an Ecce-homo,
the snow so pallid, such a red red sun!
How, human brothers,
not to tell you that I can't stand anymore and
I can't stand anymore with so múch drawer,
So múch minute, so múch
newt and so
múch inversion, so múch far, so múch thirst for more
    thirst!

Mister Minister of Health: what to do?
Ah! unfortunately, human men,
brothers, there is much too much to do.

'A man walks by with a loaf of bread on his shoulder'

A man walks by with a loaf of bread on his shoulder.
I'm going to write, after that, about my double?

Another sits, scratches, gets a louse out of his armpit,
cracks it. How dare one speak about psychoanalysis?

Another has entered my chest with a stick in his hand.
After that chat with the doctor about Socrates?

A cripple walks by arm in arm with a child.
After that I'm going to read André Breton?

Another shakes from cold, hacks, spits blood.
Is it possible to even mention the profound I?

Another searches in the mud for bones, rinds.
How write after that about the infinite?

A bricklayer falls from the roof, dies, and no longer
eats lunch.
After that innovate the trope, the metaphor?

A merchant cheats a customer out of a gram.
After that talk about the fourth dimension?

A banker falsifies his balance.
With what face to cry in the theatre?

An outcast sleeps with his foot behind his back.
After that, not talk about Picasso?

Someone goes to a burial sobbing.
How then enter the Academy?

Someone cleans a rifle in his kitchen.
How dare one speak about the beyond?

Someone walks by counting on his fingers.
How speak of the not-I without crying out?

'Another touch of calm, comrade'

Another touch of calm, comrade;
an immense northern complete ferocious
much of small calm,
in less service each triumph
facing the daring servitude of the disaster.

You've highs to spare, and there's not
so much madness in the mind, as in this
your muscular reasoning, and there's no
more rational error than your experience.

But, speaking more clear
and thinking it in gold, you are steel
on condition you are not
stupid and refuse to
delight because of death truly
and because of life, in your one tomb.

You must learn to
contain your volume without running, without hanging
    yourself up,
your entire molecular reality –
and beyond that, the march of your 'vivas'
and closer home, your legendary 'down withs'.

You are steel, as they say,
providing you don't tremble and don't
explode, godbrother
of my calculation, emphatic godson
of my luminous salts!

Go right ahead; solve,
consider your crisis, add, carry,
trim it, diminish it, crumple it up;
destiny, the intimate energies, the fourteen
versicles of bread; how many diplomas
and powers at the authentic brink of your start!
How múch detail in synthesis with you!
How múch identical pressure at your feet!
How múch rigidity and how much patronage!

It's idiotic
that method of enduring,
that modulated virulent light,
if with only the calm you flash serious
signs, fatal characteristics.

Let's see, man;
let me know what's happening to me,
for I'm always, even though I shout, at your command.

The wretched of the Earth

The day's going to come; wind
up your arm, look under
your mattress, stand again
on your head to walk straight.
The day's going to come, put on your coat.

The day's going to come; grip
your large intestine tight in your hand, reflect

before you meditate, for it's awful
when your wretchedness hits and sinks
on and on in you a tooth.

    You have to eat, but I keep telling myself
don't grieve, for grief and graveside
sobbing don't belong to the poor;
pull yourself together, remember,
confide in your white thread, smoke, check
your chain and keep it behind your portrait.
The day's going to come, put on your soul.

    The day's going to come; they pass,
they've opened up an eye in the hotel
whipping and beating it with a mirror that's yours . . .
are you trembling? It's the remote state of the forehead
and this recent nation of the stomach.
They're still snoring. . . . What universe puts up with
    this snore!
How your pores hang on, indicting it!
With so many twos, ay! you're so alone!
The day's going to come, put on your dream.

    The day's going to come, I repeat
through the oral organ of your silence
and urge you to move further left with hunger
further right with thirst; in any case
stop being poor with the rich,
poker
your cold, for in it is mixed my warmth, beloved victim.
The day's going to come, put on your body.

    The day's going to come;
morning, sea, meteor
pursue your weariness with banners,
and through your classic pride, the hyenas
count their steps to the beat of the ass,
the baker's wife thinks about you,

the butcher thinks about you, fingering
the cleaver in which steel
iron and metal are imprisoned; never forget
that during Mass there are no friends.
The day's going to come, put on your sun.

   The day comes; double
your breathing, triple
your rancorous goodwill
and elbow fear, link and emphasis,
for you, as anyone can see in your crotch the evil
being, ay! immortal,
you've dreamed tonight you were living
on nothing and dying from everything . . .

HUGH MACDIARMID
b. 1892

✻

The skeleton of the future

Red granite and black diorite, with the blue
Of the labradorite crystals gleaming like precious stones
In the light reflected from the snow; and behind them
The eternal lightning of Lenin's bones.

Second hymn to Lenin

Ah, Lenin, you were richt. But I'm a poet
(And you cu'd mak allowances for that!)
Aimin' at mair than you aimed at
Tho' yours comes first, I know it.

An unexamined life is no' worth ha'in'.
Yet Burke was richt; owre muckle concern
Wi' Life's foundations is a sure
Sign o' decay; tho' Joyce in turn

Is richt, and the principal question
Aboot a work o' art is frae hoo deep
A life it springs – and syne hoo faur
Up frae't it has the poo'er to leap.

And hoo muckle it lifts up wi' it
Into the sunlicht like a saumon there,
Universal Spring! for Morand's richt –
It su'd be like licht in the air –

159

Are my poems spoken in the factories and fields,
  In the streets o' the toon?
Gin they're no', then I'm failin' to dae
  What I ocht to ha' dune.

Gin I canna win through to the man in the street,
  The wife by the hearth,
A' the cleverness on earth'll no' mak' up
  For the damnable dearth.

'Haud on, haud on; what poet's dune that?
  Is Shakespeare read,
Or Dante or Milton or Goethe or Burns?'
  — You heard what I said.

— A means o' world locomotion,
The maist perfected and aerial o' a'.
Lenin's name's gane owre the haill earth,
But the names o' the ithers? — Ha!

What hidie-hole o' the vineyard d'they scart
Wi' minds like the look on a hen's face,
Morand, Burke, Joyce, and the rest
That e'er wrote; me noo in like case?

Great poets hardly onybody kens o'?
Geniuses like a man talkin' t'm sel'?
Nonsense! They're nocht o' the sort.
Their character's easy to tell.

They're nocht but romantic rebels
Strikin' dilettante poses;
Trotsky — Christ, no' wi' a croon o' thorns
But a wreath o' paper roses.

A' that's great is free and expansive.
What ha' they expanded tae?
They've affected nocht but a fringe
O' mankind in ony way.

Barbarian saviour o' civilization
Hoo weel ye kent (we're owre dull witted)
Naething is dune save as we ha'e
Means to en's transparently fitted.

Poetry like politics maun cut
The cackle and pursue real ends,
Unerringly as Lenin, and to that
Its nature better tends.

Wi' Lenin's vision equal poet's gift
And what unparalleled force was there!
Nocht in a' literature wi' that
Begins to compare.

Nae simple rhymes for silly folk
But the haill art, as Lenin gied
Nae Marx-withoot-tears to workin' men
But the fu' course insteed.

Organic constructional work,
Practicality, and work by degrees;
First things first; and poetry in turn
'll be built by these.

You saw it faur off when you thocht
O' mass-education yet.
Hoo lang till they rise to Pushkin?
And that's but a fit!

>   *Oh, it's nonsense, nonsense, nonsense,*
>   *Nonsense at this time o' day*
>   *That bried-and-butter problems*
>   *Su'd be in ony man's way.*
>
>   *They su'd be like the tails we tint*
>   *On leavin' the monkey stage;*
>   *A' maist folk fash aboot's alike*
>   *Primaeval to oor age.*

We're grown-up folk that haena yet
Put bairnly things aside
– A' that's material and moral –
And oor new state descried.

Sport, love, and parentage,
Trade, politics, and law
S'ud be nae mair to us than braith
We hardly ken we draw.

Freein' oor poo'ers for greater things,
And fegs there's plenty o' them
Tho' wha's still trammelt in alow
Canna be tenty o' them –

In the meantime Montéhus' sangs –
But as you were ready to tine
The Russian Revolution to the German
Gin that ser'd better syne,

Or foresaw that Russia maun lead
The workers' cause, and then
Pass the lead elsewhere, and aiblins
Fa' faur backward again,

Sae here, twixt poetry and politics,
There's nae doot in the en'.
Poetry includes that and s'ud be
The greatest poo'er among men.

– It's the greatest, *in posse* at least,
That men ha'e discovered yet
Tho' nae doot they're unconscious still
O' ithers faur greater than it.

You confined yoursel' to your work
– A step at a time;
But, as the loon is in the man,
That'll be ta'en up in the rhyme,

Ta'en up like a pool in the sands
Aince the tide rows in,
When life opens its hert and sings
Withoot scruple or sin.

Your knowledge in your ain sphere
Was exact and complete
But your sphere's elementary and sune by
As a poet maun see't.

For a poet maun see in a' thing,
Even what looks trumpery or horrid,
A subject equal to ony
– A star for the foreheid!

A poet has nae choice left
Betwixt Beaverbrook, say, and God,
Jimmy Thomas or you,
A cat, carnation, or clod.

He daurna turn awa' frae ocht
For a single act o' neglect
And straught he may fa' frae grace
And be void o' effect.

> *Disinterestedness,*
> *Oor profoundest word yet,*
> *But hoo faur yont even that*
> *The sense o' onything's set!*
>
> *The inward necessity yont*
> *Ony laws o' cause*
> *The intellect conceives*
> *That a'thing has!*

Freend, foe; past, present, future;
Success, failure; joy, fear;
Life, Death; and a'thing else,
For us, are equal here.

Male, female; quick or deid,
Let us fike nae mair;
The deep line o' cleavage
Disnae lie there.

> *Black in the pit the miner is,*
> *The shepherd reid on the hill,*
> *And I'm wi' them baith until*
> *The end of mankind, I wis.*

> *Whatever their jobs a' men are ane*
> *In life, and syne in daith*
> *(Tho' its sma' patience I can ha'e*
> *Wi' life's ideas o' that by the way)*
> *And he's no poet but kens it, faith,*
> *And ony job but the hardest's ta'en.*

> *The sailor gangs owre the curve o' the sea.*
> *The hoosewife's thrang in the wash-tub,*
> *And whatna rhyme can I find but hub,*
> *And what else can poetry be?*

> *The core o' a' activity,*
> *Changin't in accordance wi'*
> *Its inward necessity*
> *And mede o' integrity.*

Unremittin', relentless,
Organized to the last degree,
Ah, Lenin, politics is bairns' play
To what this maun be!

5 *In the children's hospital*

'*Does it matter? Losing your legs?*' Siegfried Sassoon

Now let the legless boy show the great lady
How well he can manage his crutches.

It doesn't matter though the Sister objects,
'He's not used to them yet', when such is
The will of the Princess. Come, Tommy,
Try a few desperate steps through the ward.
Then the hand of Royalty will pat your head
And life suddenly cease to be hard.
For a couple of legs are surely no miss
When the loss leads to such an honour as this!
One knows, when one sees how jealous the rest
Of the children are, it's been all for the best! –
But would the sound of your sticks on the floor
Thundered in her skull for evermore!

Lo! A child is born

I thought of a house where the stones seemed suddenly
    changed
And became instinct with hope, hope as solid as
    themselves,
And the atmosphere warm with that lovely heat,
The warmth of tenderness and longing souls, the smiling
    anxiety
That rules a home where a child is about to be born.
The walls were full of ears. All voices were lowered.
Only the mother had the right to groan or complain.
Then I thought of the whole world. Who cares for its
    travail
And seeks to encompass it in like lovingkindness and
    peace?
There is a monstrous din of the sterile who contribute
    nothing
To the great end in view, and the future fumbles,
A bad birth, not like the child in that gracious home
Heard in the quietness turning in its mother's womb,
A strategic mind already, seeking the best way
To present himself to life, and at last, resolved,

Springing into history quivering like a fish,
Dropping into the world like a ripe fruit in due time –
But where is the Past to which Time, smiling through her
 tears
At her new-born son, can turn crying: 'I love you'?

Another epitaph on an army of mercenaries[1]

It is a God-damned lie to say that these
Saved, or knew, anything worth any man's pride.
They were professional murderers and they took
Their blood money and impious risks and died.
In spite of all their kind some elements of worth
With difficulty persist here and there on earth.

Ballad of Aun, King of Sweden

Surely Hell burns a deeper blue
With each noble boast of men like you.

With each noble boast of men like you
– Such men as all but all men it's true.

See what I'm doing for England, you cry,
Or for Christendom, civilization, or some other lie.

And no one remembers the story of Aun,
The Swedish king, who sent son after son

To death, buying with each another span
Of life for himself, the identical plan

All governments, all patriots, self-righteously pursue.
How many sons have *you* given, and *you*, and you?

1. In reply to A. E. Housman's.

Nine sons in succession was the grim
Record of Aun, till the people rose and slew *him*.

But when will the people rise and slay
The ubiquitous Aun of State Murder today?

Realizing murder is foulest murder no matter
What individual or body for what end does the slaughter!

To nearly everybody in Europe today

A war to save civilization, you say?
Then what have *you* to do with it, pray?
Some attempt to acquire it would show truer love
Than fighting for something you know nothing of.

KUO MO-JO
b. 1893

✳

On the summit of Mount Hekilitsuyama

O pulse of the great city!
Throbs of life!
Beating, blowing and shouting,
Gushing, flying and jumping ...
The horizon is veiled in mist!
My heart leaps out of my mouth!
O, waves of mountains, waves of roofs
Swelling and surging!
A symphony of myriad melodies
The hymen of nature and human life to celebrate!
The coast is curved like Cupid's bow:
Men's lives are arrows whizzing over the sea!
In the dark harbour steamers anchored,
    steamers moving, steamers innumerable!
On every chimney blooms a coal-black peony.
Illustrious flower of this century!
O fatherhood of modern civilization!

ERNST TOLLER
1893–1939

❋

To the living

It is not seemly for you to
Mourn,
It is not seemly for you to
Delay;
You have received a legacy
Soaked
In the heart's blood of your brothers.
The pregnant deed
Waits
For you.

The time,
Burdensome,
Presses upon your necks.
Wide burst
The gates
Of bright morning!

MAO TSE-TUNG
b. 1893

✳

Ch'angsha

Alone in the autumn cold
I scan the river
   that flows northward
Past the Orange Islet
And the mountains crimson
With the red leaves of the woods.
On this broad stream
   of rich green water
A hundred boats
   race with the currents.
Eagles dart
   across the wide sky,
Fish swim
   in the shallows –
All display their freedom
   in the frosty air.
Bewildered by the immensity,
I ask the vast grey earth:
'Who decides men's destinies?'

I brought hither
   hundreds of companions
In those turbulent
   months and years.
We were fellow students
Then in our lissom youth.
In the true manner of scholars

We accused without fear or favour,
Pointed at these rivers and ranges,
And wrote vibrant words,
Valuing marquisates
  as dust.
Do you not remember
How in mid-stream
  our boats struck currents
And were slowed down by torrents?

Chingkang Mountain

At the foot of the mountain
  waved our banners.
Upon its peak
  sounded our bugles and drums.
A myriad foes
  were all around us.
But we stood fast
  and gave no ground.

Our defence was strong
  as a mighty wall.
Our wills united
  to form a fortress.
From Huangyangchieh[1]
  came the thunder of guns.
And the army of our foes
  had fled into the night!

1. Huangyangchieh: in 1928 Mao and Chu Te defeated the first
Kuomintang attack at Huangyangchieh.

New Year's Day 1929

Ninghua! Ch'ingliu! Kweihua![1]
Narrow the path, deep the woods
   and the moss slippery.
Where are we bound today?
Straight to the foot of Wuyi Mountain.
The foot of the mountain,
   the foot of the mountain,
There the wind will unfurl,
   like a scroll,
     our scarlet banner.

Advance to Fukien

A sudden wind gathers clouds
As warlords renew their clashes
And a pillow of dreams of fortune,
Only to spread hatred among men.

Over the Ting River
And straight to Lungyen and Shanghang
Are carried the crimson banners.
A part of the realm has been recovered
And the land is being actively redistributed.

March on Chian

Seeing under the sky only white,
   no green of cypress,
The troops march in the snow.
Peaks tower above them.

1. Places in Fukien province.

The wind unfurls the red flags,
As they climb over the mountain pass.

Where are they going?
To the Kan River where wind sweeps up snow.
The order of yesterday
To a lac of workers and peasants
  was to take Chian.

Attack on Nanch'ang

June: the peerless troops attack
  the corrupt and villainous,
Seeking to bind the cockatrice
  with a rope a myriad ells in length.
On the far side of the Kan River
  a patch of ground has turned red,
Thanks to the wing
  under the command of Huang Kung-lüeh.

The million elated workers and peasants
Roll up Kiangsi like a mat
  and thrust straight on to Liang Hu.
The heartening *Internationale*,
  like a hurricane,
Whirls down on me from heaven.

Tapoti

Red, orange, yellow,
  green, blue, indigo, violet –
Who is dancing in the sky,
  whirling this ribbon of colour?

After the rain
   the sun has returned to set,
And the pass and the lines of hills
   are blue.

A desperate battle
   raged here once.
Bullet holes
   pit the walls of the village.
They are an embellishment
And today the hills
   seem yet more fair.

Loushan Pass

Cold blows the west wind,
Far off in the frosty air
   the wild geese call
   in the morning moonlight.
In the morning moonlight
Horse's hoofs ring out sharply
And the bugle's note
   is muted.

Do not say
   that the pass is defended with iron.
This very day
   at one step
   we shall cross over it.
We shall cross over it.
The hills are blue like the sea,
And the dying sun is like blood.

The Long March

The Red Army fears not the trials of the Long March
And thinks nothing of a thousand mountains and rivers.
The Wuling Ridges spread out like ripples;
The Wumeng Ranges roll like balls of clay.
Warmly are the cliffs wrapped in clouds
    and washed by the Gold Sand;
Chilly are the iron chains lying across
    the width of the Great Ferry.
A thousand acres of snow on the Min Mountains delight
My troops who have just left them behind.

Snow

The northern scene:
A thousand leagues locked in ice,
A myriad leagues of fluttering snow.
On either side of the Great Wall
Only one vastness to be seen.
Up and down this broad river
Torrents flatten and stiffen.
The mountains are dancing silver serpents
And hills, like waxen elephants, plod on the plain,
Challenging heaven with their heights.
A sunny day is needed
For seeing them, with added elegance,
In red and white.

Such is the beauty of these mountains and rivers
That has been admired by unnumbered heroes –
The great emperors of Ch'in and Han
Lacking literary brilliance,
Those of T'ang and Sung
Having but few romantic inclinations,

And the prodigious Gengis Khan
Knowing only how to bend his bow
   and shoot at vultures.
All are past and gone!
For men of vision
We must seek among the present generation.

Return to Shaoshan

On 25 June 1959 I returned to Shaoshan,
after an absence of thirty-two years.

I curse the time that has flowed past
   Since the dimly-remembered dream of my departure
From home, thirty-two years ago.
With red pennons, the peasants lifted their lances;
In their black hands, the rulers held up their whips.
Lofty emotions were expressed in self-sacrifice:
So the sun and moon were asked to give a new face to
   heaven.
In delight I watch a thousand waves of growing rice and
   beans,
And heroes everywhere going home in the smoky sunset.

Inscription on a photograph of women militia

These well-groomed heroines carry five-foot rifles,
On this parade ground in the first rays of the sun,
Daughters of China have uncommon aspirations,
Preferring battle-tunics to red dresses.

Reply to Kuo Mo-jo

Kuo:

Only among the cross-currents of this vast sea
Does the greatness of man become manifest.
The six hundred million,
Having consolidated their unity,
Hold fast to their tenets.
When the sky falls, raise it;
When the world goes wrong, right it.
Listen to the cockcrow
As dawn breaks in the east.

The sun comes out
And ice drips on the mountains.
But pure gold
Is never consumed by flames.
The four majestic volumes[1]
Set a standard for the people.
It is absurd that a rogue's dogs should bark at a saint,
And there should be no news of the clay oxen that went
    overseas.
Unfurl the red flags into the east wind
To turn the world scarlet.

Mao:

In this small world
A few flies knock against walls.
The noise they make
Is sometimes spine-chilling
And sometimes like sobbing.
Ants climbing up an ash tree brag about a great country,

1. Mao's books.

But it is easy to say that beetles can shake the roots of a
    stout tree.
In Ch'angan, when leaves were falling in the west wind,
The signal was given.

There have always been
Many things that were urgent.
Although the world spins on
Time is short.
Millennia are too long:
Let us dispute about mornings and evenings.
The four seas are tempestuous as clouds and waters show
    their wrath;
The five continents are shaken as gales and thunder rage.
Pests should be stamped out
So that we may become invincible.

VLADIMIR MAYAKOVSKY

1893–1930

✳

From '*The cloud in trousers*'

Your thought,
musing on a sodden brain
like a bloated lackey on a greasy couch,
I'll taunt with a bloody morsel of heart;
and satiate my insolent, caustic contempt.

No grey hairs streak my soul,
no grandfatherly fondness there!
I shake the world with the might of my voice,
and walk – handsome,
twentytwoyearold.

Tender souls!
You play your love on a fiddle,
and the crude club their love on a drum.
But you cannot turn yourselves inside out,
like me, and be just bare lips!

Come and be lessoned –
prim officiates of the angelic league,
lisping in drawing-room cambric.

You, too, who leaf your lips like a cook
turns the pages of a cookery book.

If you wish,
I shall rage on raw meat;

or, as the sky changes its hue,
if you wish,
I shall grow irreproachably tender:
not a man, but a cloud in trousers!

I deny the existence of blossoming Nice!
Again in song I glorify
men as crumpled as hospital beds,
and women as battered as proverbs.

Order no. 2 to the army of the arts

This is for you –
the fleshy baritones
who, since the days
of Adam,
have shaken those dens called theatres
with the arias of Romeos and Juliets.

This is for you –
the *peintres*,
grown as robust as horses,
the ravening and neighing beauty of Russia,
skulking in ateliers
and, as of old, imposing Draconian laws on flowers
and bulking bodies.

This is for you –
who put on little fig leaves of mysticism,
whose brows are harrowed with wrinkles –
you, little futurists,
imaginists,
acmeists,
entangled in the cobweb of rhymes.
This is for you –
who have exchanged rumpled hair
for a slick hairdo,

bast shoes for lacquered pumps,
you, men of the Proletcult,
who keep patching
Pushkin's faded tailcoat.

This is for you –
who dance and pipe on pipes,
sell yourselves openly,
sin in secret,
and picture your future as academicians
with outsized rations.
I admonish you,
I –
genius or not –
who have forsaken trifles
and work in Rosta,[1]
I admonish you –
before they disperse you with rifle-butts:
Give it up!

Give it up!
Forget it.
Spit
on rhymes
and arias
and the rose bush
and other such mawkishness
from the arsenal of the arts.
Who's interested now
in – 'Ah, wretched soul!
· How he loved,
how he suffered ...'?
Good workers –
these are the men we need
rather than long-haired preachers.

1. Rosta: The Russian Telegraphic Agency, where Mayakovsky
was employed drawing posters and cartoons, the slogans for which
became famous.

Listen!
The locomotives groan,
and a draft blows through crannies and floor:
'Give us coal from the Don!
Metal workers
and mechanics for the depot!'
At each river's outlet, steamers
with an aching hole in their side,
howl through the docks:
'Give us oil from Baku!'
While we dawdle and quarrel
in search of fundamental answers,
all things yell:
'Give us new forms!'

There are no fools today
to crowd, open-mouthed, round a 'maestro'
and await his pronouncement.
Comrades,
give us a new form of art –
an art
that will pull the republic out of the mud.

My university

From '*I Love*'

French you know.
You divide.
Multiply.
You decline wonderfully.
Well, decline then!
But tell me –
can you sing in tune
with a house?

Do you understand the idiom of tramcars?
The human fledgling –
barely out of the egg –
grasps at a book,
at quires of exercise paper.
But I learned my alphabet from signboards,
Leafing through pages of iron and tin.
People take the earth,
trim
and strip it –
and they teach you a lesson.
It's just a tiny globe.
But I
learned my geography with my ribs –
no wonder I
flop down to earth
for my night's rest!
Painful questions torment the Ilovaiskys:[1]
Did Barbarossa have a red beard? –
What if he did!
I do not rummage in dust-laden rubbish –
I know all the histories in Moscow!
They take Dobrolyubov (to hate evil),[2]
but the name objects,
the family whimpers.
Since childhood,
I've always hated
the overfed,
for I always had to sell myself
for a meal.
They learn
to sit down –
to please a lady;
their trifling thoughts clink against tinpot foreheads.

1. Ilovaiskys: D. I. Ilovaisky, author of history textbooks used in Russian schools.
2. Dobrolyubov: Nicholas Dobrolyubov (1836–61), radical literary critic whose name means 'a lover of good'.

But I
talked
only to houses.
Water towers were my only company.
Listening closely with their dormer windows,
the roofs caught what I threw in their ears.
Afterwards,
they prattled
about the night
and about each other,
wagging their weathercock tongue.

Back home!

Thoughts, go your way home.
Embrace,
        depths of the soul and the sea.
In my view,
      it is
         stupid
to be
   always serene.
My cabin is the worst
          of all cabins –
all night above me
         thuds a smithy of feet.
All night,
     stirring the ceiling's calm,
dancers stampede
        to a moaning motif:
'Marquita,
     Marquita,
Marquita, my darling,
why won't you,
     Marquita,
why won't you love me . . .'

But why
          should Marquita love me?!
I have
      no francs to spare.
And Marquita
                (at the slightest wink!)
for a hundred francs
                    she'd be brought to your room.
The sum's not large –
                    just live for show –
no,
    you highbrow,
                    ruffling your matted hair,
you would thrust upon her
                          a sewing machine,
in stitches
          scribbling
                    the silk of verse.
Proletarians
            arrive at communism
                              from below –
by the low way of mines,
                          sickles,
                                  and pitchforks –
but I,
      from poetry's skies,
                        plunge into communism,
because
        without it
                  I feel no love.
Whether
        I'm self exiled
                        or sent to mamma –
the steel of words corrodes,
                            the brass of the bass tarnishes.
Why,
      beneath foreign rains,
must I soak,

rot,
       and rust?
Here I recline,
       having gone oversea,
in my idleness
       barely moving
          my machine parts.
I myself
       feel like a Soviet
          factory,
manufacturing happiness.
I object
       to being torn up,
like a flower of the fields,
          after a long day's work.
I want
       the Gosplan to sweat[1]
          in debate,
assigning me
       goals a year ahead.
I want
       a commissar
          with a decree
to lean over the thought of the age.
I want
       the heart to earn
its love wage
       at a specialist's rate.
I want
       the factory committee
          to lock
my lips
       when the work is done.
I want
       the pen to be on a par
          with the bayonet;

1. Gosplan: the State Planning Commission, responsible for drawing up the national economic plan.

and Stalin
   to deliver his Politbureau
reports
  about verse in the making
as he would about pig iron
      and the smelting of steel.
'That's how it is,
   the way it goes ...
        We've attained
the topmost level,
    climbing from the worker's bunks:
in the Union
   of Republics
      the understanding of verse
now tops
   the prewar norm ...'[1]

At the top of my voice

My most respected
     comrades of posterity!
Rummaging among
    these days'
      petrified crap,
exploring the twilight of our times,
you,
  possibly,
    will inquire about me too.
And, possibly, your scholars
      will declare,
with their erudition overwhelming
       a swarm of problems;

1. Originally the poem ended: 'I want to be understood by my country,/but if I fail to be understood –/what then?/I shall pass through my native land/to one side,/like a shower/of slanting rain.' Patricia Blake (*The Bedbug and Selected Poetry*) says the present ending was substituted 'at the last minute'.

once there lived
                 a certain champion of boiled water,
and inveterate enemy of raw water.
Professor,
            take off your bicycle glasses!
I myself will expound
                those times
                     and myself.
I, a latrine cleaner
               and water carrier,
by the revolution
                 mobilized and drafted,
went off to the front
                  from the aristocratic gardens
of poetry –
            the capricious wench.
She planted a delicious garden,
the daughter,
              cottage,
                 pond
                    and meadow.
Myself a garden I did plant,
myself with water sprinkled it.
Some pour their verse from water cans;
others spit water
               from their mouth –
the curly Macks,
             the clever Jacks –
but what the hell's it all about!
There's no damming all this up –
beneath the walls they mandoline:
'Tara-tina, tara-tine,
tw-a-ng . . .'
It's no great honour, then,
                 for my monuments
to rise from such roses
above the public squares,
                 where consumption coughs,

where whores, hooligans, and syphilis
                                        walk.
Agitprop[1]
            sticks
                    in my teeth too,
and I'd rather
                compose
                            romances for you –
more profit in it
                    and more charm,
But I
      subdued
                myself,
                        setting my heel
on the throat
                of my own song.
Listen,
        comrades of posterity,
to the agitator,
                    the rabble-rouser.
Stifling
          the torrents of poetry,
I'll skip
          the volumes of lyrics;
as one alive,
                I'll address the living.
I'll join you
                in the far communist future,
I, who am
            no Esenin super-hero.
My verse will reach you
                            across the peaks of ages,
over the heads
                of governments and poets.
My verse
          will reach you

1. Agitprop: the Agitation and Propaganda Section of the Central Committee of the Communist Party.

not as an arrow
           in a cupid-lyred chase,
not as worn penny
           reaches a numismatist,
not as the light of dead stars reaches you.
My verse
     by labour
          will break the mountain chain of years,
and will present itself
           ponderous,
              crude,
                tangible,
as an aqueduct,
           by slaves of Rome
constructed,
           enters into our days.
When in mounds of books,
              where verse lies buried,
you discover by chance the iron filings of lines,
touch them
     with respect,
           as you would
some antique
        yet awesome weapon.
It's no habit of mine
         to caress
           the ear
              with words;
a maiden's ear
        curly-ringed
will not crimson
        when flicked by smut.
In parade deploying
           the armies of my pages,
I shall inspect
        the regiments in line.
Heavy as lead,
      my verses at attention stand,

ready for death
                    and for immortal fame.
The poems are rigid,
                    pressing muzzle
to muzzle their gaping
                    pointed titles.
The favourite
            of all the armed forces,
the cavalry of witticisms,
                    ready
to launch a wild hallooing charge,
reins its chargers still,
                    raising
the pointed lances of the rhymes.
And all
        these troops armed to the teeth,
which have flashed by
                    victoriously for twenty years,
all these
        to their very last page,
I present to you,
                the planet's proletarian.
The enemy
        of the massed working class
is my enemy too,
                inveterate and of long standing.
Years of trial
            and days of hunger
                    ordered us
to march
        under the red flag.
We opened
        each volume
                of Marx
as we would open
            the shutters
                in our own house;
but we did not have to read

                              to make up our minds
which side to join,
                        which side to fight on.
Our dialectics
              were not learned from Hegel.
In the roar of battle
                      it erupted into verse,
when,
      under fire,
                  the bourgeois decamped
as once we ourselves
                    had fled
                          from them.

Let fame
        trudge
              after genius
like an inconsolable widow
                          to a funeral march –
die then, my verse,
                  die like a common soldier,
like our men
            who nameless died attacking!
I don't care a spit
                  for tons of bronze;
I don't care a spit
                  for slimy marble.
We're men of a kind,
                  we'll come to terms about our fame;
let our
        common monument be
socialism
          built
              in battle.
Men of posterity
                examine the flotsam of dictionaries:
out of Lethe
            will bob up
                        the debris of such words

as 'prostitution',
                    'tuberculosis',
                                    'blockade'.
For you,
        who are now
                    healthy and agile,
the poet,
        with the rough tongue
                                of his posters,
has licked away consumptives' spittle.
With the tail of my years behind me,
                                    I begin to resemble
those monsters,
                excavated dinosaurs.
Comrade life,
            let us
                    march faster,
march
        faster through what's left
                                    of the five-year plan.
My verse
        has brought me
                            no roubles to spare:
no craftsmen have made
                        mahogany chairs for my house.
In all conscience,
                I need nothing
except
        a freshly laundered shirt.
When I appear
                before the C.C.C.[1]
                                    of the coming
                                            bright years,
by way of my Bolshevik party card,
                                    I'll raise
above the heads

1. C.C.C.: the Central Control Commission of the Soviet Communist
Party.

        of a gang of self-seeking
                        poets and rogues,
all the hundred volumes
                of my
                    communist-committed books.

From 'Lenin'

When I sieve through
                  what I've lived through,
When I summarize:
              which the best,
                    which the worst day –
There it is,
        the best,
              the 25th,
                  the first day.
Bayonets
        clashing,
              flashing out
                  lightning.
Sailors playing
            with bombs,
                like balls,
Smolny rocking
            with the crash
                of the fighting,
Machine-gunners
            dashing
              down
                its halls.
'Comrades!
        Press on!
              What have you stopped for?
Man the armoured cars!
            Make

for Post Office!

A host of us
            pitched
                        against a handful
                                    of Junkers!'
'Righto!'
            A right-about
                        and out of sight
                                    in the night.
On the sailor's cap
                        the letters 'Aurora'
                                    like golden flora
                                                bloomed in the light.
Here men giving orders,
                        three men in discussion,
Reports,
            applications,
                        affadavits
                                    to send in.
At the end
            of the corridor,
                        amid all this rushing,
Quiet,
      intent,
            inconspicuous –
                        Lenin.
All night
            he pondered
                        the world situation.
In the morning
            he issued
                        a proclamation:
To all!
      To all!
            To all!
To all
      who are wallowing
                        in the trenches!

To all
      who are sweating
                  at benches!
To slaves
      all and sundry!
Power to the Soviets!
Bread to the hungry!
Land to the peasants!
Peace to the nation!
Bread to the hungry!

6 nuns

With small baked-potato
                  faces
                        looking up,
blacker
      than negroes
                  who have never used soap,
six pious Catholic sisters
climb the Espagne's
                  gangplank
                        and board the boat.
Their fronts
      and backs
                  as straight as a string,
their habits
      hang from their shoulders
                        as from pegs,
and their faces
            are haloed
                  by the whitest frills
like the trimmings
                  at Easter
                        on little pig's legs.
If only

I remember
               this marvel
when my time is ripe
                   and I'm the next to go,
a yawn
        will rip open
                my mouth
wider than the Gulf of Mexico.
Temperate
           antiseptic –
                     like boric acid.
A squad,
          they sit down to eat – all
                        at once.
Having eaten,
             they hide in a toilet.
One yawns;
           five yawn in response.
Instead of symmetrical
                  places where women
should have curves – they have caves,
                        which do not satisfy us.
In one cave there
               is a silver cross;
in another – medals
               with Leo and Pius.
In Paradise
         (Someday!)
                   they will sleep overtime,
but, still sleepy-eyed,
                and as early as possible,
like an orchestra without a conductor,
now they take out
              six pocket
                 Gospels.
You meet them at night.
They pray all right.
The dawn spreads its roses –

they pray, holy moses!
At night,
            at day, mornings and noons,
they sit
        and they pray –
                        the lord's buffoons.
And if
    the day
            grows a
                    little darker,
they go down to their cabin,
                            get out twelve galoshes,
put them on together
                    and go out again,
and again
        they continue
                    their unctuous hogwashes.
Would
    I could
            speak Spanish!
                            I would ask in rage:
'Angelitas,
        give this poet
                    a simple reply.
If you
    are people,
            then who
                    are crows?
And if
    you are crows,
                why don't you fly?'
Propagan-Com!
                Here's your dish.
Though you search
                all earth and nature
the greatest
        atheist couldn't
find a more profane

caricature.
Crucified Jesus, rejoice!
Don't get off
of the nails on your tree;
at your second coming
keep your nose
out of here,
or you'll hang yourself
from ennui!

A poem about my Soviet passport

I would gnaw out
red tape
like a wolf.
Show papers, no;
respect, none.
Other documents
may go straight
to the devil
and all my mothers,
but not this one ...
Along the long line
of cabins
and compartments
a polite official
moves in this direction.
All hand him their passports
and I
give him my
purple booklet
for inspection.
For some passports –
there's a look down his nose.
For others
a smile broadly written.

Yet for others,
                for instance,
                            respect
for the double-bedded
                        Leo from Britain.
Eating
        the kind uncle with his eyes,
with such bowing that
                        he may disjoint his hips,
he takes
        the passports
                        of Americans
as if they were tips.
He looks
        at the Poles'
                    like a goat at a sign.
At the Poles'
                his eyes bulge in a blind
bureaucratic
                idiocy –
as if saying:
            what's this? And where did you find
this geographical novelty?
Never showing
                emotion,
never turning
                his cabbage
                            head without brains,
never blinking an eye,
                        he just takes
                                    the passports of the Swedes
and all
        other
            Danes.
And suddenly,
                as if a burn
                            made
                                the gentleman's

mouth
     distort –
this
   is Mister Official
                   taking
my red-skinned
                piece of passport . . .
As if it
     were a porcupine,
                as if it
                    were a bomb;
a razor-like
         super-sharp blade,
like a seven-foot
           twenty-fang
                 venomous snake
rattling
     a cannonade.
The redcap
        winks
           significantly:
he will carry
        your bags for free.
The inspector
         and a detective
               exchange glances
bruskly
     and questioningly.
What joy it would be
              for this coppers' clique
to nail me and whip me
         and crush me,
because my hands hold
           the hammer-and-sicklehood
of a passport
       of Soviet Russia!
I would gnaw out
       red tape

like a wolf.

Show papers, no;

respect, none.

Other documents

may go straight

to the devil

and all mothers

but not this one ...

So

I take it

from my wide pants

as a symbol

of precious weight.

Read it

with envy:

I'm a citizen

of the Soviet State.

Past one o'clock[1]

Past one o'clock. You must have gone to bed.
Night's Milky Way flows like a silver stream.
No rush. I'll not wake you, bothering your head
With lightning telegrams to crush your dream.
As they say, that's the end of the story,
The boat of love has smashed against life's reefs.
We are quits and we don't need an inventory
Of our mutual hurtings, insults and griefs.
And see how the world lies in quietness
The sky pays Night with a rash of stars from its purse.
In hours like these, one gets up to address
All Time and History and Universe!

1. This poem was found in Mayakovsky's pocket after his suicide
in 1930. Probably his last piece of writing.

WILFRED OWEN
1893–1918

✳

Disabled

He sat in a wheeled chair, waiting for dark,
And shivered in his ghastly suit of grey,
Legless, sewn short at elbow. Through the park
Voices of boys rang saddening like a hymn,
Voices of play and pleasure after day,
Till gathering sleep had mothered them from him.

About this time Town used to swing so gay
When glow-lamps budded in the light blue trees,
And girls glanced lovelier as the air grew dim, –
In the old times, before he threw away his knees.
Now he will never feel again how slim
Girls' waists are, or how warm their subtle hands;
All of them touch him like some queer disease.

There was an artist silly for his face,
For it was younger than his youth, last year.
Now, he is old; his back will never brace;
He's lost his colour very far from here,
Poured it down shell-holes till the veins ran dry,
And half his lifetime lapsed in the hot race,
And leap of purple spurted from his thigh.

One time he liked a blood-smear down his leg,
After the matches, carried shoulder-high.
It was after football, when he'd drunk a peg,
He thought he'd better join. – He wonders why.

Someone had said he'd look a god in kilts,
That's why; and may be, too, to please his Meg;
Aye, that was it, to please the giddy jilts
He asked to join. He didn't have to beg;
Smiling they wrote his lie; aged nineteen years.
Germans he scarcely thought of; all their guilt,
And Austria's, did not move him. And no fears
Of Fear came yet. He thought of jewelled hilts
For daggers in plaid socks; of smart salutes;
And care of arms; and leave; and pay arrears;
Esprit de corps; and hints for young recruits.
And soon, he was drafted out with drums and cheers.

Some cheered him home, but not as crowds cheer Goal.
Only a solemn man who brought him fruits
Thanked him; and then inquired about his soul.

Now, he will spend a few sick years in Institutes,
And do what things the rules consider wise,
And take whatever pity they may dole.
Tonight he noticed how the women's eyes
Passed from him to the strong men that were whole.
How cold and late it is! Why don't they come
And put him into bed? Why don't they come?

The parable of the old man and the young

So Abram rose, and clave the wood, and went,
And took the fire with him, and a knife.
And as they sojourned both of them together,
Isaac the first-born spake and said, My Father,
Behold the preparations, fire and iron,
But where the lamb for this burnt-offering?
Then Abram bound the youth with belts and straps,
And builded parapets and trenches there,
And stretchèd forth the knife to slay his son.

When lo! an angel called him out of heaven,
Saying, Lay not thy hand upon the lad,
Neither do anything to him. Behold,
A ram, caught in a thicket by its horns;
Offer the Ram of Pride instead of him.
But the old man would not so, but slew his son,
And half the seed of Europe, one by one.

JOE CORRIE
1894–1968

❋

Women are waiting tonight

Women are waiting tonight on the pit-bank,
Pale at the heart with dread,
Watching the dead-still wheels
That loom in the mirky sky,
The silent wheels of Fate,
Which is the system under which they slave.
They stand together in groups,
As sheep shelter in storm,
Silent, passive, dumb.
For in the caverns under their feet,
The coffin seams of coal
'Twixt the rock and the rock,
The gas has burst into flame,
And has scattered the hail of Death.
Cold the night is, and dark,
And the rain falls in a mist.
Their shawls and their rags are sodden,
And their thin, starved cheeks are blue,
But they will not go home to their fires,
Tho' the news has been broken to them
That a miracle is their only hope.
They will wait and watch till the dawn,
Till the wheels begin to revolve,
And the men whom they loved so well,
The strong, kind, loving men,
Are brought up in canvas sheets,

To be identified by a watch,
Or a button,
Or, perhaps, only a wish.
And three days from now,
They will all be buried together,
In one big hole in the earth.
And the King will send his sympathy,
And the Member of Parliament will be there,
Who voted that the military be used
When last these miners came on strike
To win a living wage.
His shining black hat will glisten over a sorrowful face,
And his elegantly shod feet will go slowly behind the
    bier.
And the director of the company will be there,
Who has vowed many a time
That he would make the miner eat grass.
And the parson, who sits on the Parish Council,
Starving the children and saving the rates,
Will pray in a mournful voice,
And tear the very hearts of the bereaved.
He will emphasize in godly phrase,
The danger of the mine,
And the bravery and valour of the miner.
And the Press
That has spilled oceans of ink
Poisoning the public against the 'destroyers of industry',
Will tell the sad tale,
And the public will say, 'How sad.'
But a week today all will be forgotten,
And the Member of Parliament,
The coalowner,
The parson,
The Press,
And the public,
Will keep storing up their venom and their hatred,
For the next big miners' strike.

Women are waiting tonight at the pit-bank,
But even God does not see
The hypocrisy and the shame of it all.

Eat more

'Eat more fruit!' the slogans say,
    'More fish, more beef, more bread!'
But I'm on Unemployment pay
    My third year now, and wed.

And so I wonder when I'll see
    The slogan when I pass,
The only one that would suit me, –
    'Eat More Bloody Grass!'

Working man, I have faith in you

Working man, I have faith in you,
    Tho' you're such a damned fool in my eyes,
I know, full well, how they've wasted you,
    And clotted your brain with their lies.
I've heard the sleek parsons preach to you,
    I've studied the dope of the Press,
And tho' they have made such a mess of you,
    I have faith in you, nevertheless.

For working man, there is none but you
    Can think in the vital way,
Can look at life from the level of you,
    And fight for equality.
There's that which I find in the soil in you,
    That brings the seed to flower,
And, working man, I have faith in you
    In this world's most piteous hour.

'How few there are . . .'

How few there are with unsoiled hands,
   And educated tongues,
Who'll stand by us, my working friends,
   And help to right our wrongs.

They go a certain length with us,
   But faint of heart return
When we meet someone with a cross,
   Bearing a crown of thorn.

JAROSLAW IWASZKIEWICZ
b. 1894

*

The brotherhood of Man

O Wanderer, if ever you approach the banks of river
    Seine,
the Place d'Alma in Paris,
you will observe a figure cut of bronze, standing upon a
    column.
The figure is not tall,
his coat is borne aloft by the breath of wind, and he
    extends his arm:
Thus stands, forever going somewhere, Mickiewicz – our
    prophet,
turned into a wind,
a wind that blows across the wastes.
It is our father, Adam,
who heralded to all the peoples of the earth eternal love
and brotherhood.
When tempests rage upon the ocean, and many-storied
    waves clap
against each other,
    emitting sounds like many thousands clapping hands,
    and toss ships and fishing boats against the rocks,
    and cast men upon the waters of the sea, their heads
    bobbing
like wooden logs from shipwrecks –
    then suddenly the clouds are rent asunder, like grey
    curtains upon
the stage, and a solitary ray falls,
    like a gigantic arrow, or a chord that joins the sky

with sea, and
the sea is calmed, and the vessels creep to their ports,
　lowering their
tattered sails.
　as a mother standing over her son's grave drops her
　arms.
　And the ray upon the turgid but already clearer wave
　draws the word: pax, pax, pax . . .
　Thus we too await for heavens to draw open and to
　give a sign
to all of us, to clasp our hands,
　and to exclaim as that ray of sun:
　pax.
　Why are you waiting, boys and girls? Why are you
　standing in
rows before the highstands? Why are your hearts
　pounding – and for
what reason? Why are all your eyes fixed on one spot,
　where the flag
is hoisted on the mast, climbing like a longshoreman?
　Why does the
sea of your heads fill the vast stadium in silence?
　Why
　do you not shout all together, white, black, and yellow
　men: pax, pax, pax?
　I glance at you with fear. Perhaps there are those
　among you
whose bodies and souls are touched by the plague?
　Perhaps there are those who hide their sharpened
　knives under
their white cloaks?
　Or those who in their hearts still worship the serpents
　of hate,
　those who wake up with malice,
　those who are sworn
　to vengeance?
　Look, I draw the curtain
　and show to you a flat and spacious land, a valley

through which flows Vistula, stretching her neck like a
swan at night,
   a valley which slumbers in autumn mists, and falls
into the drifts of winter snow,
   and at times awakens, red with fiery sunsets,
   the land covered with manifold grain
   and forests –
The grain of this land is the hiding place for beasts and
men, for the man who grew among the tall rye,
   and trod upon the poppies and corn-flowers.
The forests whose shadows covered the men who
fought for every harbour of peace, every anchor of hope,
and every shred of life.
   This is the brotherhood of Man!

You see those tall chimneys and the smoke above?
Here are men who burn other men, here the conquerors –
   those who have no chance to fight even for a single
breath.
   No traitors' bodies hang from pear trees in the fields.
   Judas, the conqueror, hangs upon the knotted trees
those men who couldn't even die.
   The endless roads of this land
   are trod by the iron heel of the trained rabble who
trample human brains and skulls, torn bowels, limbs;
who trample on the cries and thoughts of men, their
lives and hopes, illusions and impatiences and pain –
   This is the brotherhood of Man!

Upon overgrown plateaux those who are dying of
thirst groan pitifully,
   the blue tunics of soldiers press into the breadtree
shadows,
   and black corpses in the coffee groves
   and green flies like leaven on faces
   buzzing like poor fiddles
   murmuring like water which isn't there, which isn't
there.

The chieftains of fabulous lands – peeled mango fruits,
hang like ducks impaled on spits,
and soldiers with torn bellies
buzz with moans like flies!
In the thicket of lianas and roots, beneath the man-
grove shadow gleam the petals of orchids and victoria
regina:
hearts ripped and dripping with blood,
eyes open and plucked with the knife of terror
from the festering orbs of ignorance.

Murdered man, murdered woman, murdered people,
buried alive, shot, killed, strangled, executed, knived,
gassed –
This is the brotherhood of Man!
In the deserts, steppes, taiga, forests, jungles, icy
expanse and stretches of sand;
in hovels, houses, palaces, shelters, mud huts, cellars.
on all the earth,
fear now dwells and whispers into everybody's ear
ever more terrifying thoughts,
ever more gruesome visions:
eyes covered with sores, babies born like monsters, the
flowers of black death blooming in the armpits, dried
blood on lips, vermin feeding on living bodies
and on the bodies of the dead.
Fear for everything: the houses, gardens, souls,
existence, for seas lest they dry out, for mountains lest
they cave in, for trees lest they burn,
for children,
for our children, grandchildren, and great-grand-
children.
This is the brotherhood of Man!

You, handsome, white, strong men! You who resemble
the eternal gods of Hellas! You, whose eyes and souls
shine like sparks
when you stand thus

and when the swarm of your eyes flies like bees towards
the spot where the flag crawls up the mast like a sailor,
when the sea of your heads fills the gigantic stadium as
black and white grapes fill a wicker basket,
 when you open your mouths, to give out the words of
joy
 like round balloons soaring into the sky,
 like golden fish floating in dark-blue oceans,
 like the fragrance of flowers borne by summer breeze,
 think of all those who could not cry out before they
died!
 Think of those whose mouths were sealed with plaster,
and of those felled by bullets before they could cry out,
of those whose eyes were filled with blood and who could
not cast a glance upon the sky,
 as you look upon it now,
 nor on the victorious banner,
 because they died in degradation –
 and think about the brotherhood of Man!

 And if you cannot fight for man
 and if you too take to swords and rifles
 and kill your brothers –
 mankind shall not attain salvation.

 Think, think of this now.
 Think of happiness and freedom.
 For only the struggle for good can win goodness
 and only the degradation of evil can elevate goodness
 and only the brotherhood of man can raise upon the
mast
 the Olympic flag, great as the world.

 Take each other's hand and sing:
 pax, pax, pax –
 To signify the brotherhood of Man.

PAUL ÉLUARD
1895–1952

❋

Honest justice

It is the burning law of men
From grapes they make wine
From coal they make fire
From kisses they make men

It is the unkind law of men
To keep themselves whole in spite
Of war and misery
In spite of the dangers of death

It is the gentle law of men
To change water into light
Dreams into reality
Enemies into brothers

A law old and new
A self-perfecting system
From the depths of the child's heart
Up to the highest judgement.

Stupid and evil

Coming from within
Coming from without
These our enemies

Coming from above
Coming from below
From near and far
From right and left
Dressed in green
Dressed in grey
The blouse too short
The overcoat too long
The cross askew
Their rifles long
Their knives short
Proud of their spies
Strong in their butchers
And heavy with dismay
Armed to the earth
Armed in the earth
Stiff with salutes
And stiff with fear
Before their shepherds
Beer-soaked
Moon-soaked
Gravely singing
The song of boots
They have forgotten
The joy of being loved
When they say yes
All answer no
When they speak of gold
All turns to lead
But against their shadow
All will turn to gold
All will grow young again
Let them leave let them die
Their death suffices us

We love men
They shall escape
We shall take care of them

On the morning of glory
Of a new world
Of a world set right.

The same day for all

I

The sword we do not sink in the heart of the guilty's
    masters
We sink in the heart of the poor and innocent

The first eyes are of innocence
The second of poverty
We must know how to protect them

I will condemn love only
If I do not kill hate
And those who have inspired me with it

2

A small bird walks in the vast regions
Where the sun has wings

3

Her laughter was about me
About me she was naked

She was like a forest
Like a multitude of women
About me
Like an armour against wilderness
Like an armour against injustice
Injustice struck everywhere

Unique star inert star of thick sky which is the privation
   of light
Injustice struck the innocent the heroes and the madmen
Who shall one day know how to rule

For I heard them laugh
In their blood in their beauty
In misery and torture
Laugh of a laugh to come
Laughter at life and birth in laughter.

Liberty

On my schoolboy's notebooks
On my desk and on the trees
On sand on snow
I write your name

On all pages read
On all blank pages
Stone blood paper or ash
I write your name

On gilded images
On the weapons of warriors
On the crowns of kings
I write your name

On jungle and desert
On nests on gorse
On the echo of my childhood
I write your name

On the wonders of nights
On the white bread of days
On betrothed seasons
I write your name

On all my rags of azure
On the pool musty sun
On the lake living moon
I write your name

On fields on the horizon
On the wings of birds
And on the mill of shadows
I write your name

On each puff of dawn
On the sea on ships
On the demented mountain
I write your name

On the foam of clouds
On the sweat of storm
On thick insipid rain
I write your name

On shimmering shapes
On bells of colour
On physical truth
I write your name

On awakened pathways
On roads spread out
On overflowing squares
I write your name

On the lamp that is lit
On the lamp that burns out
On my reunited houses
I write your name

On the fruit cut in two
Of the mirror and my chamber
On my bed empty shell
I write your name

On my dog greedy and tender
On his trained ears
On his awkward paw
I write your name

On the springboard of my door
On familiar objects
On the flood of blessed fire
I write your name

On all tuned flesh
On the foreheads of my friends
On each hand outstretched
I write your name

On the window of surprises
On the attentive lips
Well above silence
I write your name

On my destroyed refuges
On my crumbled beacons
On the walls of my weariness
I write your name

On absence without desire
On naked solitude
On the steps of death
I write your name

On health returned
On the risk disappeared
On hope without memory
I write your name

And by the power of a word
I start my life again
I was born to know you
To name you

Liberty.

The last night

I

This murderous little world
Is oriented toward the innocent
Takes the bread from his mouth
Gives his house to the flames
Takes his coat and his shoes
Takes his time and his children

This murderous little world
Confounds the dead and living
Whitens the mud pardons traitors
And turns the word to noise

Thanks midnight twelve rifles
Restore peace to the innocent
And it is for the multitudes to bury
His bleeding flesh his black sky
And it is for the multitudes to understand
The frailty of murderers.

2

The wonder would be a light push against the wall
It would be being able to shake this dust
It would be to be united.

3

They had skinned his hands bent his back
They had dug a hole in his head
And to die he had to suffer
All his life.

4

Beauty created for the happy
Beauty you run a great risk

These hands crossed on your knees
Are the tools of an assassin

This mouth singing aloud
Serves as a beggar's bowl

And this cup of pure milk
Becomes the breast of a whore.

5

The poor picked their bread from the gutter
Their look covered light
No longer were they afraid at night
So weak their weakness made them smile
In the depths of their shadow they carried their body
They saw themselves only through their distress
They used only an intimate language
And I heard them speak gently prudently
Of an old hope big as a hand

I heard them calculate
The multiplied dimensions of the autumn leaf
The melting of the wave on the breast of a calm sea
I heard them calculate
The multiplied dimension of the future force.

6

I was born behind a hideous façade
I have eaten I have laughed I have dreamed I have been
    ashamed
I have lived like a shadow
Yet I knew how to sing the sun
The entire sun which breathes
In every breast and in all eyes
The drop of candour which sparkles after tears.

7

We throw the faggot of shadows to the fire
We break the rusted locks of injustice
Men will come who will no longer fear themselves
For they are sure of all men
For the enemy with a man's face disappears.

Greatness of yesterday and today

The walls in waves the absent look of children
Grey plaster of dead houses
Dead stone around unprofitable doors
Children brought down in life the walls go with them
As with the brilliant waters mud in spring
As with some virgin beauty the dull smile
A longing to be sick rolls round and dreams in the grass.

2

Two shades upon the purblind earth
The evil word
And evil night

The shell of flesh under the sliding linen
Of crouching fear

Two shades on the cold earth
Where worms keep snug and warm
Better than wheat

On the cold earth where speech declines
Where woman is the end of man

Two shades one single night
A final night the renegades
Reasoned with reason

Filthy windows captured fire
Broken windows scattered fire
Poverty deprived of hope.

3

Nothing poorer than a child
Nothing poorer than its mother
Nothing poorer than a soldier
Than a dog than a bank clerk

O confusion purblind earth
One eye out for seeing nothing
One sky-gazing for forgetting
Winter murders everywhere at random like a miser

His heart burns out it is too late
To glorify his former life
And his beginnings in a cellar
His golden age under his rags and wrinkles
Under his special cares under a weight his own.

4

And suddenly I feel a lord of speech
And clearer more alive more proud and better
And nearer to the sun and sure to last
A child is born in me not of today

A child of always from one single kiss
More carefree than a first-come butterfly
At dawn the spring-time grants a second to him
Death conquered from the ruins comes a child

Behind him ruins and the night fade out

Seasons

1

The centre of the world is everywhere and where we live

A road self-offered to the sun
Where was it and it weighed how much
Laid out in the imploring light
Of winter born of lesser love

Of winter of a pauper child
With her accompaniment of rags
With all her retinue of fears
And cold feet walking over tombs

In the mild desert of the road.

2

The centre of the world is everywhere and where we live

Then suddenly the welcomed earth
Became a fortune-bringing rose
In bright blond mirrors visible
Where like an open rose all sang

With white of metals green of leaves
Sticky with drunkenness and heat
And gold yes gold that earth will bear
This pressing multiplicity

This good this overwhelming life.

Our movement

We live oblivious of our transformations
The day is indolent but night is active
Night strains and uses midday's bowl of air
Night does not leave its dusty trail on us

This echo though rolling through all our day
Outside the time of anguish or caresses
This brutish linking of insipid worlds
And of responsive worlds their sun is double

Are we far off or near our consciousness
Where are our boundaries our roots our aims

Yet the long pleasure of our transformations
Skeletons come to life in rotted walls
The assignation with inanimate forms
Ingenious flesh and with the blind who see

The meeting made by full-face with its profile
By malady with health and by the light
With forests by the mountain with the valley
The pit with flowers and a pearl with sun

We are side by side of earth we stand on earth
We are born of everywhere are limitless.

ANTONI SLONIMSKI
b. 1895

❊

All

In Toulouse or Ankara, in Hungary or Scotland,
Lisbon, or Dakar or London, the wave is carrying us
    forward,
Further and further from our way back to our homes.
For what are we fighting, for what are we longing?
What treasures tremendous have we lost?
Not for glory nor riches are we wandering in pain,
For a greater and more sacred cause.
Not at world domination we aim; we dream of freedom

To enjoy the calm of big, old shadowy trees,
The peaceful hours of sunset in our dear village-home,
Lost in listening the soft humming of bees,
The neigh of horses grazing on meadows,
When the dark night is approaching . . .

We don't want to rule over others, we want to share
    bread
In all justice with our own people, at home,
We dream to walk freely through our well-known roads,
And look happily into the deep, starry sky
And sleep in peace under its blue vault
It's so little, and yet it's *all*.

ANTONI SLONIMSKI

He is my brother

This man, who his own fatherland forgets
When of the shedding of Czech blood he hears,
Who, as a brother feels for Yugoslavia,
Who in the pain of Norway's people shares,

Who with the Jewish mother wrings his hands
In grief and bends with her above her slain.
Who Russian is, when Russia falls and bleeds,
And with Ukrainian weeps for the Ukraine.

This man, with heart to all compassionate,
French, when France suffers in captivity,
Greek, when Greeks in cold and hunger perish,
He is my brother – man. He is Humanity.

LOUIS ARAGON
b. 1897

❋

Santa Espina

I remember a tune we used to hear in Spain
And it made the heart beat faster, and we knew
Each time as our blood was kindled once again
Why the blue sky above us was so blue

I remember a tune like the voice of the open sea
Like the cry of migrant birds, a tune which stores
In the silence, after the notes, a stifled sob
Revenge of the salt seas on their conquerers

I remember a tune which was whistled at night
In a sunless time, an age with no wandering knight
When children wept for the bombs and in catacombs
A noble people dreamt of the tyrants' doom

It bore in its name the sacred thorns which pierced
The brow of a god as he hung upon the gallows
The song that was heard in the ear and felt in the flesh
Reopened the wound in his side and revived his sorrows

No one dared to sing to the air they hummed
All the words were forbidden and yet I know
Universe ravaged with inveterate pox
It was your hope and your month of Sundays. O

Vainly I seek its poignant melody
But the earth has now but operatic tears
The memory of its murmuring waters lost
The call of stream to stream, in these deaf years

O Holy Thorn, Holy Thorn, begin again
We used to stand as we heard you long ago
But now there is no one left to renew the strain
The woods are silent, the singers dead in Spain

I would like to believe that there is music still
In that country's heart, though hidden underground
The dumb will speak and the paralytics will
March one fine day to the cobla's triumphant sound

The crown of blood, the symbol of anguish and sorrow
Will fall from the brow of the Son of Man that hour
And man will sing loudly in that sweet tomorrow
For the beauty of life and the hawthorn tree in flower.

Richard Coeur-de-Lion

If the universe is like this gaol where now
At Tours in France we are as prisoners penned,
If strangers put our clover under plough
If today is empty of an end

Must I mark up each hour upon a chart
As time to hate, who never had the will?
One has no home now – even in the heart,
O my country, are you my country still?

Not for me now to watch the swallow fly
Who speaks to heaven a language under ban
Nor watch the unreliable cloud go by,
Old ferryman of dreams that have had their span.

Not for me now to say what I am thinking
Nor hum this air that haunts my heart and brain;
I cannot face the silence without shrinking
And sunlight is as ill as fog or rain.

They are brute force and we are only legion;
You sufferers, we know where we belong.
Why make the night a yet more sombre region?
A prisoner can still compose a song.

A song as pure as running water, white
As bread before the war, a song to rise
Above the manger clear into the night
And high enough to catch the shepherds' eyes

O all the shepherds, sailors, and Wise Men,
Carters and dons and butchers and the race
Of image-makers, tricksters with the pen,
And queues of women in the market-place

People in business and commercial roles
Men who make steel or textiles, also men
Whose job in life is scaling telegraph poles
And the black miners – all shall listen again

All Frenchmen are Blondel, in each he sings:[1]
Whatever name we called her at the start
Freedom – like a whispering of wings –
Answers the song of Richard Lionheart.

Song for a barrel organ

The refugees the bombers stopped
Turned and came back in broad daylight
Touched in the head, so tired they dropped
    Turned and came back in broad daylight
    Under their loads the women bent
    The men were crazy with their plight

1. Blondel was a troubadour and Richard's companion. In legend
he wandered through Germany to find the castle where Richard was
imprisoned and sang a ballad outside the window to reveal his
presence.

Under their loads the women bent
And children crying for lost toys
Looked without knowing what it meant
  And children crying for lost toys
  Opened their eyes too wide upon
  The shattered world of little boys
Opened their eyes too wide upon
The bakery at the corner burned
The crossroads with a Hotchkiss gun

  At the corner where the bakery burned
  Soldiers who count in an undertone
  And a colonel looking unconcerned
The soldiers count in an undertone
Their dead and wounded one by one
From the schoolhouse comes a single groan
  The dead and wounded one by one
  Their girls at home, what will they do?
  Oh, sweetheart, if I were not gone

The girls at home, what will they do?
The men sleep with their photographs
The sky outlasts the swallows too
  The men sleep with their photographs
  On canvas stretchers head by head
  Each with a pictured girl who laughs
On canvas stretchers head by head
We'll take them away, the young men
Whose skin is grey, whose bellies red

  We'll take them away, the young men
  But who knows if it's worth our while
  Look, Sergeant, they'll be dead by then
And who knows if it's worth our while
Should they arrive at Saint-Omer
What will they find with every mile?
  Should they arrive at Saint-Omer
  The tanks have cut us from the sea
  They'll find the enemy is there

The tanks have cut us from the sea
We hear they've taken Abbeville
May all our sins forgiven be
  'We hear they've taken Abbeville'
  So said the gunners who passed by
  Seeing civilians at their heel
So said the gunners who passed by
Like painted ghosts, they were so pale
The wild head and the starting eye

  Like painted ghosts they were so pale
  A fellow who came into view
  Laughed like a savage at their tale
A fellow who came into view
He was as dark as the mines
As dark as life itself in hue
  He was as dark as the mines
  This giant going home again
  To Méricourt or Sallaumines

This giant going home again
Cried, 'We return, no matter what
If it is bombs or only rain'
  Cried, 'We return no matter what
  Better by far die where you are
  With one or two shots in the gut
Better by far die where you are
Than go into a strange country
Better a hundred times in war

  Die than go to a strange country.
  We're turning back, we're going home
  The heart full, the stomach empty
We're turning back, we're going home
All hope we lack and tears and arms
We found we're not allowed to roam
  All hope we lack and tears and arms
  Little they care in safety there
  Those people chased us with gendarmes

Little they care in safety there
They sent us back beneath the bombs
"You can't get by", they told us. "Bear
   Your lot. Go back beneath the bombs"
   We're going while as yet we live
   No need for us to dig our tombs
We're going while as yet we live
Still with our children, with our wives
Thanks to no one. No thanks we give'

   Still with their children, with their wives
   Saint Christophers of the hard road
   They walked the way that cut like knives
Back to the flames, the burnt abode
Saint Christophers of the hard road
Giants outlined as they went by
   No staff in hand to help the load
   Giants outlined as they went by
   Against the white rage of the sky.

BERTOLT BRECHT
1898–1956

✳

Nanna's song

Good Sirs, at seventeen summers
I went to Lechery Fair
And plenty of things it's taught me.
Many a heartache,
That's the chance you take.
But I've wept many times in despair.
(After all I'm a human being, too.)
Thank God it's all over with quickly,
All the love and the grief we must bear.
Where are the tears of yesterevening?
Where are the snows of yesteryear?

As the years pass by it gets easy,
Easy in Lechery Fair.
And you fill your arms with so many.
But tenderness
Grows strangely less
When you spend with so little care.
(For every stock runs out in the end.)
Thank God it's all over with quickly,
All the love and the grief we must bear.
Where are the tears of yesterevening?
Where are the snows of yesteryear?

And, though you may learn your trade well,
Learn it at Lechery Fair,
Bartering lust for small change
Is a hard thing to do.

Well, it comes to you.
But you don't grow younger there.
(After all you can't stay seventeen forever.)
Thank God it's all over with quickly,
All the love and the grief we must bear.
Where are the tears of yesterevening?
Where are the snows of yesteryear?

Praise of learning

Learn the simplest things. For you
whose time has already come
it is never too late!
Learn your A B C's, it is not enough,
but learn them! Do not let it discourage you,
begin! You must know everything!
You must take over the leadership!

Learn, man in the asylum!
Learn, man in prison!
Learn, wife in the kitchen!
Learn, man of sixty!
Seek out the school, you who are homeless!
Sharpen your wits, you who shiver!
Hungry man, reach for the book: it is a weapon.
You must take over the leadership.

Don't be afraid of asking, brother!
Don't be won over,
see for yourself!
What you don't know yourself,
you don't know.
Add up the reckoning.
It's you who must pay it.
Put your finger on each item,
ask: how did this get here?
You must take over the leadership.

Song of the patch and the overcoat

Whenever our overcoat is ragged
you come running up and say: this can't continue,
you must be helped in every possible manner.
And, full of zeal, you run off to the bosses
while we who freeze are waiting.
And you come back and in triumph
show us what you have won for us:
a little patch.
            Fine, that's a patch all right
            but where is
            the whole coat?

Whenever we cry aloud from hunger
you come running up and say: this can't continue,
you must be helped in every possible manner.
And, full of zeal, you run to the bosses
while we who starve are waiting.
And you come back and in triumph
show us what you have won for us,
a crumb of bread.
            Fine, that's the breadcrumb
            but where is
            the whole loaf?

We need much more than patches,
we need the whole overcoat, too;
we need much more than the breadcrumb,
we need the loaf itself.
We need much more than a job,
we need the whole factory and the coal and the ore and
power in the state
            Fine, that's what we all need
            but what
            do you offer us?

All of us or none

Slave, who is it who shall free you?
Those in deepest darkness lying,
Comrade, these alone can see you,
They alone can hear you crying.
Comrade, only slaves can free you.
    Everything or nothing. All of us or none.
    One alone his lot can't better.
    Either gun or fetter.
    Everything or nothing. All of us or none.

You who hunger, who shall feed you?
If it's bread you would be carving,
Come to us, we too are starving.
Come to us and let us lead you.
Only hungry men can feed you.
    Everything or nothing. All of us or none.
    One alone his lot can't better.
    Either gun or fetter.
    Everything or nothing. All of us or none.

Beaten man, who shall avenge you?
You, on whom the blows are falling,
Hear your wounded brothers calling.
Weakness gives us strength to lend you.
Comrade, come, we shall avenge you.
    Everything or nothing. All of us or none.
    One alone his lot can't better.
    Either gun or fetter.
    Everything or nothing. All of us or none.

Who, O wretched one, shall dare it?
He who can no longer bear it
Counts the blows that arm his spirit,
Taught the time by need and sorrow,
Strikes today and not tomorrow.

Everything or nothing. All of us or none.
One alone his lot can't better.
Either gun or fetter.
Everything or nothing. All of us or none.

The mask of evil

On my wall hangs a Japanese carving,
The mask of an evil demon, decorated with gold
  lacquer.
Sympathetically I observe
The swollen veins of the forehead, indicating
What a strain it is to be evil.

Songs for children, Ulm 1592

Bishop, I can fly,
The tailor said to the Bishop.
Just watch how it works.
And he climbed with things
That looked like wings
To the broad, broad roof of the church.
The Bishop passed by.
It's all a lie,
Man is no bird,
No one will ever fly,
The Bishop said of the tailor.

The tailor is done for,
The people said to the Bishop.
It was the talk of the fair.
His wings were smashed
And he was dashed
On the hard, hard stones of the square.

Toll the bells in the steeple,
It was all a lie,
Man is no bird,
No one will ever fly,
The Bishop said to the people.

The solution

After the Uprising on June 17th
The Secretary of the Authors' Union
Had leaflets distributed in the Stalinallee
Which said that the people
Had forfeited the government's confidence
And could only win it back
By redoubled labour. Wouldn't it
Be simpler in that case if the government
Dissolved the people and
Elected another?

WILLIAM SOUTAR
1898–1943

❋

The children

Upon the street they lie
Beside the broken stone:
The blood of children stares from the broken stone.

Death came out of the sky
In the bright afternoon:
Darkness slanted over the bright afternoon.

Again the sky is clear
But upon earth a stain:
The earth is darkened with a darkening stain:

A wound which everywhere
Corrupts the hearts of men:
The blood of children corrupts the hearts of men.

Silence is in the air:
The stars move to their places:
Silent and serene the stars move to their places:

But from earth the children stare
With blind and fearful faces:
And our charity is in the children's faces.

ILYA SELVINSKY
1899–1968

✳

A rabbit made strong by decree

A FABLE

The Lion once gathered the beastly throng.
And he decreed, without a stuttering habit,
That from now on the one most strong
   Would be simply – the Rabbit.
The little Rabbit went into the wood,
And there was dancing, there was singing there!
But from where a birch tree stood
   Climbed down a Bear.
'Get out of my way', the Rabbit squeaked, 'You
   dummy!
   Don't you see who's coming?'
The Bear guffawed ('How ludicrous and grim!')
He whacked the bunny in the midst of laughter
And not one spot was left of him
   – Not even any fur thereafter.
But from an oak the Owl raised up a fuss
With its prophetic voice, 'You'll rue this blunder.
   The Rabbit was the strongest among us,
   According to the Lion's law we're under.
He told us when we met, the wood's aristocracy.'

And here the Bear began to cry – repeating
'O heaven, how could I know about the Rabbit? See,
   I wasn't at the meeting.'

AVRAHAM SHLONSKY

b. 1900

✳

Work

The palm of our hand is small and five are its fingers,
Thin fingers of wax and all too fragile,
A pulse at their roots, their tips – nails.
What will be done to our fingers on the day we employ
   them?
Throb mightily, my pulse. Wildly grow, my nails –
We are going to work.

O fortunate fingers, holding the sickle in harvest,
Hugging the clod covered with nettles,
Tell us:
What will be done to these fingers so tender?

O sweat,
O beaded benedictions gliding from the height of my
   forehead
As dew from the lucid heavens.
Behold, my flesh is pure and hairy,
Its hair is dusky grass.
O sweat, salt sweat,
Make my flesh dewy, turgid as fields in the morning.
Praise, Halelujah.

The morning skies lift the thick boughs of an oak,
Absalom's head, golden, curly,
Hangs high in the branches above –
Sun, O Sun!

I will stoop to the sands.
Beneath the heavy concrete, dunes gasp:
O Man, why did you come to the deserts
To anchor the bit in our mouths?
A wind lashes suddenly from the east
And like herds of wild unbroken camels
Sweep down on the suburb in building –
Sands!

They gallop like hail on road and foundations;
With lilliput shoes
The granular sand-hoofs
Pellet my face.
Vengeance!
Now behold – they wheel – they shriek:
To the deserts, the deserts!

Slow my hand –
The spade in my hand is grey with cement –
The roads twist in pursuit: Follow after!
The hands stretch:
Crush them! Cramp them!
Harness the deserts,
Tighten the reins of the roads
For it is I sitting high at the wheel
I – work.

Huge fists crouch in the sands:
Houses – houses – houses –

I sense:
It is I who is caught in the branches of dawn.
As a ray in my hand gleams a spade.
And the unfinished suburb grins at me, laughs:
Sun, O Sun!

Dress me, mother dear, in a coat of splendid colours
And lead me to work with dawn.

My country is wrapped in a *talith* of light.
The houses project like frontlets –
Like *tefillin* thongs dip the roads bedded by our hands.
The lovely suburb chants a psalm of dawn to its Maker,
And among the makers – your son, Avraham,
Poet-Roadbuilder in Israel.

Father will return from his sufferings with dusk
And murmur his pleasure in prayer:
Avraham is my one dear son,
Just skin and sinew and bone –
Praise! Halelujah!

Dress me, mother dear, with a coat of splendour,
And at dawn lead me
To work.

OKAMOTO JUN
b. 1901

✿

A wind-swept bridge

a long river bank
the wind-swept dam
it is strange: only motor-hearses
go crossing that long wind-swept bridge

A vanished bridge

War has broken the bridge
and the ditch was filled in:
the bridge is no longer there.
No one cares about the disappearance
of the bridge, however, and people
are walking in a stream along the busy streets.

A bridge

Incendiary bombs were dropped,
bombs were dropped,
and both your home
and you
are gone.
Only a pier is left
in the vast barren ruins now
and the flowing water is rapping its foot.

RAFAEL ALBERTI
b. 1902

❋

Nocturne

When one suffers sleepless, listening to rage
Running through the veins its lonely course,
When hate trembles sharply in the bones
And vengeance through the marrow continuously burns,
Then words make no sense: they are only words.

Bullets. Bullets.

Misty impressions and clouds of forgotten smoke
Are the manifestos and the speeches;
An anguish of paper for the wind to brush away.
A sorrow of ink for the waters to erase.

Bullets. Bullets.

Now I suffer poverty, meanness and despair,
The unfortunate and dead with throat like an abyss
Filled with language that desired to cry aloud
But was forever silent, for this was not possible.

Bullets. Bullets.

Tonight it seems that words are wounds in me of death.

Country recruits

They march flintily forward, the colour of bark
slashed by the axe's aggression, immutable.
Like splinters of adamant, the heads and the faces are
   dark,
but a glow flashes out of their dream like the husk of a
   fruit.

An odour of clothing goes up: lamb's wool rank with
   the rain –
a reek as of burlap and gathered potatoes that moves
over mud and manure and clings to whatever remains
in the mash of their boot soles and hardens the leather
   like hooves.

Their sound in the darkness is obdurate: mule teams and
   burros
fanning out in the streets and blocking the doors and
   the gutters,
they pour from the fields like a mountain of wheat in the
   kernel
and plant themselves deep in the trenches like seeds in a
   furrow.

They know nothing, have little to say. Their conviction
   is this:
to advance with all possible speed on the threatened
   assault of their star,
to labour from sunrise to sunrise in another employment
dealing death to their deaths and winning their lives in a
   war.

To 'Misty', my dog

Misty, you could never conceive it: though your ears
    ring with the truth
of it – all that innocent tobacco of your gaze, now a
    little demented;
all the pathless magnificence left on the slope of the
    mountain
where you bound like the supplest of rays that uncoils on
    a breeze.

Those castaway mongrels, now grown wary, or mad:
    look
at them well: they bolt from a rent in the fog, placing paw
after paw, with the timid estrangement of dogs, to pluck
out the heart of a mystery: a house that was theirs, in the
    rubble.

Despite all that panic cortège, the unceremonious
queuing of cars that carry their death in a box
in the barest of woods; or a child looking up at a lark
of a fight in the clouds that might batter him down as he
    looks –

For all the friends fallen, the pick of a lifetime now lost,
or that last desolation of all: a family cold
to all I would have them weigh well and conceive at all
    costs;
or the turncoats recoiled from our love, and sold out –

nevertheless, Misty, dog at my heels, nevertheless,
for all you can never conceive, without knowing why,
at the heart of heroical anguish and endless bom-
    bardment,
ours is the faith in a world that is joy! that is joy! that is
    joy!

Corporeal sonnets: 7

The stilled heat grows in the groin; in the silence
of surf, a flicker of spray turning over.
The tulip's magnificence that thrives in a hardness of
  wicker,
bends back in its drought and continues, alive and
  exhausted.

A power lives on in the blood: a kindling vagary,
uneasy, insistent, belligerent, granting no quarter.
All that was lost to the flower or forgotten in lethargy
breaks out of sleep and forces its roots toward the water.

The very cobbles leap up: out of the clay of its entrails,
resins unload, wellsprings, the green of the poplars.
All trembles and crackles, strains forward, lashes out,
  and explodes.

Life cleaves to life, splits asunder to magnify life.
And however death forces its forfeits or gains its
  advantage,
the fields lie before us for battle, and the battle is
  jubilant.

NAKANO SHIGEHARU
b. 1902

❋

The Imperial Hotel

I

Here, it's the West:
The dogs talk English.
Here, manners are the West's:
The dogs invite you to Russian opera.
Here, it's the West, the West's bazaar:
A junkshop of Japanese fly-blown clothes and curios.

Here, too, is a gaol:
The warder twiddles his keys.
Yes, here a dank and cheerless gaol:
Warder and prisoner speak to no man.
Prisoners are known by numbers:
A warder stands by the door.

Here, it's a cheap bar:
Fat men get tight.

Here, it's a whorehouse:
Whores parade in the nude.

Here, it's a nothing
Black and stinking.

Huge nothing
Huge whorehouse
Huge bar parlour
Huge dank gaol.
A seedy junkshop of Japan
Squats in the heart of Tokyo
And vomits a vile stink
Over all our heads.

Farewell before dawn

We have our work.
To work, we must talk,
But if we talk
The police come and batter in our faces.

So we switched our upper room,
With an eye to a back alley and escape route.
Six young men asleep here
And, beneath, a couple and their baby.
I don't know the past of these six;
I only know they think as I do.
I don't know the names of the people below;
I only know they gladly rented their upper room.

Dawn any moment.
Moving on again,
Our bags all ready.
There'll be a secret meeting
And slowly our work will go forward.
Tomorrow, sleeping again in hired blankets.
Dawn any moment.
Good-bye, tiny room,
Nappies on the line,

Naked, grimy light,
Celluloid toys,
Hired blankets,
Bugs.
Good-bye!
That thoughts may flower –
Ours,
The couple's,
The baby's –
All, at once, and savagely.

LANGSTON HUGHES
1902–67

❋

I, too, sing America

I, too, sing America.

I am the darker brother.
They send me to eat in the kitchen
When company comes,
But I laugh,
And eat well,
And grow strong.

Tomorrow,
I'll sit at the table
When company comes.
Nobody'll dare
Say to me,
'Eat in the kitchen',
Then.

Besides,
They'll see how beautiful I am
And be ashamed –

I, too, am America.

Dream variation

To fling my arms wide
In some place of the sun,
To whirl and to dance
Till the white day is done.

Then rest at cool evening
Beneath a tall tree
While night comes on gently,
    Dark like me –
That is my dream!

To fling my arms wide
In the face of the sun,
Dance! whirl! whirl!
Till the quick day is done.
Rest at pale evening . . .
A tall, slim tree . . .
Night coming tenderly
    Black like me.

The Weary Blues

Droning a drowsy syncopated tune,
Rocking back and forth to a mellow croon,
    I heard a Negro play.
Down on Lenox Avenue the other night
By the pale dull pallor of an old gas light
    He did a lazy sway . . .
    He did a lazy sway . . .
To the tune o' those Weary Blues.
With his ebony hands on each ivory key
He made that poor piano moan with melody.
    O Blues!

Swaying to and fro on his rickety stool
He played that sad raggy tune like a musical fool.
   Sweet Blues!
Coming from a black man's soul.
   O Blues!
In a deep song voice with a melancholy tone
I heard that Negro sing, that old piano moan—
   'Ain't got nobody in all this world,
   Ain't got nobody but ma self.
   I's gwine to quit ma frownin'
   And put ma troubles on the shelf.'
Thump, thump, thump, went his foot on the floor.
He played a few chords then he sang some more—
   'I got the Weary Blues
   And I can't be satisfied.
   Got the Weary Blues
   And can't be satisfied—
   I ain't happy no mo'
   And I wish that I had died.'
And far into the night he crooned that tune.
The stars went out and so did the moon.
The singer stopped playing and went to bed
While the Weary Blues echoed through his head.
He slept like a rock or a man that's dead.

Song for a dark girl

   Way Down South in Dixie
      (Break the heart of me)
   They hung my dark young lover
      To a cross-roads tree.

   Way Down South in Dixie
      (Bruised body high in air)
   I asked the white Lord Jesus
      What was the use of prayer.

Way Down South in Dixie
  (Break the heart of me)
Love is a naked shadow
  On a gnarled and naked tree.

Merry-go-round

Coloured child at carnival

Where is the Jim Crow section
On this merry-go-round,
Mister, cause I want to ride?
Down South where I come from
White and coloured
Can't sit side by side.
Down South on the train
There's a Jim Crow car.
On the bus we're put in the back –
But there ain't no back
To a merry-go-round!
Where's the horse
For a kid that's black?

Mother to son

Well, son, I'll tell you:
Life for me ain't been no crystal stair.
It's had tacks in it,
And splinters,
And boards torn up,
And places with no carpet on the floor –
Bare.
But all the time
I'se been a-climbin' on,
And reachin' landin's,

257

And turnin' corners,
And sometimes goin' in the dark
Where there ain't been no light.
So, boy, don't you turn back.
Don't you set down on the steps
'Cause you finds it's kinder hard.
Don't you fall now
For I'se still goin', honey,
I'se still climbin',
And life for me ain't been no crystal stair.

The Negro speaks of rivers

I've known rivers:
I've known rivers ancient as the world and older than the
    flow of human blood in human veins.

My soul has grown deep like the rivers.

I bathed in the Euphrates when dawns were young.
I built my hut near the Congo and it lulled me to sleep.
I looked upon the Nile and raised the pyramids above it.
I heard the singing of the Mississippi when Abe Lincoln
    went down to New Orleans, and I've seen its muddy
    bosom turn all golden in the sunset.

I've known rivers:
Ancient, dusky rivers.

My soul has grown deep like the rivers.

Cross

My old man's a white man
And my old mother's black.
If ever I cursed my white old man
I take my curses back.

If ever I cursed my black old mother
And wished she were in hell,
I'm sorry for that evil wish
And now I wish her well.

My old man died in a fine big house,
My ma died in a shack.
I wonder where I'm gonna die,
Being neither white nor black?

NAZIM HIKMET
1902–63

✣

Advice to our children

Be naughty, that's all right.
Climb up sheer walls,
   up towering trees.
Like an old captain let your hands direct
the course of your bicycle.
And with the pencil which draws the cartoons
   of the master of Religious Knowledge,
   demolish the pages of the Koran.
You must know how to build your own paradise
   on this black soil.
With your geology text-book
you must silence the man who teaches you
that creation began with Adam.
You must recognize
   the importance of the Earth,
you must believe
   that the Earth is eternal
Distinguish not between your mother
and your mother Earth.
You must love it
   as much as you love her.

✒ *Since I was thrown into this hole*

Since I was thrown into this hole
the Earth has gone round the sun ten times.
If you ask the Earth, it will say,
  'Doesn't deserve mention
  such a microscopic amount of time.'
If you ask me, I'll say,
  'Ten years off my life.'

The day I was imprisoned
  I had a small pencil
which I used up within a week.
If you ask the pencil, it will say,
  'My whole lifetime.'
If you ask me, I'll say,
  'So what? Only a week.'

Osman, serving a sentence for murder
  when I first came into this hole,
  left after seven years and a half;
  enjoyed life outside for a time
  then came back for smuggling
  and left at the end of six months.
  Someone heard yesterday, he's married
  he'll have a child come spring.

The children conceived
  the day I was thrown into this hole
are now celebrating their tenth year.
The foals born on that very day
  trembling on their thin, long legs
must by now have become
  lazy mares shaking their wide rumps.
But the young olive shoots are still young,
  still growing.

They tell me new squares have been built
  in my own town since I came here.
And my family of that little house
  are now living
      in a street I do not know
        in another house I cannot see.

The bread was white as virgin cotton
the year I was thrown into this hole
and then it was rationed.
Here, in the cells,
  people killed one another
    for a handful of black crumbs.
Now things are a little better
but the bread we have, has no taste.

The year I was thrown into this hole
  the Second World War had not started;
in the concentration camps of Dachau
the gas ovens had not been built;
the atom had not exploded in Hiroshima.
Oh, the time has just flowed
  like the blood of a massacred baby.
Now that's all over
  but the American dollar
    is already talking
      of a Third World War ...

All the same, the day is brighter now
  than it was
      when I was thrown into this hole.
Since that day
  my people have raised themselves
    halfway up on their elbows;
the Earth has gone round the sun
  ten times ...
But I repeat with the same fervent yearning
  what I wrote for my people
    ten years ago today:

'You are as plenty
   as the ants in the Earth
     as the fish in the sea
       as the birds in the sky;
you may be coward or brave
   illiterate or literate.
And since *you* are the makers
   or the destroyers
     of all deeds,
only *your* adventures
   will be recorded in songs.'

And the rest,
   such as my ten years' suffering,
     is simply idle talk.

That's how it goes

Am in the middle of a spreading light,
my hands inspired, the world beautiful.
   Cannot stop looking at trees:
   they're so hopeful and so green.
A sunny pathway stretches beyond the mulberries,
I stand before the window in the prison hospital,
   cannot smell the smell of medicine:
   somewhere carnations must be in bloom.
That's how it goes, my friend.
The problem is not falling a captive,
it's how to avoid surrender.

A sad state of freedom

You waste the attention of your eyes,
the glittering labour of your hands,

and knead the dough enough for dozens of loaves
   of which you'll taste not a morsel;
you are free to slave for others –
you are free to make the rich richer.

The moment you're born
   they plant around you
mills that grind lies
lies to last you a lifetime.
You keep thinking in your great freedom
   a finger on your temple
      free to have a free conscience.

Your head bent as if half-cut from the nape,
your arms long, hanging,
you saunter about in your great freedom:
   you're free
      with the freedom of being unemployed.

You love your country
as the nearest, most precious thing to you.
But one day, for example,
   they may endorse it over to America,
and you, too, with your great freedom –
you have the freedom to become an air-base.

You may proclaim that one must live
not as a tool, a number or a link
but as a human being –
then at once they handcuff your wrists.
You are free to be arrested, imprisoned
   and even hanged.

There's neither an iron, wooden
   nor a tulle curtain
      in your life;
there's no need to choose freedom:
you are free.
But this kind of freedom
   is a sad affair under the stars.

EDVARD KOCBEK
b. 1904

❈

The parrots

Termites attacked the area,
Eating away bridges and monuments.
Tables and beds fell away to dust.
Bacilli infiltrated the laboratories
And settled on the sterile instruments,
Incidentally deceiving the experts.
It all happened so horribly quietly.

With us there was a plague of parrots;
Green and yellow, they screamed
In gardens, houses and kitchens,
Greedy, dirty and vulgar
They invaded the bathrooms and bedrooms
And finally settled inside people.
It all happened so horribly loudly.

Not one of us can lie any more;
Not one of us can tell the truth –
We speak the tongue of an unknown tribe;
We shout, curse, howl and roar,
We draw back our lips, our eyes pop out,
Even the court jester has gone mad
And screams like all the rest.

Yet somewhere in the circle stand men
Mutely gazing into the still centre.

Motionless they stand, blissfully silent,
Their shoulders growing broader and broader
Under the ancient burden of silence.
At the moment when they turn round,
The parrots in us will die.

PABLO NERUDA
b. 1904

※

From CANTO GENERAL

Some beasts

It was the twilight of the iguana.
From the rainbow-arch of the battlements,
his long tongue like a lance
sank down in the green leaves,
and a swarm of ants, monks with feet chanting,
crawled off into the jungle,
the guanaco, thin as oxygen
in the wide peaks of cloud,
went along, wearing his shoes of gold,
while the llama opened his honest eyes
on the breakable neatness
of a world full of dew.
The monkeys braided a sexual
thread that went on and on
along the shores of the dawn,
demolishing walls of pollen
and startling the butterflies of Muzo
into flying violets.
It was the night of the alligators,
the pure night, crawling
with snouts emerging from ooze,
and out of the sleepy marshes
the confused noise of scaly plates
returned to the ground where they began.

The jaguar brushed the leaves
with a luminous absence,
the puma runs through the branches
like a forest fire,
while the jungle's drunken eyes
burn from inside him.
The badgers scratch the river's
feet, scenting the nest
whose throbbing delicacy
they attack with red teeth.

And deep in the huge waters
the enormous anaconda lies
like the circle around the earth,
covered with ceremonies of mud,
devouring, religious.

The Heights of Macchu Picchu, III[1]

The human soul was threshed out like maize in the endless

granary of defeated actions, of mean things that happened,

to the very edge of endurance, and beyond,

and not only death, but many deaths, came to each one:

each day a tiny death, dust, worm, a light

flicked off in the mud at the city's edge, a tiny death with coarse wings

pierced into each man like a short lance

and the man was besieged by the bread or by the knife,

the cattle-dealer: the child of sea-harbours, or the dark captain of the plough,

or the rag-picker of snarled streets:

1. Macchu Picchu, the ancient Inca city, was built *c.* 3000 B.C. and lies some 12,000 feet above sea-level in the Peruvian Andes. Its existence was unknown until it was uncovered and excavated by Hiram Bingham in 1912.

everybody lost heart, anxiously waiting for death, the
   short death of every day:
and the grinding bad luck of every day was
like a black cup that they drank, with their hands shaking

The head on the pole[1]

Balboa, you brought death and claws
everywhere into the sweet land
of Central America, and among those hunting dogs
your dog was your soul:
with his blood-stained jowls Lioncub
picked up the slave escaping,
sank his Spanish teeth
into the panting throats;
pieces of flesh slipped from
the dogs' jaws into martyrdom
and the jewel fell in the pocket.

A curse on dog and man,
the horrible howl in the unbroken
forest, and the stealthy
walk of the iron and the bandit.
And a curse on the spiny crown
of the wild thornbush
that did not leap like a hedgehog
to protect the invaded cradle.

But the justice of knives,
the bitter branch of envy,
rose in the darkness
among the bloody captains.

1. Vasco Nuñez de Balboa (c. 1475–1517), the Spanish conquista-
dor who discovered the Pacific Ocean, was Admiral of the Pacific
and Governor of Panama; later imprisoned and executed.

And when you got back, the man
named Pedrarias stood
in your way like a rope.

They tried you surrounded by the barkings
of dogs that killed Indians.
Now you are dying, do you hear
the pure silence, broken
by your excited dogs?
Now you are dying in the hands
of the stern authorities,
do you sense the precious aroma
of the sweet kingdom smashed forever?

When they cut off Balboa's
head, it was stuck up
on a pole. His dead eyes
let their lightning rot
and descended along the pole
as a large drop of filth
which disappeared into the earth.

Toussaint L'Ouverture[1]

Out of its own tangled sweetness
Haiti raises mournful petals,
and elaborate gardens, magnificent
structures, and rocks the sea
as a dark grandfather rocks
his ancient dignity of skin and space.

1. Pierre Dominique Toussaint L'Ouverture (*c.* 1746–1803), a
Haitian slave who joined the insurrection of 1791, helped the French
abolish slavery, and became C.-in-C. of Santo Domingo in 1796; opp-
osed the French re-imposition of slavery, was captured and died in
prison in France.

Toussaint L'Ouverture knit together
the vegetable kingdom,
the majesty chained,
the monotonous voice of the drums
and attacks, cuts off retreats, rises,
orders, expels, defies
like a natural monarch,
until he falls into the shadowy net
and they carry him over the seas,
dragged along and trampled down
like the return of his race,
thrown into the secret death
of the ship-holds and the cellars.
But on the island the boulders burn,
the hidden branches speak,
hopes are passed on,
the walls of the fortress rise.
Liberty is your own forest,
dark brother, don't lose
the memory of your sufferings,
may the ancestral heroes
have your magic sea-foam in their keeping.

The United Fruit Co.

When the trumpet sounded, it was
all prepared on the earth,
the Jehovah parcelled out the earth
to Coca Cola, Inc., Anaconda,
Ford Motors, and other entities:
The Fruit Company, Inc.
reserved for itself the most succulent,
the central coast of my own land,
the delicate waist of America.
It rechristened its territories

as the 'Banana Republics'
and over the sleeping dead,
over the restless heroes
who brought about the greatness,
the liberty and the flags,
it established the comic opera:
abolished the independencies,
presented crowns of Caesar,
unsheathed envy, attracted
the dictatorship of the flies,
Trujillo flies, Tacho flies,
Carias flies, Martines flies,
Ubico flies, damp flies
of modest blood and marmalade,
drunken flies who zoom
over the ordinary graves,
circus flies, wise flies
well trained in tyranny.

Among the blood-thirsty flies
the Fruit Company lands its ships,
taking off the coffee and the fruit;
the treasure of our submerged
territories flow as though
on plates into the ships.

Meanwhile Indians are falling
into the sugared chasms
of the harbours, wrapped
for burial in the mist of the dawn:
a body rolls, a thing
that has no name, a fallen cipher,
a cluster of dead fruit
thrown down on the dump.

The dictators

An odour has remained among the sugar cane:
a mixture of blood and body, a penetrating
petal that brings nausea.
Between the coconut palms the graves are full
of ruined bones, of speechless death-rattles.
The delicate dictator is talking
with tophats, gold braid, and collars.
The tiny palace gleams like a watch
and the rapid laughs with gloves on
cross the corridors at times
and join the dead voices
and the blue mouths freshly buried.
The weeping cannot be seen, like a plant
whose seeds fall endlessly on the earth,
whose large blind leaves grow even without light.
Hatred has grown scale on scale,
blow on blow, in the ghastly water of the swamp,
with a snout full of ooze and silence.

Cristobal Miranda

(Shoveller at Tocopilla)

I met you on the broad barges
in the bay, Cristobal, while the sodium nitrate
was coming down, wrapped in a burning
November day, to the sea.
I remember the ecstatic nimbleness,
the hills of metal, the motionless water.
And only the bargemen, soaked
with sweat, moving snow.
Snow of the nitrates, poured
over painful shoulders, dropping
into the blind stomach of the ships.

Shovellers there, heroes of a sunrise
eaten away by acids, and bound
to the destinies of death, standing firm,
taking in the floods of nitrate.
Cristobal, this memento is for you,
for the others shovelling with you,
whose chests are penetrated by the acids
and the lethal gases,
making the heart swell up
like crushed eagles, until the man drops,
rolls toward the streets of town,
toward the broken crosses out in the field.
Enough of that, Cristobal, today
this bit of paper remembers you, each of you,
the bargemen of the bay, the man
turned black in the boats, my eyes
are moving with yours in this daily work
and my soul is a shovel which lifts
loading and unloading blood and snow
next to you, creatures of the desert.

I wish the wood-cutter would wake up

West of the Colorado River
there's a place I love.
I take refuge there with everything alive
in me, with everything
that I have been, that I am, that I believe in.
Some high red rocks are there, the wild
air with its thousand hands
has turned them into human buildings.
The blind scarlet rose from the depths
and changed in these rocks to copper, fire, and energy.
America spread out like a buffalo skin,
light and transparent night of galloping,
near your high places covered with stars
I drink down your cup of green dew.

Yes, through acrid Arizona and Wisconsin full of knots,
as far as Milwaukee, raised to keep back the wind and
    the snow
or in the burning swamps of West Palm,
near the pine trees of Tacoma, in the thick odour
of your forests which is like steel,
I walked weighing down the mother earth,
blue leaves, waterfalls of stones,
hurricanes vibrating as all music does,
rivers that muttered prayers like monasteries,
geese and apples, territories and waters,
infinite silence in which the wheat could be born.

I was able there, in my deep stony core, to stretch my
    eyes, ears, hands,
far out into the air until I heard
books, locomotives, snow, battles,
factories, cemeteries, footsteps, plants,
and the moon on a ship from Manhattan,
the song of the machine that is weaving,
the iron spoon that eats the earth,
the drill that strikes like a condor,
and everything that cuts, presses, sews:
creatures and wheels repeating themselves and being
    born.

I love the farmer's small house. New mothers are asleep
with a good smell like the sap of the tamarind, clothes
just ironed. Fires are burning in a thousand homes,
with drying onions hanging around the fireplace.
(When they are singing near the river the men's voices
are deep as the stones at the river bottom;
and tobacco rose from its wide leaves
and entered these houses like a spirit of the fire.)
Come deeper into Missouri, look at the cheese and the
    flour,
the boards aromatic and red as violins,
the man moving like a ship among the barley,

the blue-black colt just home from a ride smells
the odour of bread and alfalfa:
bells, poppies, blacksmith shops,
and in the rundown movies in the small towns
love opens its mouth full of teeth
in a dream born of the earth.
What we love is your peace, not your mask.
Your warrior's face is not handsome.
North America, you are handsome and spacious.
You come, like a washerwoman, from
a simple cradle, near your rivers, pale . . .
Built up from the unknown,
what is sweet in you is your hive-like peace.
We love the man with his hands red
from the Oregon clay, your negro boy
who brought you the music born
in his country of tusks: we love
your city, your substance,
your light, your machines, the energy
of the West, the harmless
honey from hives and little towns,
the huge farmboy on his tractor,
the oats which you inherited
from Jefferson, the noisy wheel
that measures your oceanic earth,
the factory smoke and the kiss,
the thousandth, of a new colony:
what we love is your workingman's blood:
your unpretentious hand covered with oil.

For years now under the prairie night
in a heavy silence on the buffalo skin
syllables have been asleep, poems
about what I was before I was born, what we were.
Melville is a sea fir, the curve of the keel
springs from his branches, an arm
of timber and ship. Whitman impossible to count
as grain, Poe in his mathematical

darkness, Dreiser, Wolfe,
fresh wounds of our own absence,
Lockbridge more recently, all bound to the depths,
how many others, bound to the darkness:
over them the same dawn of the hemisphere burns,
and out of them what we are has come.
Powerful foot-soldiers, blind captains,
frightened at times among action and leaves,
checked in their work by joy and by mourning,
under the plains crossed by traffic,
how many dead men in the fields never visited before:
innocent ones tortured, prophets only now published,
on the buffalo skin of the prairies.

From France, and Okinawa, and the atolls
of Leyte (Norman Mailer has written it out)
and the infuriated air and the waves,
almost all the men have come back now,
almost all . . . The history of mud and sweat
was green and sour; they did not hear
the singing of the reefs long enough
and perhaps never touched the islands, those wreaths of
   brilliance and perfume,
except to die:
                    dung and blood
hounded them, the filth and the rats,
and a fatigued and ruined heart that went on fighting.
But they have come back,
                         you have received them
into the immensity of the open lands
and they have closed (those who came back) like a flower
with thousands of nameless petals
to be reborn and forget.

(1948)

Letter to Miguel Otero Silva, in Caracas (1948)

Nicolas Guillén brought me your letter, written
invisibly, on his clothes, in his eyes.
How happy you are, Miguel, both of us are!
In a world that ulcers have almost hidden
there is no one left aimlessly happy but us,
I see the crow go by; there's nothing he can do.
You watch the scorpion, and polish your guitar.
Writing poetry, we live among the wild beasts, and when
    we touch
a man, the stiff of someone in whom we believed,
and he goes to pieces like a rotten pie,
you in the Venezuela you inherited gather together
whatever can be salvaged, while I cup my hands
around the live coal of life.

                        What happiness, Miguel!
Are you going to ask where I am? I'll tell you –
giving only details useful to the State –
that on this coast scattered with wild rocks,
the sea and the fields come together, the waves and the
    pines,
petrels and eagles, meadows and foam.
Have you ever spent a whole day close to seabirds,
watching how they fly? They seem
To be carrying the letters of the world to their destination.
The pelicans go by like sailing ships,
other birds go by like arrows, carrying
messages from dead kings, viceroys
buried with strands of turquoise on the andean coasts,
and seagulls, so magnificently white,
they are constantly forgetting what their messages are.
How clear life is, Miguel, like the sky, when we put
loving and fighting in it, words that are bread and wine,
words they have not been able to degrade even now,
because we walk out in the street with poems and guns.
They don't know what to do with us, Miguel.

What can they do but kill us; and even that
wouldn't be a good bargain – nothing to do
but rent a room across the street, and tail us
so they can learn to laugh and cry like us.
When I was writing my love poems, which sprouted out
    from me
on all sides, and I was dying from depression,
nomadic, abandoned, gnawing on the alphabet,
they said to me: 'What a great man you are, Theocritus!'
I am not Theocritus: I took life,
and faced her, and kissed her and won her,
and then went through the tunnels of the mines
to see how other men live.
And when I came out, my hands stained with garbage
    and sadness,
I held my hands up and showed them to the generals,
and said: 'I am not a part of this crime.'
They started to cough, showed disgust, left off saying
    hello,
gave up calling me Theocritus, and ended by insulting me
and assigning the entire police force to arrest me,
because I didn't continue to be occupied exclusively with
    metaphysical subjects.
But I have brought joy over to my side.
From then on I started getting up to read the letters
the seabirds carry from so far away,
letters that arrive moist, messages I translate
phrase by phrase, slowly and confidently: I am
    punctilious
as an engineer in this strange duty.
I go to the window all at once. It is a square
of pure light, there is a clear horizon
of grasses and crags, and I go on working here
among the things I love: waves, rocks, wasps,
with an oceanic and drunken happiness.
But no one cares if we are happy or not; and they cast
you in a genial role: 'Now do not exaggerate, don't
    worry,'

and they want to lock me in a cricket cage, where there
    would be tears,
and I would drown, and they themselves could give
    speeches on my grave.
I remember one day in the sandy acres
of the nitrate flats; there were five hundred men
on strike. It was a scorching afternoon
of Tarapaca. And after the faces had absorbed
all the sand and the bloodless dry sun of the desert,
I saw coming into me, like a cup that I hate,
my old depression. At this (critical) point,
in the desolation of the salt flats, in that weak moment
of the fight, when we could have been beaten,
a little pale girl who had come from the mines
spoke a poem of yours in a brave voice
that had glass in it and steel, an old poem of yours that
    moves among the wrinkled eyes
of all the workers of my country, of America.
And this small piece of your poetry blazed suddenly
like a purple blossom in my mouth,
and went down to my blood, filling it
with a luxuriant joy born from your poem.
I thought of you, and also of your bitter Venezuela.
Years ago I saw a student who had marks on his ankles
from chains ordered on him by a general,
and he told me of the chaingangs that work on the roads
and the jails where people disappear forever. Because
    that is what our America has been:
long stretches with destructive rivers and constellations
of butterflies (in some places the emeralds are heavy as
    apples)
but along the whole length of the night and the rivers
there are always bleeding ankles, at one time near the oil
    wells,
now near the nitrate, in Pisagua, where a rotten leader
has put the best men of my country under the earth to die,
    so he can sell their bones.

That is why you write poetry, so the disgraced and
  wounded America
can someday let its butterflies tremble and collect its
  emeralds
without the terrifying blood of beatings, coagulated
on the hands of the executioners and the business men.
I guessed how full of joy you would be, by the Orinoco,
  writing,
probably, or perhaps buying wine for your house,
taking your part in the fight and the exaltation,
with broad shoulders, like the poets of our age –
with light clothes and walking shoes.
Ever since that time, I wanted to write to you,
and when Guillén arrived, running over with stories of
  you,
which were coming loose everywhere out of his clothes
they poured out under the chestnuts of my house –
I said to myself: 'Now!', and even then I didn't start a
  letter to you.
But today has been too much for me: not only one sea
  bird,
but thousands have gone past my window,
and I have picked up the letters no one reads, that they
  take along
to all the shores of the world until they lose them.
Then in each of those letters I read words of yours
and they resembled the words I write, and dream of, and
  put in poems,
and so I decided to send this letter to you, which I end
  here,
so I can watch through the window the world that is ours.

They receive instructions against Chile

But we have to see behind all these, there is something
behind the traitors and the gnawing rats,
an empire which sets the table,
and serves up the nourishment and the bullets.
They want to repeat their great success in Greece.
Greek playboys at the banquet, and bullets
for the people in the mountains: we'll have to destroy the
    flight
of the new Victory of Samothrace, we'll have to hang,
kill, lose men, sink the murderous knife
held to us from New York, we'll have to use fire
to break the spirit of the man who was emerging
in all countries as if born
from the earth that had been splashed with blood.
We have to arm Chiang and the vicious Videla,
give them money for prisons, wings
so they can bomb their own populations, give them
a hand-out, a few dollars, and they do the rest,
they lie, bribe, dance on the dead bodies
and their first ladies wear the most expensive minks.
The suffering of the people does not matter: copper
executives need this sacrifice: facts are facts:
the generals retire from the army and serve
as vice-presidents of the Chuquicamata Copper Firm,
and in the nitrate works the 'chilean' general
decides with his trailing sword how much the natives
may mention when they apply for a raise in wages.
In this way they decide from above, from the roll of
    dollars,
in this way the dwarf traitor receives his instructions,
and the generals act as the police force,
and the trunk of the tree of the country rots.

The enigmas

You've asked me what the lobster is weaving there with
  his golden feet?
I reply, the ocean knows this.
You say, what is the ascidia waiting for in its transparent
  bell? What is it waiting for?
I tell you it is waiting for time, like you.
You ask me whom the Macrocustic alga hugs in its arms?
Study, study it, at a certain hour, in a certain sea I know.
You question me about the wicked tusk of the narwhal,
  and I reply by describing
how the sea-unicorn with the harpoon in it dies.
You inquire about the kingfishers' feathers,
which tremble in the pure springs of the southern tides?
Or you've found in the cards a new question touching on
  the crystal architecture
of the sea anemone, and you'll deal that to me now?
You want to understand the electric nature of the ocean
  spines?
  The armoured stalactite that breaks as it walks?
  The hook of the angler fish, the music stretched out
  in the deep places like a thread in the water?

I want to tell you the ocean knows this, that life in its
  jewel boxes
is endless as the sand, impossible to count, pure,
and among the blood-coloured grapes time has made the
  petal
hard and shiny, made the jellyfish full of light
and untied its knot, letting its musical threads fall
from a horn of plenty made of infinite mother-of-pearl.

I am nothing but the empty net which has gone on ahead
of human eyes, dead in those darknesses,
of fingers accustomed to the triangle, longitudes
on the timid globe of an orange.

I walked around as you do, investigating
the endless star,
and in my net, during the night, I woke up naked,
the only thing caught, a fish trapped inside the wind.

Friends on the road (1921)[1]

Then I arrived at the capital, vaguely saturated
with fog and rain. What streets were those?
The garments of 1921 were breeding
in an ugly smell of gas, coffee, and bricks.
I walked among the students without understanding,
pulling the walls inside me, searching
each day into my poor poetry for the branches,
the drops of rain, and the moon, that had been lost.
I went deep into it for help, sinking
each evening into its waters, grasping
energies I could not touch, the seagulls of a deserted sea,
until I closed my eyes and was shipwrecked in the middle
of my own body.
                        Were these things dark shadows,
were they only hidden damp leaves stirred up from the
    soil?
What was the wounded substance from which death was
    pouring out
until it touched my arms and legs, controlled my smile,
and dug a well of pain in the streets?

I went out into life: I grew and was hardened,
I walked through the hideous back-alleys
without compassion, singing out on the frontiers
of delirium. The walls filled with faces:
eyes that did not look at light, twisted waters
lit up by a crime, legacies

1. This describes the poet's schooldays in Santiago, when he was
seventeen.

of solitary pride, holes
filled with hearts that had been condemned and torn
    down.
I walked with them: it was only in that chorus
that my voice refound the solitudes
where it was born.

I finally became a man
singing among the flames, accepted
by friends who find their place in the night,
who sang with me in the taverns,
and who gave me more than a single kindness,
something they had defended with their fighting hands,
which was more than a spring,
a fire unknown elsewhere, the natural foliage
of the places slowly falling down at the city's edge.

C. DAY LEWIS

b. 1904

✳

The magnetic mountain: 25

Consider these, for we have condemned them;
Leaders to no sure land, guides their bearings lost
Or in league with robbers have reversed the signposts,
Disrespectful to ancestors, irresponsible to heirs.
Born barren, a freak growth, root in rubble,
Fruitlessly blossoming, whose foliage suffocates,
Their sap is sluggish, they reject the sun.

The man with his tongue in his cheek, the woman
With her heart in the wrong place, unhandsome,
    unwholesome;
Have exposed the new-born to worse than weather,
Exiled the honest and sacked the seer.
These drowned the farms to form a pleasure-lake,
In time of drought they drain the reservoir
Through private pipes for baths and sprinklers.

Getters not begetters; gainers not beginners;
Whiners, no winners; no triers, betrayers;
Who steer by no star, whose moon means nothing.
Daily denying, unable to dig:
At bay in villas from blood relations,
Counters of spoons and content with cushions
They pray for peace, they hand down disaster.

They that take the bribe shall perish by the bribe,
Dying of dry rot, ending in asylums,
A curse to children, a charge on the state.
But still their fears and frenzies infect us;
Drug nor isolation will cure this cancer:
It is now or never, the hour of the knife,
The break with the past, the major operation.

The magnetic mountain: 32

You that love England, who have an ear for her music,
The slow movement of clouds in benediction,
Clear arias of light thrilling over her uplands,
Over the chords of summer sustained peacefully;
Ceaseless the leaves' counterpoint in a west wind lively,
Blossom and river rippling loveliest allegro,
And the storms of wood strings brass at year's finale:
Listen. Can you not hear the entrance of a new theme?

You who go out alone, on tandem or on pillion,
Down arterial roads riding in April,
Or sad beside lakes where hill-slopes are reflected
Making fires of leaves, your high hopes fallen:
Cyclists and hikers in company, day excursionists,
Refugees from cursed towns and devastated areas;
Know you seek a new world, a saviour to establish
Long-lost kinship and restore the blood's fulfilment.

You who like peace, good sorts, happy in a small way
Watching birds or playing cricket with schoolboys,
Who pay for drinks all round, whom disaster chose not;
Yet passing derelict mills and barns roof-rent
Where despair has burnt itself out – hearts at a standstill,
Who suffer loss, aware of lowered vitality;
We can tell you a secret, offer a tonic; only
Submit to the visiting angel, the strange new healer.

You above all who have come to the far end, victims
Of a run-down machine, who can bear it no longer;
Whether in easy chairs chafing at impotence
Or against hunger, bullies and spies preserving
The nerve for action, the spark of indignation –
Need fight in the dark no more, you know your enemies.
You shall be leaders when zero hour is signalled,
Wielders of power and welders of a new world.

YI YUK-SA

1905–44

✳

The summit

Whipped by the bitter season's scourge,
At last I am driven to this north.

I stand upon the sword-blade frost,
Where numb circuit and plateau merge.

I know not where to bend my knees,
Nor where to place my vexed steps.

Naught but to close my eyes
And think of winter as a steel rainbow.

ATTILA JÓZSEF
1905-37

❋

Night in the suburbs

The light smoothly withdraws
its net from the yard, and as water
gathers in the hollow of the ditch,
darkness has filled our kitchen.

Silence. – The scrubbing-brush sluggishly
rises and drags itself about;
above it, a small piece of wall is in
two minds to fall or not.

The greasy rags of the sky
have caught the night; it sighs;
it settles down on the outskirts;
it sets off through the square, going where?
It kindles a dim moon for a fire.

The workshops stand
like a ruin;
within
the thickest gloom
a plinth for silence to assume.

On the windows of the textile factory
the bright moon now climbs
in a cluster of light,
the moon's soft light

is a thread at the boards of the looms,
and all through the idle night
the darkened machines weave the dreams
of the weaver-girls – the unravelled dreams.

Farther on, iron-works, nut-and-bolt-works
and cement-works, bounded by a graveyard.
Family vaults alive with echoes.
The factories sleep with their arms over
the sombre secret of their resurrection.
A cat comes poking a paw through the railings.
The superstitious watchman catches
a will-o-the-wisp – a flash of
brilliance – the cold
glitter of beetle-backed dynamos.

A train-whistle.

The damp explores the greyness,
probes the leaves of splintered trees,
lays the dust more heavily
along the streets.

On the street a policeman, a muttering workman.
A comrade rushes down
with leaflets in his hand:
sniffs ahead like a dog,
looks over his shoulder like a cat,
the lamp-posts watch him pass.

The tavern mouth ejects a sour glare;
puddles vomit from the window-sill;
the lamp inside shakes, gasping for air.
A solitary labourer stares.
The host is asleep, he snores.
The other one grinds his teeth by the wall,
his wretchedness gushes and weeps down the stair.
He hymns the revolution still.

The water cracks, goes stiff
like chilled metal, the wind
wanders about like a dog,
its huge tongue dangles
as it slobbers up the water.

Swimming like rafts on the stream
of the voiceless night, paillasses –

The warehouse is a grounded boat,
the foundry an iron barge,
while the foundryman sees a pink baby
taking shape in the iron mould.

Everything wet, everything heavy.
A musty hand maps the countries
of misery. There, on the barren fields,
on ragged grass – paper, and rags.
If only the paper could fly up! It stirs
slightly, weakly. See it try
to get on its way . . .

Filthy sheets are fluttering round
in your slapping wind, your wetting wind,
O night!
You cling to the sky as unthreaded
cambric clings to the rope, as sadness
clings to life, O night!
Night of the poor! Be my coal,
and the smoke at my heart's core,
cast me in your ore,
make me a seamless forge,
and make me a hammer that labours and rings,
and make my blade strike till it sings,
O night!

Grave night, heavy night.
My brothers, I too must turn out the light.
May misery be a brief lodger in our soul.
May the lice leave our body whole.

Keep going!

Mandarins hanged in Peking,
the dead man liked his cocaine.
– Go to sleep, you're rustling the straw.
The dead man liked his cocaine.

What does the poor man watch
through the window? Till and cash.
– Go to sleep, you're rustling the straw.
Through the window? Till and cash.

Buy yourself sausage and bread,
keep hardy, keep your head.
– Go to sleep, you're rustling the straw.
Keep hardy, keep your head.

You'll find the woman of gold,
she'll cook and never scold.
– Go to sleep, you're rustling the straw.
She'll cook and never scold.

'What reader . . .'

What reader would I most want to have
but the one who can understand me through love
and sees the future written in the present –
for his steps are like mine, at large in the emptiness

of a great patience, and only he is able
to give a human form to what is still silent,
and only in him – as in me – is it no fable
to see the deer stand safely by the tiger.

They'd love me

I don't meditate on good and evil.
I work, and I suffer: that's all.

I make screw-propeller boats, crockery,
badly in bad times, well in ordinary.

Numberless my works! Only my love,
being aware of them, takes stock of them, my love

takes stock of them all, my love has faith
but is silent before creed or oath.

Make me a tree, and the crow, I believe,
would only nest if there was no tree near.

Make me a field, and the old farmer's hoe
will turn up nothing but the weeds I've grown.

You'd have to water potatoes with sweat
to see them thrive on my thankless earth.

I'm water? A marsh begins to form.
Fire? I'm ash. But if I was transformed

to a god, in place of the god they know,
men would love me in truth, with all their soul.

March 1937

Soft rain is drifting like a smoke
across the tender fuzz of wheat.
As soon as the first stork appears
winter shrivels in retreat.

Spring comes, tunnelling a path
mined with exploding spikes of green.
The hut, wide open to the sun,
breathes hope and wood-dust sharp and clean.

The papers say that mercenaries
are ravaging the face of Spain.
A brainless general in China
chases peasants from hill to plain.
The cloth we use to wipe our boots
comes laundered back in blood again.
All round, big words bemuse and smooth
the voiceless miseries in men.

My heart is happy as a child's.
Flora loves me. But oh what arms
the beauty of love? For us, for all,
war stirs its withering alarms.
The bayonet contends in zeal
with the assaulting tank. Alone
I draw to us the force I need
against the fear I can't disown.

Men – women – all have sold themselves.
A heart? They keep it close as sin.
Hearts torn by hate – I pity you,
I shudder to see hatred win.
A little life on earth I have,
yet here I watch all life unfold –
O Flora, in this blaze of love
nothing surrenders to the cold!

May our daughter be beautiful
and good, our son be fearless, keen.
May they transmit some sparks beyond
star-clusters you and I have seen.
When this sun loses its great fire,
the children of our illumination
will launch towards infinity
their own galactic exploration.

ZOLTÁN ZELK

b. 1906

*

Nightmare and dawn

DEATH'S LIKENESS

The moment's shattered – but not the ear,
the heart in panic pants.
The minute splits, and swarms apart,
a thousand agitated ants.
In sleep I stir, my being's vague,
not sleeping, not awake;
bat wings of darkness, raspingly,
bring in the outer dark.
Silence thickens without, within,
but oil drops from the moon
drip, drip, falling, pattering
on leaves of trees that swoon;
as in a cell where water drops
tap out insanity . . .
The prisoner sees, not hears the sound,
eyes it whimperingly . . .
Cell of the world! Cell of the night!
The consciousness, in despair,
longs to break through bars that seem
likeness of death. – Out there
under the sunk, despondent sky
what shades in agony dangle high?
It is I! hanging from every tree!

RESURRECTION

Wicker-warble quickens, golden wires,
bright bird-choirs warble, on golden wires
creation's cradle swings, my waking
world rocks. It appears
I *was* asleep, deep under
three blessed hours long.
I swim as from the sea-floor up
to surface in bird-song:
wire over gold mesh, warbled, weaves
a fabric of bright sound,
till murk and muffled shapes dissolve,
till marsh is solid ground.
Gardens, streetcars, factories
step out under the sun.
Up then! perhaps the Day may yet
accept me as its own,
the world of day, the daylight world.
Can I perhaps, so soiled
with sin, go reconciled,
washed clean? With work to do
I might work with a will, renew
my bond with this skewered, askew,
battered, yet braced and valiantly
astir and straining, bound-to-be-free
old world!

LÉOPOLD SÉDAR SENGHOR

b. 1906

✳

In memoriam

It is Sunday.
I fear the crowd of my brothers with stony faces.
From my tower of glass filled with pain, the nagging
 Ancestors
I gaze at roofs and hills in the fog
In the silence – the chimneys are grave and bare.
At their feet sleep my dead, all my dreams are dust
All my dreams, the liberal blood spills all along the streets
 mixing with the blood of the butcheries.
And now, from this observatory as from a suburb
I watch my dreams float vaguely through the streets, lie
 at the hills' feet
Like the guides of my race on the banks of Gambia or
 Saloum,
Now of the Seine, at the feet of these hills.
Let me think of my dead!
Yesterday it was Toussaint, the solemn anniversary of
 the sun
And no remembrance in any cemetery.
Ah, dead ones who have always refused to die, who have
 known how to fight death
By Seine or Sine, and in my fragile veins pushed the
 invincible blood,
Protect my dreams as you have made your sons,
 wanderers on delicate feet.
Oh Dead, protect the roofs of Paris in the Sunday fog
The roofs which guard my dead

That from the perilous safety of my tower I may descend
  to the streets
To join my brothers with blue eyes
With hard hands.

Totem

I must hide him in my innermost veins
The Ancestor whose stormy hide is shot with lightning
  and thunder
My animal protector, I must hide him
That I may not break the barriers of scandal:
Protecting my naked pride against
Myself and the scorn of luckier races.

The dead

They are lying out there beside the captured roads, all
  along the roads of disaster
Elegant poplars, statues of sombre gods draped in their
  long cloaks of gold,
Senegalese prisoners darkly stretched on the soil of
  France.
In vain they have cut off your laughter, in vain the
  darker flower of your flesh.
You are the flower in its first beauty amid a naked
  absence of flowers
Black flower with its grave smile, diamond of immemorial
  ages.
You are the slime and plasma of the green spring of the
  world
Of the first couple you are the flesh, the ripe belly the
  milkiness

You are the sacred increase of the bright gardens of
    paradise
And the invincible forest, victorious over fire and
    thunderbolt.
The great song of your blood will vanquish machines and
    cannons.
Your throbbing speech evasions and lies.
No hate in your soul void of hatred, no cunning in your
    soul void of cunning.
O Black Martyrs immortal race, let me speak the words
    of pardon.

Luxembourg 1939

This morning at the Luxembourg, this autumn at the
    Luxembourg, as I lived and relived my youth
No loafers, no water, no boats upon the water, no
    children, no flowers.
Ah! the September flowers and the sunburnt cries of
    children who defied the coming winter.
Only two old boys trying to play tennis.
This autumn morning without children – the children's
    theatre is shut!
This Luxembourg where I cannot trace my youth, those
    years fresh as the lawns.
My dreams defeated, my comrades despairing, can it be
    so?
Behold them falling like leaves with the leaves, withered
    and wounded trampled to death the colour of blood
To be shovelled into what common grave?
I do not know this Luxembourg, these soldiers mounting
    guard.
They have put guns to protect the whispering retreat of
    Senators,
They have cut trenches under the bench where I first
    learnt the soft flowering of lips.

That notice again! Ah yes, dangerous youth!
I watch the leaves fall into the shelters, into the ditches,
   into the trenches
Where the blood of a generation flows
Europe is burying the yeast of nations and the hope of
   newer races.

Prayer to masks

Black mask, red mask, you black and white masks,
Rectangular masks through whom the spirit breathes,
I greet you in silence!
And you too, my pantherheaded ancestor.
You guard this place, that is closed to any feminine
   laughter to any mortal smile.
You purify the air of eternity, here where I breathe the
   air of my fathers.
Masks of maskless faces, free from dimples and wrinkles,
You have composed this image, this my face that bends
   over the altar of white paper.
In the name of your image, listen to me!
Now while the Africa of despotism is dying – it is the
   agony of a pitiable princess
Just like Europe to whom she is connected through the
   navel,
Now turn your immobile eyes towards your children
   who have been called
And who sacrifice their lives like the poor man his last
   garment
So that hereafter we may cry 'here' at the rebirth of the
   world being the leaven that the white flour needs.
For who else would teach rhythm to the world that has
   died of machines and cannons?
For who else should ejaculate the cry of joy, that arouses
   the dead and the wise in a new dawn?
Say, who else could return the memory of life to men
   with a torn hope?

They call us cotton heads, and coffee men, and oily men,
They call us men of death.
But we are the men of the dance whose feet only gain
    power when they beat the hard soil.

MIKLÓS RADNÓTI
1907–44

※

Spain, Spain

For two days it has poured like this, and as I open
my window the roofs of Paris shine,
a cloud settles on my table
and moist light blows over my face.

From above houses, standing far down in gutters,
the rain-beaten soot cries on me
and I am ashamed of this dusk, dirty
with loose mud and news.

O black-winged war, whipping us,
terror flies across the border,
no one sows, no one reaps on the other side.
Grapes aren't picked anymore.

The young bird doesn't sing, the sun doesn't
burn in the sky, mothers don't have sons
anymore. Spain, only your bloody rivers
run and boil.

But new armies will come, if need be from nothingness
like mad tornadoes,
armies starting from deep
mines and wounded fields.

Freedom, men cry about your fate!
This afternoon, their song carried you up.
With heavy words, the wet-faced poor
of Paris sang about this.

At an impatient hour

I lived high in the air, in the wind, where the sun was.
Hungary, how you lock up your broken son in valleys!
   You dress me in shadows, and in the evening landscape
   the sunset's fire doesn't comfort me.

Rocks above me, the white sky far away,
I live in the depths among mute stones.
   Maybe I should be silent too. What makes me
   Write poems today? Tell me, is it death? Who asks,

Who asks about life,
and about this poem – mere fragments?
   Know that there won't even be one cry
   that they won't bury you, that the valley won't hold
      you.

The wind will scatter you. But before long
a stone will echo
what I say, and young men and young women,
grown tall, will understand it.

Fires

Fires break out and slowly die forever.
Soldiers' ghosts fly to the bright meridians – one soul!
Oh, it doesn't matter who this one or that one was
while the heat bends repeatedly here, and the frost
   screams there –
sailors at the guns of torn ships, drunk on homesickness,
vomiting in their yellow fear!
Mines burst everywhere, sensitively death watches
and sometimes, at high tide with a slippery body, it
   crawls ashore.

Dead men follow it and dolphins ripped apart.
Dawn wakes too but no one needs it.
A plane roars across. Its shadow
follows it silently on the fox-eyed sea.
A whirlpool hisses at it. Signals cross on the water,
blood flowers on the reef instead of coral,
the plague howls all day, oil leaks over the fine machines
while blind insanity and fear hide behind them.
Then the sun drowns in smoke and, like a long-stemmed
    pain,
the moon bends repeatedly on the other side
and fires break out, and slowly die forever,
and soldiers' ghosts fly to the bright meridians.

GUNNAR EKELÖF
1907–68

❋

Each person is a world

Each person is a world, peopled
by blind creatures in dark revolt
against the I, the king, who rules them.
In each soul thousands of souls are imprisoned,
in each world thousands of worlds are hidden
and these blind and lower worlds
are actual and living, though not full-born,
as truly as I am living. And we kings
and barons of the thousand potential creatures within us
are citizens ourselves, imprisoned
in some larger creature, whose personality
we understand as little as our master
his master. From their death and their love
our own feelings have received a colouring.
As when a great liner passes by
far out below the horizon where the sea lies
so still at dusk. And we know nothing of it
until a swell reaches us on the shore,
first one, then one more, and then many
washing and breaking until it all goes back
as before. Yet it is all changed.

So we shadows are seized by a strange unrest
when something tells us that people have left,
that some of the possible creatures have gotten free.

RENÉ CHAR
b. 1907

✳

The inventors

They have come, the people from the other side, total
    strangers, alien to our ways.
They have come in hordes.
At the place where the cedars part from the old
Harvest-field, now green and irrigated, a crowd of them
    appeared.
The long march had made them sweat.
Their caps were pulled over their eyes, and their weary
    feet foundered.
They stopped dead when they saw us.
Obviously they didn't expect to find us there,
On the fine earth and well-kept furrows,
Utterly indifferent to an audience.
We gave them a nod and encouraged them.

The most erudite approached, then another just as
    rootless and slow.
We are here, they said, to warn you of the coming
    hurricane, your most inexorable enemy.
We know about it, like you, only
By hearsay, and from the stories of the old men.
But why are we now inconceivably happy before you and
    overcome with child-like euphoria?

We thanked them and asked them to leave.
But first something to drink, and their hands trembled
    and their eyes sparkled in their cups.

Men of timber and the axe, built for facing adversity, but inept at mastering water or building houses or painting these with glowing colours.

Ignorant of the winter garden or the brevity of joy.

Of course, we could have educated them and conquered them.

For the fear of the hurricane is profound.

And the hurricane was on its way;

But was that worth wasting words on, did it justify altering the future?

Where we are, there is no pressing fear.

W. H. AUDEN
b. 1907

✳

Musée des Beaux Arts

About suffering they were never wrong,
The Old Masters: how well they understood
Its human position; how it takes place
While someone else is eating or opening a window or just
    walking dully along;
How, when the aged are reverently, passionately waiting
For the miraculous birth, there always must be
Children who did not specially want it to happen,
    skating
On a pond at the edge of the wood:

They never forgot
That even the dreadful martyrdom must run its course
Anyhow in a corner, some untidy spot
Where the dogs go on with their doggy life and the
    torturer's horse
Scratches its innocent behind on a tree.

In Breughel's *Icarus*, for instance: how everything turns
    away
Quite leisurely from the disaster; the ploughman may
Have heard the splash, the forsaken cry,
But for him it was not an important failure; the sun shone
As it had to on the white legs disappearing into the
    green
Water; and the expensive delicate ship that must have
    seen
Something amazing, a boy falling out of the sky,
Had somewhere to get to and sailed calmly on.

The shield of Achilles

> She looked over his shoulder
>   For vines and olive trees,
> Marble well-governed cities
>   And ships upon untamed seas,
> But there on the shining metal
>   His hands had put instead
> An artificial wilderness
>   And a sky like lead.

A plain without a feature, bare and brown,
  No blade of grass, no sign of neighbourhood,
Nothing to eat and nowhere to sit down,
    Yet, congregated on its blankness, stood
    An unintelligible multitude.
A million eyes, a million boots in line,
Without expression, waiting for a sign.

Out of the air a voice without a face
  Proved by statistics that some cause was just
In tones as dry and level as the place:
    No one was cheered and nothing was discussed;
    Column by column in a cloud of dust
They marched away enduring a belief
Whose logic brought them, somewhere else, to grief.

> She looked over his shoulder
>   For ritual pieties,
> White flower-garlanded heifers,
>   Libation and sacrifice,
> But there on the shining metal
>   Where the altar should have been,
> She saw by his flickering forge-light
>   Quite another scene.

Barbed wire enclosed an arbitrary spot
  Where bored officials lounged (one cracked a joke)

And sentries sweated for the day was hot:
  A crowd of ordinary decent folk
  Watched from without and neither moved nor spoke
As three pale figures were led forth and bound
To three posts driven upright in the ground.

The mass and majesty of this world, all
  That carries weight and always weighs the same
Lay in the hands of others; they were small
  And could not hope for help and no help came:
  What their foes liked to do was done, their shame
Was all the worst could wish; they lost their pride
And died as men before their bodies died.

     She looked over his shoulder
       For athletes at their games,
     Men and women in a dance
       Moving their sweet limbs
     Quick, quick, to music,
       But there on the shining shield
     His hands had set no dancing-floor
       But a weed-choked field.

A ragged urchin, aimless and alone,
  Loitered about that vacancy, a bird
Flew up to safety from his well-aimed stone:
  That girls are raped, that two boys knife a third,
  Were axioms to him, who'd never heard
Of any world where promises were kept.
Or one could weep because another wept.

     The thin-lipped armourer,
       Haphaestos hobbled away,
     Thetis of the shining breasts
       Cried out in dismay
     At what the god had wrought
       To please her son, the strong
     Iron-hearted man-slaying Achilles
       Who would not live long.

YANNIS RITSOS
b. 1909

✳

Romiosyne

I

These trees cannot be accommodated beneath a lesser
    sky,
These stones are not content beneath an alien heel,
These faces cannot be accommodated except beneath the
    sun,
These hearts are not content with anything short of
    justice.

This landscape is as merciless as silence;
It hugs the scorching stones against its body
And presses in its light the orphaned olive-trees and
    vines.
Its teeth are clenched. No water here. Light only.
And the road is lost in light, and the shadow of the
    sheepfold is iron.

Trees and streams and voices
Have turned to marble in the quicklime of the sun.
The root trips on the marble. The dustladen lentisk.
The mule and the boulder. All panting. There is no
    water.
All parched. For years now they have all been chewing
    at a mouthful of sky to choke down their bitterness.

Their eyes are bloodshot through lack of sleep;
A deep furrow is wedged between their brows, like a
    cypress between two hills at sunset.

Their hand is welded to the rifle,
The rifle an extension of their arm,
And their arm is a projection of their soul.
Their lip is curled in anger, and the anguish
From deep inside their eyes
Gleams like a star in a salt-basin.

When they tighten their grip the sun
    is certain of the world;
When they smile a tiny swallow rises
    from the thicket of their beards;
When they sleep twelve stars tumble from their empty
    pockets;
When they are killed, life
Sweeps uphill with pounding drums and pennants flying.

For so many years they have starved and thirsted, died,
Besieged by land and sea;
Their fields have been scorched by the noonday heat,
    the brine has washed through their homes;
The winds have blown down their doors and the clump
    of lilac bushes in the square.
Death comes and goes through the tatters of their coats,
And their tongues have gone acrid as cypress cones.
Their dogs have perished, wrapped in their shadows.
And the rain beats down on their bones.

They sit transfixed high in their outposts
    smoking horse-dung and the night,
Scanning the tormented ocean, where
The broken mast of the moon has sunk.

They have run out of bread, exhausted their munitions,
So now they load their hearts into their cannons.

So many years besieged by land and sea
They have been starving, they have been slaughtered,
    yet none has perished.

High in their outposts their eyes shine —
A huge flag, a huge bright fire —
And from their hands each dawn a thousand doves
Soar out to the four gates of the horizon.

2

Evenings, when the thyme is sizzled in
   the rock's embrace,
There is a drop of water, which has eaten its way through
   the ages into the marrow of silence;
And there is a bell hanging from the ancient plane-tree,
   which calls out the years.

Sparks doze in the embers of the wilderness,
And the rooftops dream of the golden down
   on the upper lip of July —
Down, yellow as the plume on the corncob, smoked in
   the longing of the west.

The Virgin lies among the myrtle shrubs, her wide
   skirts stained with grape-juice.
A child cries in the lane, and from the valley
The ewe that has lost her lambs responds.

Tree shadows round the spring. Cold moisture on the
   barrel;
The blacksmith's daughter with her soaking feet;
The bread and olives on the table;
The evening star strung inside the climbing vine.
And high up there, turning on its spit, the galaxy,
Fragrant with garlic and pepper and burnt fat.

Oh, what a muslin of stars is needed still
For the pine-needles to embroider
   'This, too, will pass,'
On the scorched sheepfold of the summer!

How much longer must the mother with the seven
    butchered sons
Wring her heartstrings on their graves,
Before the light can find its own path
    up the steep slope of her soul?

This bone emerging from the earth
Measures the land out league by league, and the echoes
    of the clarinet,
And the clarinet and violin from sundown to sunrise
Speak their pain and yearning to the rosemary
    and pine,
And the rigging on the caiques sings like the lýra,
And the sailor drinks the bitter sea from the winecup
    of Odysseus.

Who will barricade the passes, and what sword
    will cleave through courage,
And what key will lock your heart up when with both
    its shutters open wide
It gazes up at God's star-laden orchards?

The hour is big like a Saturday night in May
    at the sailors' tavern,
The night is big as an oven-dish hanging on
    the tin-smith's wall,
The song is big like the loaf on the sponge-diver's table.
And see where the Cretan moon runs through its pulleys:
Thump! Crack! Twenty rows of cleats in its high-boots.
And there are the men mounting the steps of Náfplion,
Filling their pipes with coarse-flaked leaves of darkness,
Their moustachios thick like star-splashed thyme
    in Roúmeli,
And their tooth sunk deep as pine-root in the rock and
    salt of the Aegean.

They have been through fire and steel, they have
    conversed with stones;

They have treated Death to wine served in the skull-
 bones of their grandpas,
And they have met with Dighenēs
 on those same threshing-floors
And sat themselves to feast there,
Slicing their anguish in two just as they broke their
 barley-loaves across their knees.

Come mistress with the salt-flaked eyelashes and the hand
Bronzed by the anxiety that haunts the poor
And the burden of the years:
Love awaits you in the lentisk,
The seagull hangs your blackened icon in his cave,
And the embittered sea-urchin honours your foot with
 kisses.

In the black nipple of the grape the must boils brilliant-
 red,
The shoot of holly boils on the burnt-out ilex,
Beneath the ground the dead man's root seeks water to
 throw a pine into the air,
And the mother firmly grips a knife in the furrow on
 her brow.

Come mistress brooding on the golden eggs of thunder –
When will the seablue day arrive when you will toss
 your headscarf off
And take up arms again,
And the hail that falls in May will beat upon your brow,
And the sun will break open like a pomegranate in the
 lap of your homespun dress,
And you will share him out to your dozen orphans
 grain by grain,
And the sea will shimmer all around like the blade of
 the sword and the snow in April,
And the rock-crab emerge from hiding and cross his
 claws
And bask under the sun?

3

Here the sky never for a moment saps the oil-drop in
 our eye,
Here the sun takes on his shoulder half the weight of the
 stone on our back,
The rooftops crack without a groan on the knee of the
 midday heat,
And the men advance before their shadow like dolphins
 before the caiques of Skiáthos.
Then their shadow turns into an eagle, who dyes his
 wings in the setting sun,
And perches on their head, and contemplates the stars,
While they themselves are lying on the sun-terrace
 amid the red-black raisins.

Here each door is graven with a name
Some three thousand years old,
Each rock is frescoed with a saint with wrathful eyes and
 hair like rope,
On each man's arm stitch by stitch there is tattooed a
 crimson mermaid,
Each girl boasts a handful of salted light beneath her
 skirts,
And on the children's hearts are stamped the five or six
 small crosses of their bitterness,
Like the tracks of seagulls on the sand-dunes in the
 afternoon.

No need to recollect. We know.
All paths lead to the Upper-Threshing-Floors. The air
 is sharper there.

When the Minoan fresco of sunset is frayed by distance,
And the blaze in the haystack by the shore dies out,
The old women climb up as far as this, up the steps cut
 in the rockface,

And they sit on the Great-Stone, spinning the thread of
the sea with their eyes;
They sit and count the stars as they would count
ancestral silverware, and then
They take the slow descent, to feed their grandchildren
On gunpowder from Missolónghi.

Yes, truly, the Prince of Chains has shackled hands as
sad as these,
Yet his eyebrow shifts above his bitter eye
Like a boulder on a landslide's edge.
This wave that heeds no supplication comes from deep
inside the ocean,
And from the limits of the sky this wind
With the resinated vein and sage-brush lung rolls down.

Oh, let it blow once to obliterate the orange-trees of
memory,
Let it blow twice, to strike a spark against the iron rock
like a percussion-cap,
Let it blow three times, to drive the cedar-woods of
Liákoura
Insane, and with its fist smash tyranny in pieces,
And ruff the bear-night's collar in the square so that she
dances us a tsámiko,
While the tambourine-moon thuds, till island balconies
are thronged
With raw-awakened children and Soúliot mothers.

From the Great Valley a messenger arrives each
morning.
The sweating sun glistens on his face;
Under his arm he holds on fast to Romiosýne
As the labourer holds his cap at church.
'The time has come,' he says. 'Be prepared.
Every hour now belongs to us.'

4

They pushed on into the dawn with the disdain of men
    who are hungry;
A star had crystallized in their unswerving gaze,
And they bore the stricken summer on their shoulders.

The army passed through here, their banners hugged
    against their bodies,
Their obstinacy clenched between their teeth like a
    bitter pear;
The sand of the moon filled their clumsy boots,
And the coaldust of night choked their ears and nostrils.

They crossed the earth, tree by tree, and stone by stone;
They passed into sleep with thorns for a pillow,
And they carried life like a river
Between their two parched hands.

At each stride they won a league of sky – to give away.
In their look-out nests they turned to stone like burnt-out
    trees,
And when they danced in village squares, the ceilings
    shook
And glassware clattered on the shelves.

What a song it was that shook the peaks!
They held the platter of the moon between their knees
    and ate,
And broke the back of suffering in the pincer of their
    heart,
As they would crush a louse between their thickened
    fingernails.

Who is there to bring you now the warm loaf to feed
    your dreams on in the night?
Who will stand now in the shadow of the olive to keep
    the cicada company, lest the cicada sing no more –

Now that the quicklime of noon has stained the sheepfold
   of the horizon all around,
Obliterating all their manly names?

This earth that was fragrant at dawn,
This earth that was both theirs and ours –
Their blood – how fragrant the earth was!
And how is it now that our vineyards' gates are barred
   to us,
And the light on the rooftops and trees has lessened?
Who can bear to utter it, that half of them are in the
   ground
And the other half in chains?

Think how the sunlight's million leaves are bidding you
   good-day,
And the sky gleams with a multitude of banners,
Yet some are lying in chains, and the others in the
   ground.

Be still! The bells will toll at any moment.
This earth is theirs and ours.
Under the ground, between their two crossed hands
They hold the bell-rope, waiting for the hour; they do
   not sleep, they never die!
They wait to sound the resurrection. This earth
Is theirs and ours; nobody can take it from us.

5

They sat under the olive-trees in early afternoon
Sifting the ash-grey light through thickened fingers.
They laid down their packs, and reckoned
How much sweat it took to fill the path of night,
How much bitterness was knotted in the mallow,
How much courage in the eyes of the barefoot boy who
   held the flag aloft.

In the valley the last swallow lingered on,
Weighing itself in air, like a black stripe on the sleeve of
    autumn.
Nothing else was left. Only the gutted shells of houses
    smouldered still.

The ones under the stones left us some time ago,
With their tattered shirts and the oath inscribed upon
    the fallen door.
No one wept; we had no time. Only the silence grew
    ever deeper,
And down on the shore the light was neat, like the
    kitchen of the murdered woman.

What will happen to them now, when the rain seeps
    through the earth
And the rotten plane-leaves?
What will happen to them when the sun dries out in the
    flannelsheet of clouds,
Looking like a crushed bedbug on a peasant's bed,
Or when the snow, like a stork embalmed, settles
On the chimney-stack of night?

The aged mothers scatter salt in the fire, they scatter
    earth into their hair;
They have torn up the vines of Monovasiá, lest even one
    black grape sweeten the tooth of a foe;
They have put their grandfathers' bones in a sack
    together with their cutlery,
And they search outside their homeland's walls for a
    place to put down roots at night.

It would be difficult today to find the cherry-blossom
    words,
Less powerful words, less stony –
Those hands that survived in the fields
Or on the mountains or the seabed do not forget, they
    never forget –

It will be difficult to forget their hands,
Difficult for the hands that grew calloused on a trigger to
  entreat a daisy,
To give thanks on their knees or on the book,
Or in the bodice of the starlight.

It will take time. And we must speak up
Until they find their bread and vindication.

Two oars nailed in the sand at dawn and the storm
  lashing.
  Where is the dinghy?
A plough sunk in the earth and the wind blowing,
The earth burnt. Where is the ploughman?

The olive-tree and vine and home are ashes.
The night hoards stars like money in a peasant's stocking.
Dry bayleaves and oregano in the middle cupboard on
  the wall; the fire did not touch these.
A blackened kettle in the hearth, the water in it
Boiling, unattended, in the barricaded house. They had
  no time to eat.

The veins of the forest on the smoking ruin of their
  door – blood flows in the veins.
Listen! The footstep is familiar. Who comes?
The well-known hobnailed step that echoes on the
  hillside,
The edging of the root through stone. Someone is
  coming.
The password, the response. A brother. Good-evening!

So the light will find its trees, and the tree will find its
  fruit.
The dead man's water-flask has light and water in it
  still.
Good-evening, brother, Good-evening.

The old woman of the west is selling thread and spices
    in her hovel,
But no one wants to buy. They have risen high.
They will find it hard now to descend.
They will find it hard even to tell out the stature they
    have reached.

On the threshing-floor where on a night the warriors
    dined,
The olive-stones and moon's dried blood remain
Together with the epic metre of their guns;
And round about the cypresses and laurel grove.

Next day the sparrows finished off the bread-crumbs
    they had left,
The children fashioned toys out of the matches
They had lit their cigarettes with, and the thornspikes
    of the stars.

And the stone they sat on under the olive-trees early in
    the afternoon, looking out to sea,
Tomorrow will be turned to quicklime;
The day after tomorrow we shall whitewash our homes
    with it and the steps of Saint Saviour,
And the day after that we shall plant the seed where they
    slept,
And a pomegranate-bud will burst like the child's
First peal of laughter at the sunlight's breast.

And finally we shall gather round there to read their
    heart,
And we shall be reading through the history of man
    from its beginnings.

6

When the sun smites the sea, whitewashing the opposite
    shore of day,

Confinement and the pangs of thirst are suffered over
  twice and thrice again,
The old wound bleeds afresh,
And the heart is roasted dry by the heat, like Argive
  onions spread before the door.

As time goes by, their eyes begin to look more like the
  earth;
As time goes by, their eyes begin to look more like the
  sky.

The jar is drained of oil. Only the lees remain, and the
  dead mouse.
The mother's courage too has drained away, together
  with the pitcher and the cistern;
The gums of the wilderness are acrid with gunsmoke.

Where will you find the oil now for the lamp of Santa
  Barbara?
Where is the mint to offer in your incense-burner
To the golden icon of the afternoon?
Where is a mouthful of bread for the beggar-maid
  evening
To improvise some Cretan couplets for you on the lýra
  of her stars?

In the upper fortress of the island the prickly-pears and
  asphodels have turned to ghouls;
The earth is ploughed up by cannon-fire and graves.
The ruined Headquarters gapes, patched together with
  the sky.
There is no more room for yet more dead.
Grief has no place left to pause and plait her hair.

Gutted houses stare through gouged eyesockets at an
  ocean turned to marble,
And the bullets screwed in walls,
Like the knives in the ribcage of the saint they lashed to
  a cypress.

All day long the supine dead bask in sunshine,
And only when the sun descends soldiers crawl on bellies
    over blackened stones,
Groping with their nostrils the air surrounding death,
Groping the shoes of the moon, and chewing on a piece
    of bootleather,
And smash their fist against the rockface to release the
    pent-up water there –
But on its other side the rock is hollow,
And once again they hear the whine and uproar of the
    shell exploding in the sea,
And once again they hear the wounded scream before
    the gates.

Where can you go now? Your brother is calling you.
The night is walled round with the shadows of foreign
    ships;
The roads have been blocked with fallen walls.
One path is open, but it leads only to the highest
    reaches:
So they curse the ships and bite their tongue
To feel their pain that has not yet turned to bone.

On the parapets the dead captains guard the fortress.
Their flesh is rotting in their clothes.
Hey, brother, aren't you tired yet?
The bullet in your heart has blossomed,
Five hyacinths have sprouted from the armpit of the
    boulder,
Breath by breath, the fragrance tells the story – don't
    you remember? –
Stab by stab, the wound speaks to you of life.
And from the filth in your toenail sprouts the camomile,
That speaks to you of the beauty of the world.

You take the hand. It's yours. Moistened in the brine.
The sea is yours. The figtree's bitter milk drips down as
    you uproot a hair

From the scalp of silence. At any moment now the sky
   will see you.

The evening star rolls your soul between his fingers like a
   cigarette.
That's how you should smoke your soul as you lie supine,
Wetting your left hand in the starlight,
And holding your rifle in your right as you would hold
   your girl.
Remember that the sky has not forgotten you, when you
   take his tattered letter from your pocket,
And unfold the moonlight with your burnt fingers and
   read of manliness and glory.

Then you will climb to the highest outpost of your island,
And with the star as a percussion cap fire in the air,
Over the walls and masts,
Over the mountains bent double like stricken soldiers,
Just to scare the ghouls away, and chase them into the
   blanket of the shadow.

You will fire a shot into the bosom of the sky, seeking out
   the skyblue target,
As if seeking through her blouse
The nipple of the woman who tomorrow will be suckling
   your child –
As if groping after many years for the bolt on the gate of
   your fathers' house.

7

The house, the lane, the cactus, the chickens pecking at
   the rinds of sunlight in the yard –
We know these things,
And they know us. Down here, amidst the briers,
The tree-snake has shed her yellow shirt.

Here you will find the hovel of the ant, and the fortress
   of the wasp with many battlements;

On the same olive-tree the shell of last year's cricket and
    the voice of this year's cricket;
Your shadow in the lentisk follows you like a dog,
    noiselessly, long-suffering,
A faithful dog;
At noon it sits beside your earthen sleep sniffing at the
    bitter laurels,
At night it curls up at your feet, peeping at a star.

There is a silence of pears that eggs between the thighs of
    summer,
A drowsiness of water lazing between the carob's roots;
Spring has seven orphans sleeping in her aprons,
A dying eagle in her eyes,
And high up there, beyond the pine-forest,
The chapel of St John the Eremite dries in the sun,
Like the sparrow's droppings drying in the heat on the
    mulberry's broad leaf.

This shepherd wrapped in his sheepskin
Has a dried-up river in each hair,
Forests of oak sprout from the tops of his flute,
And his staff is roughened by the selfsame knots
That roughened the first oar dipped in the waters of the
    Hellespont.

There is no need for you to recollect. The vein of the
    plane-tree shares your blood,
Together with the island asphodel and caper.

From deep the speechless well sends up a rounded voice
    of black glass and white wind.
A voice as round as ancient wine-jars – the same
    primeval voice,
And the sky rinses the stones and our eyes with indigo.

Each night in the fields the moon turns the magnificent
    dead over on their backs,

Searching their faces with savage, frozen fingers
To spot her son by the cut of his chin and the stone in
  his eyebrow;
She searches their pockets. She will always find some-
  thing. We always find something.
A locket with a splinter of the Cross. A crushed cigarette.
A key. A letter. A watch that stopped at seven.
We wind up the watch once more. The hours march on.

When tomorrow their clothing rots away,
And they remain naked, lying amidst their tunic buttons
Just as the bits of sky remain between the summer stars
And the streams remain between the shrubs of laurel
And the path between the lemon-trees in spring;
Then perhaps we'll see their name, and then perhaps
  we'll shout it out: I love.

Then. But again, these things are perhaps a little too
  remote,
Perhaps a little too immediate, as when you grasp a
  hand in greeting in the darkness
With the bitter understanding of the exile returning to his
  fathers' house,
When he is not recognized even by his kinsfolk,
Because he has encountered Death,
And he has encountered the life that comes before life
  and beyond Death –
But he recognizes them. He is not bitter. Tomorrow, he
  says.
And he is certain in his conviction that the longest road
  is the shortest road into the heart of God.

And now the hour has come when the moon kisses him
  on the cheek with some sorrow;
The seaweed, the flowerpot, the stool, the stone stairway
  bid him good-evening;
The mountains and the seas, the cities and the sky bid
  him good-evening,

And at long last, flicking his cigarette-ash from the
    lattice of the balcony,
He can weep in his assurance,
He can weep in the assurance of the trees, the certainty
    of stars,
And the testimony of his brothers.

Athens, 1945–7

TSANG K'E-CHIA
b. 1910

✻

Sinners' black hands

I

A site had been fenced in
Beside the boulevard.
In the middle of it
A church is being built.

The scaffolding is denser than a cobweb,
Resembling an endless ladder of bones and ribs.
Ten thousand hands, five thousand hearts
Pulsate on it from sunrise to sunset.

This will be the finest building in town.
Now there is no harm in describing it:
The lofty walls will cordon off human sins
And enclose only serene air.
A bird, a tree, and even a blade of grass
Will take pride in living here.

Above the gate, a huge cross will be hung
Over the heads of passers-by;
The saintly image of Christ,
Supreme and kind, will stand at a great height,
An intermediary between God and His children,
He will pass on the doctrine with this tacit message:
'Slaves, endure all there is to endure,
Hang your heads low even when suffering hunger;
Turn your right cheek
When the left is struck.

Tolerance is above all virtues,
So you must have no defiant thoughts!
How can human eyes distinguish right from wrong?
After your death, the Lord will always pass a just
    judgement.'

The rising sun will first sweep past the holy image
To fall from noble towers on to lowly roofs.
After dusk, the place will be wrapped in fearful gloom
And the satanic shadow of the spire will tumble on the
    ground.

The morning knell will sound like magic spells,
(After all, these bells are different),
That summon flocks of people
To be led in by their shepherds.
Robes will mingle with mantillas,
Dancing in a gentle breeze
As if sins were waving their limbs in the sun's brightness.
Smart and handsome men will follow
With light steps, exchanging a few whispers.
Their round, fair and shining faces
Will be forced into a grave expression.
The procession will end with a column of women
Whose perfume fills the entire courtyard
As they walk arm in arm
Like pairs of entwined garlands.

Sunshine will be seen as the Lord's love
That falls upon them and the pavement underneath.
The tempo of the chimes will quicken,
As they file into the holy church.

Some of them will have just laid down their daggers
And bear stains that are still fresh on their hands;
Some will have failed in love
And come here for comfort;

Some, not being content with this happy life,
Will be hatching plans for an even better life to come;
Some will be searching for peace in Christ,
Because their sensitive hearts are rent;
Some, having seen through their bogus lives,
Will now be asking for a moment of truth;
Others will be here, not for pardon,
But to be close to adorable women.
They will all kneel down and raise their faces,
Although their hearts are of different shades and colours.

The preacher in the pulpit
    will face his flock in an authoritative way.
With eloquent lips
And eloquent gestures
Will explain the chapter and verse as if they were truth.
He will tell them to control themselves,
Forbid them to entertain rebellious thoughts.
Fearing that this may not be enough,
He will cite example after example.

Each time before rice touches the mouth,
Man should say his prayer of thanks.
Each night before he retires,
He should search his heart.
Day in, day out, tedium continues,
Yet he never seems to weary of it.

2

But all this, all this prosperity,
Has nothing to do with our workmen.
Under the iron whip of hardship,
They hurry to finish the job before the agreed date.

From the unnerving height of several thousand feet,
Their dark shadows are cast upon the ground.

They are covered in lime
And dappled with black spots of clay.
The sparks, spurting out from under the hammer,
Are mixed with sawdust and inhaled with the wind.

Here, playing throughout the day, in the violent music
Of men's shouts and the screeching of cranes,
Listen to the crescendo!
The saw vibrates in and out of a log
While the anvil beats the tempo;
The workers, driven by the maddening melodies,
Answer the call in their hearts while they labour on.

Some crystallize their skill in the design of masonry,
Some ponder deeply over pieces of wood,
Some adroit hands are pitching bricks up to their mates,
And other sinful black ones are fashioning the holy
    image of Christ.

Their backs bear the morning sun,
Only to be broken by the day's rain and sweat.
On the ground, a thousand lamps blink in the dark
And beside them pant weary hearts.

They tease one another in coarse accents.
An occasional joke helps to banish fatigue.
The lingering flavour of rustic stories
Puffs rings of smoke that lengthen in the air,
Recalling to mind many a summer night at home in the
    backyard.
Once, twice, a thousand times – it never grows stale.
Now it is being brought to fresh life in this city landscape
To make its listeners nostalgic.
This vast building brings them together from all over
    the land;
Strangers have now become brothers.
Busy days tightly grip every heart,
Deprive them of a moment's thought of home.

Night that has been spent in sleep, happy and sound,
Dissolves into slavery at dawn.
What is Creation? To whose design?
Were they born for bitter suffering?
The sun scorches, wind and rain eat away
The steel-grey bodies whence dark clouds will rise.
Whose shoulders are cast in bronze
That they can sustain knocking against slabs of stone or
    iron?
There are also family worries and illnesses
That blur their vision of the colours of the toiling seasons.
An instant of dizziness or carelessness
Will end in a heap of blood and flesh,
Or the usual striking out of a name
From the register in Heaven!

3

Who can foresee all that can happen?
Today's rebels may have been yesterday's servants.
Who can foretell a sudden gust of wind on the sea?
After all, tidal waves may arise in this ancient well!
Wait until hunger blinds their eyes
Which will no longer see God or the 'Truth'.
Then we shall tear up the sacred pages of the past
    centuries
And start a great and sweeping rebellion!
This church will become their canteen or hostel,
So their own creation will be theirs again.
The chorus that can be heard then
Will not be mysterious or in praise of Jesus.
It will be a song of great joy,
As the sun shines on the 'sinners'.

MIGUEL HERNÁNDEZ

1910–42

❀

The winds of the people

The winds of the people sustain me,
spreading within my heart.
The winds of the people impel me,
and roar in my very throat.
Oxen may bow their heads
gentle and impotent
before their punishment;
but lions lift their heads
and with their strident claws
they punish in return.
I come not from a people of oxen,
my people are they who enthuse
over the lion's leap,
the eagle's rigid swoop,
and the strong charge of the bull
whose pride is in his horns.
Oxen were never bred
On the bleak uplands of Spain.
Who speaks of setting a yoke
On the shoulders of such a race?
Who has set yoke or shackle
on the vigorous hurricane,
or held the thunderbolt
a prisoner in a cage?

You Basques of armoured stone,
you brave Asturians,
lively Valencianos
And tempered Castillians,
worked-over like the soil
yet as airy as wings,
Andalusians like lightning,
born amidst guitars
and forged in torrential
smithies of tears,
rye-field Estramadurans,
Galicians of calm rain,
dour trustful Catalans,
pure-born of Aragon,
dynamiting Murcians
so fruitful in your race,
men of Navarre and Leon, masters
of hunger, sweat, and the axe,
kings of the mineral kingdom
and lords of the work of tillage,
you who amidst the roots,
like noble roots yourselves,
go from life to death,
go from nothing to nothing:
you men of the scant grasslands,
they would set on you a yoke,
a yoke that you must shatter
in two across *their* backs!
The twilight of the oxen
heralds a sparkling dawn.
The oxen are dying, clad
in the humble smell of the barn.
But the eagles and the lions,
and behind them the sky,
and the arrogant bulls
are calm, will not die.

The agony of oxen
is of little countenance.
That of the virile animal
travels the universe.
If I must die, then may I
with my head high at last.
Dead and twenty times dead,
My mouth in the coarse grass.
My teeth shall remain clenched
and my beard bristling.
Singing, I wait for death,
for there are nightingales that sing
above the rifles' voice
and in the battles' midst.

AI CH'ING
b. 1910

✳

She has arisen[1]

She has arisen –
From decades of humilation,
From the pit dug by her enemy.

Blood streams down her forehead,
And from her bosom,
But she smiles
– Never has she smiled like this before.

She smiles,
Her eyes glitter
As if searching
For fallen foes.

She arises.
When she arises
She will be fiercer than any beast,
And wiser than any man.

For she must be so,
For she
Must regain her own life
From her enemy's death.

1. Written in 1937, at the outbreak of the Sino-Japanese War.

A message at daybreak

The Sun Addresses the Poet

Answer my prayers,
O Poet, arise!

I beseech you to tell them all
That what they have waited for will come.

Say that I shall come, treading on dew drops,
Led by the last rays of the last star.

I shall come from the east,
From the sea on which waves roar.

Bringing light to the Earth
And warmth to man.

You, the honest man, your mouth
Will pass on my message

To those in whose anxious eyes the flame of hope burns
To the distant cities and villages submerged in misery.

Tell them to welcome me –
The herald of day and light –

By throwing open all their windows,
By flinging open all their doors,

By sounding their steam-whistles,
By blowing their bugles.

Let sweepers clean the road.
Let dust-carts take away the rubbish.

Let labouring men stride in the streets.
Let radiant columns file through the squares.

Awaken villages amid the damp mist,
Open their gates to welcome me.

Let country women let out their chickens.
Let farmers lead out their herds.

Lend me your passionate mouth to tell them all
I shall come from the far side of the hills and woods.

Let them sweep their threshing floors
And their eternally dirty courtyards.

Let them open the windows pasted with flowerpapers.
Let them open the doors adorned with red scrolls.

Please wake up hospitable ladies
And their snoring men.

Let young lovers arise.
As well as all those sleepy girls.

Please call tired mothers
And the babies in their arms.

Wake everyone –
Wake those who are sick and those about to give birth.

And the withering and ageing
And those who groan in their beds.

The wounded who fought for justice,
The refugees who have lost their homes.

Please wake up all unfortunates:
I shall give them comfort.

Please arouse those who love life:
Workers, artisans and artists,

Let singers sing their welcome
In voices blended with dew and green grass.

Let dancers dance their welcome
In morning gowns of white mist.

Please waken too the handsome and healthy:
I shall soon tap upon their window panes.

Please, Poet,
Take this comforting news to man betimes.

Tell him to prepare, tell all of them to pave the way,
For I shall arrive at the last crow of the cock.

Tell them to fix their eyes on the edge of the sky.
I shall reward those who wait for my benignest glow.

As the night is ending, please tell them
That what they have waited for will soon be here.

The sun

From primeval graves
From dark ages
From the far side of the River of Death
It shakes up the slumbering ranges
Hovers like a wheel of fire over sandy mounds –
The sun that rolls towards me . . .

Its uncontainable rays
Give breath to life
Make lofty trees and dense branches dance
And rivers rush towards it singing their turbulent songs.

When it comes, I can hear
Hibernating worms and chrysalids turning over under-
    ground,
Masses of people speaking loudly on vast plains,
Distant cities
Calling it with power and steel.

So my chest
Is ripped open by the hands of fire,
My putrefying soul
Is left on a riverbank,
My unshakable faith in man is reborn.

This winter pond

This winter pond –
Lonely like an old man's heart
That has savoured all human sadness;
This winter pond –
Dry and sunken like an old man's eyes
That have lost their lustre through hard labour;
This winter pond –
Desolate like an old man's hair
That is sparse, grey and frosted;
This winter pond –
Sullen like a sad old man
Who shrivels up under the sullen sky.

ODYSSEUS ELYTIS
b. 1911

✳

From 'Heroic and elegiac song for the lost second lieutenant of Albania'

7

The trees are of coal which the night does not kindle.
The wind runs wild beating its breast, the wind still
   beating its breast
Nothing happens. Forced to their knees the mountains
   roost
Beneath the frost. And roaring out of the ravines,
Out of the heads of the corpses rises the abyss . . .
Not even Sorrow weeps any longer. Like the mad orphan
   girl
She roams about, wearing on her breast a small cross of
   twigs
But does not weep. Surrounded only by pitch-black
   Acroceraunia
She climbs to the peak and sets the moon's disc there
Perhaps the planets will turn and see their shadows
And hide their rays
And stand poised
Breathless with amazement at the chaos . . .

The wind runs wild beating its breast, the wind still
   beating its breast
The wilderness is muffled in its black shawl
Crouching behind months of cloud it listens
What is there to listen for, so many cloud-months away?

With a tangle of hair on her shoulders – ah, leave her
    alone –
Half a candle half a flame a mother weeps – leave her
    alone –
In the empty frozen rooms where she roams leave her
    alone!
For fate is never a widow
And mothers are here to weep, husbands to fight
Orchards for the breasts of girls to blossom
Blood to be spent, waves to break into foam
And freedom to be born always in the lightning flash!

FAIZ AHMAD FAIZ
b. 1911

❋

Freedom's dawn

(AUGUST 1947)

This leprous daybreak, dawn night's fangs have mangled,
– This is not that long-looked-for break of day,
Not that clear dawn in quest of which our comrades
Set out, believing that in heaven's wide void
Somewhere must be the stars' last halting-place,
Somewhere the verge of night's slow-washing tide,
Somewhere the anchorage of the ship of sorrow.

When they set out, those friends, taking youth's secret
Pathways, how many hands plucked at their sleeves!
From panting casements of the land of beauty
Soft arms invoked them, flesh cried out to them;
But dearer was the lure of dawn's bright cheek,
More precious shone her robe of shimmering rays;
Light-winged their longing, feather-light their toil.
But now, word goes, the birth of day from darkness
Is finished, wandering feet stand at their goal;
Our leaders' ways are altering, festive looks
Are all the fashion, discontent reproved.
Yet still no physic works on unslaked eye
Or heart fevered by absence, any cure:
Where did that fine breeze, that the wayside lamp
Has not once felt, blow from – where has it fled?
Night's heaviness is unlessened still, the hour
Of mind and spirit's ransom has not struck;
Let us go on, our goal is not reached yet.

This hour of chain and gibbet

On every pathway broods this hour of waiting,
No hour that strikes is the longed hour of spring;
And daily cares lie heavy on our souls –
This is the touchstone hour to try love's spells.

Blest minute that brings a dear face back to sight,
Blest hour that brings rest to a restless heart!
Wine-cup and cup-filler denied, in vain
That hour when cool clouds walk across the mountain,
Or cypress or chenar leaf, when no comrades
Share with us its green hour of dancing shades.

These scars ached long ago, a little – not
As this hour does that keeps all friends apart,
This hour of chain and gibbet and rejoicing,
Hour of necessity and hour of choice.

At your command the cage, but not the garden's
Red rose-fire, when its freshest hour begins;
No noose can catch the dawn-wind's whirling feet,
The spring's bright hour falls prisoner to no net.

Others will see, if I do not, that hour
Of singing nightingale and splendid flower.

A prison nightfall

Step by step by its twisted stairway
Of constellations night descends;
Close, as close as a voice that whispers
Tendernesses, a breeze drifts by;
Trees of the prison courtyard, exiles
With drooping head, are lost in broidering
Arabesques on the skirt of heaven.

Graciously on that roof's high crest
The moonlight's exquisite fingers gleam;
Star-lustre swallowed into the dust,
Sky-azure blanched into one white glow,
Green nooks filling with deep-blue shadows,
Waveringly, like separation's
Bitterness eddying into the mind.

One thought keeps running in my heart –
Such nectar life is at this instant,
Those who mix the tyrants' poisons
Can never, now or tomorrow, win.
What if they put the candles out
That light love's throneroom? let them put out
The moon, then we shall know their power.

LEAH GOLDBERG
b. 1911

✳

Will days indeed come

Will days indeed come with their gift of forgiveness and
    blessing
And then, with a light heart and mind as a wayfarer goes,
You'll walk in the field, with the clover-leaves gently
    caressing
Your bare feet and stubble deliciously stinging your toes?

Or rain overtake you, its throng of drops beating aloud
On your bare, fragrant head, on your neck, on your
    shoulders and chest,
And will there expand in you, as in the skirts of a cloud,
A sunlight of quiet and rest?

And breathing the smell of the furrow that lies over
    yonder
You'll see the sun's rays in the puddle, a mirror of gold.
And things are so simple, alive, and a pleasure to fondle,
To love and to hold.

Alone you will walk there, unscorched by the fires, nor
    stumble
On highways that bristle with horror and blood; and
    again
In pureness' embrace you shall be meek and humble
As a blade of grass, as mere man.

MIGJENI
1911–38

✳

Sons of the new age

We, the sons of this new age
Quit our elders' patronage,
Raise our fists to fight and win,
Life of freedom to begin.

We, the sons of this new age,
Nourished by this land of rage,
Toiling under whip and yoke,
Will no more in bondage choke.

We, the sons of this new age,
Brothers born in mourn, engage
In a just and righteous cause
Nobler than our elders' laws.

In this bloody world contest,
Triumph is with those oppressed;
Triumph full of strength and zeal,
Free to think and free to feel.

Youth is fierce and strong and brave,
Can no longer live as slave;
No more sobs or tears or toil
For the sons born of this soil.

We, the sons of this new age,
In fresh battles shall engage,
And for freedom pay the price
With our dearly cherished lives.

AIMÉ CÉSAIRE
b. 1913

✻

'Upright now, my country and I . .'[1]

Upright now, my country and I, hair in the wind, my
hand small in its enormous fist and our strength not in-
side us but above in a voice that bores through the night
and its listeners like the sting of an apocalyptic wasp.
And the voice declares that for centuries Europe has
stuffed us with lies and crammed us with plague,
for it is not true that:
the work of man is finished
we have nothing to do in the world
we are the parasites of the world
our job is to keep in step with the world.
The work of man is only just beginning
it remains for him to conquer
at the four corners of his fervour
every rigid prohibition.
No race holds a monopoly of beauty, intelligence and
    strength
there is room for all at the meeting-place of conquest
we know now
that the sun revolves round our earth illuminating the
    plot
which we alone have selected
that every star falls at our command from the sky to the
    earth
without limit or cease.

1. From *Return to my native land.*

Now I see what the ordeal means: my country is the 'spear of the night' of my ancestral Bambaras. It shrinks and its desperate blade retracts if it is offered chicken-blood; its temper wants the blood of man, the fat of man, the liver of man, the heart of man and not the blood of chickens.

Thus I too seek for my country not hearts of dates but hearts of men pumping manly blood so that men may enter the silver cities by the great trapezoidal gate, my eyes sweep the acres of my native country and I count the wounds with a kind of gladness as I pile them on top of one another like rare species and the account is constantly lengthened by the contemptible being unexpectedly and newly minted.

There are those who never get over being made in the likeness of the devil and not in the likeness of God, there are those who think that to be a Negro is like being a second-grade clerk, waiting for better things but with no prospect of promotion; there are those who have capitulated before themselves, there are those who live in a corner of a deep pit inside themselves; those who say to Europe: 'See, I know how to scrape and bow as well as you, and like you I can pay my respects, I am different from you in nothing; pay no attention to my black skin: it's the sun that has burnt it.'

There is the Negro pimp and the Negro Askari: all zebras shake themselves in their own fashion so that their stripes may fall into a dew of fresh milk. And in the midst of all this I say Hurrah! my grandfather is dying. Hurrah! little by little the old negritude is turning into a corpse. There's no denying it: he was a good nigger. The Whites say he was a good nigger, a really good nigger, his good master's good Negro.
And I say Hurrah!
He was a very good nigger.
Misery beat him front and back, they shoved into his

poor brain the idea that he could never trick his own
oppressive fate, that he had no power over his own des-
tiny; that an unkind Lord had for all eternity written
prohibitions into the nature of his pelvis. To be a good
nigger he must believe honestly in his unworthiness and
never feel any perverse curiosity to check those fateful
hieroglyphics

He was a very good nigger

And it did not occur to him that he might ever hoe and
dig and cut anything except the insipid cane

he was a very good nigger.

And they threw stones at him, bits of scrap iron, broken
bottle ends, but neither these stones nor this iron nor
those bottles . . .

O quiet years of God on this clod of an earth

and the whip argued with the swarming flies over the
    sweet dew of our wounds.

I say Hurrah! more and more the old negritude
is turning into a corpse
the undone horizon is pushed back and stretched
Between the torn clouds a sign by lightning:
the slave-ship is splitting open . . . . Its belly in spasm
    ringing with noises.
The cargo of this bastard suckling of the seas is gnawing
    at its bowels like an atrocious tapeworm
Nothing can drown the threat of its growling intestines
in vain the joy of the sails filled out like a purse full of
    doubloons
in vain the tricks allowed by the fatal stupidity of the
    police frigates
in vain does the captain have the most troublesome

nigger hanged from the yard-arm, or thrown overboard,
or fed to his mastiffs.
In their spilt blood
the niggers smelling of fried onion
find the bitter taste of freedom
and they are on their feet the niggers

the sitting-down niggers

unexpectedly on their feet
on their feet in the hold
on their feet in the cabins
on their feet on deck
on their feet in the wind
on their feet beneath the sun
on their feet in blood
on their feet
   and
    free
on their feet and in no way distraught
free at sea and owning nothing
veering and utterly adrift
surprisingly
on their feet
on their feet in the rigging
on their feet at the helm
on their feet at the compass
on their feet before the map
on their feet beneath the stars
on their feet
   and
    free
and the cleansed ship advances fearless upon the caving
 waters

VITTORIO SERENI
b. 1913

✳

A dream

I was just going to pass through the bridge
across the river – it could have been the Magra
where I spend my summer, or the Tresa
in my part of the country between Germignaga and
    Luino.
A leaden faceless figure stood in my way.
'Take out your papers', he ordered. 'What papers?' I
    said.
'Produce your papers', he snapped, seeing me
    nonplussed.
I tried to calm him. 'I have hopes,
someone waiting for me in a small town,
a few memories, some friends still alive,
some dead and decently buried.'
'Nonsense', he snarled, 'one cannot pass
without a programme,' and weighed
the few papers I had. I pleaded again.
'I'll pay on my return,
if you let me pass, if you let me work.'
But in vain. There was no way
of coming to terms with him.
'Have you made up your ideological choice?'
he kept blustering.
We strove hard in utter solitude
at the parapet of the bridge,
and the fight goes on still to my shame,
and I don't know who will end up in the river.

MATEJ BOR
b. 1913

✳

Vision

Telegraphed to the 1961 disarmament conference

Town.
Town on the earth's globe.
And bombs
Heavier than the earth's globe.
Bombs. Bombs.

Through the triumphal arches of dreams,
Crumbling arches,
Retreats the rearguard of mankind.
Bare-eyed
And blind-footed.
At the head
A General
With no head –
And his voice:

Who wants to drink
May not drink;
In the water is death.

Who wants to eat
May not eat;
In the bread is death.

Who wants to think
May not think;
In thought is death.

Who wants to live
May not live;
In life is death.

The rearguard of mankind
And at the head
The General
With no head –

Where to?

T'IEN CHIEN
b. 1914

✳

/ *Different time-tables*

Some people, letting their hair turn white,
Stand still forever.
Others, in a single day,
Have conquered many peaks,
Walked deep into an ancient wood,
And discovered the hidden treasure.

DAVID ROKEAH
b. 1914

❋

The wall

The tottering wall has underground thoughts
and moss lining the cracks.
Tomorrow or the next day – a border flare-up
a parchment scroll
in an unearthed jar.

While there is still time, the sentries will sing for summer
that flutters in dug-outs like the wind in hedges.
They shut the night, and nights that will follow it
in barbed-wire cages, in the bereavement of lapsed time
in an instant of hatred
stretched to a generation. They mutter
Amen to a jackal
that violates the border. Thorns
flowering as a last hope for no-man's land.

NICANOR PARRA
b. 1914

✳

The vices of the modern world

Modern delinquents
Are authorized to convene daily in parks and gardens.
Equipped with powerful binoculars and pocket watches
They break into kiosks favoured by death
And install their laboratories among the rosebushes in
    full flower.
From there they direct the photographers and beggars
    that roam the neighbourhood
Trying to raise a small temple to misery
And, if they get a chance, having some woebegone
    shoeshine boy.
The cowed police run from these monsters
Making for the middle of town
Where the great year's end fires are breaking out
And a hooded hero is robbing two nuns at gun point.
The vices of the modern world:
The motor car and the movies,
Racial discrimination,
The extermination of the Indian,
The manipulations of high finance,
The catastrophe of the aged,
The clandestine white-slave trade carried on by
    international sodomites,
Self-advertisement and gluttony,
Expensive funerals,
Personal friends of His Excellency,
The elevation of folklore to a spiritual category,

The abuse of soporifics and philosophy,
The softening-up of men favoured by fortune,
Auto-eroticism and sexual cruelty,
The exaltation of the study of dreams and the sub-
    conscious to the detriment of common sense,
The exaggerated faith in serums and vaccines,
The deification of the phallus,
The international spread-legs policy patronized by the
    reactionary press,
The unbounded lust for power and money,
The gold rush,
The fatal dollar dance,
Speculation and abortion,
The destruction of idols,
Overdevelopment of dietics and pedagogical psychology,
The vices of dancing, of the cigarette, of games of chance,
The drops of blood that are often found on the sheets of
    newlyweds,
The madness for the sea,
Agoraphobia and claustrophobia,
The disintegration of the atom,
The gory humour of the theory of relativity,
The frenzy to return to the womb,
The cult of the exotic,
Aeroplane accidents,
Incinerations, mass purges, retention of passports,
All this just because,
To produce vertigo,
Dream-analysis,
And the spread of radiomania.

As has been demonstrated
The modern world is composed of artificial flowers
Grown under bell jars like death,
It is made of movie stars
And blood-smeared boxers fighting by moonlight
And nightingale-men controlling the economic lives of
    the nations

With certain easily explained devices;
Usually they are dressed in black like precursors of autumn
And eat roots and wild herbs.
Meanwhile the wise, gnawed by rats,
Rot in the crypts of cathedrals
And souls with the slightest nobility are relentlessly persecuted by the police.

The modern world is an enormous sewer,
The chic restaurants are stuffed with digesting corpses
And birds flying dangerously low.
That's not all: the hospitals are full of impostors,
To say nothing of those heirs of the spirit who found colonies in the anus of each new surgical case.

Modern industrialists occasionally suffer from the effects of the poisoned atmosphere.
They are stricken at their sewing machines by the terrifying sleeping sickness
Which eventually turns them into angels, of a sort.
They deny the existence of the physical world
And brag about being poor children of the grave.
And yet the world has always been like this.
Truth, like beauty, is neither created nor lost
And poetry is in things themselves or is merely a mirage of the spirit.
I admit that a well-planned earthquake
Can wipe out a city rich in traditions in a matter of seconds,
And that a meticulous aerial bombardment
Smashes trees, horses, thrones, music,
But what does it matter
If, while the world's greatest ballerina
Is dying, poor and abandoned, in a village in southern France,
Spring restores to man a few of the vanished flowers.

What I say is, let's try to be happy, sucking on the
    miserable human rib.
Let's extract from it the restorative liquid,
Each one following his personal inclinations.
Let's cling to this divine table-scrap!
Panting and trembling,
Let's suck those maddening lips.
The lot is cast.
Let's breathe in this enervating and destructive perfume
And for one more day live the life of the elect.
Out of his armpits man extracts the wax he needs to
    mould the faces of his idols
And out of woman's sex the straw and the mud for his
    temples.

Therefore
I grow a louse on my tie
And smile at the imbeciles descending from the trees.

Litany of the little bourgeois

If you want to get to the heaven
Of the little bourgeois, you must go
By the road of Art for Art's sake
And swallow a lot of saliva:
The apprenticeship is almost interminable.

A list of what you must learn how to do:
Tie your necktie artistically
Slip your card to the right people
Polish shoes that are already shined
Consult the Venetian mirror
(Head-on and in profile)
Toss down a shot of brandy
Tell a viola from a violin
Receive guests in your pyjamas

Keep your hair from falling
And swallow a lot of saliva.

Best to have everything in your kit.
If the wife falls for somebody else
We recommend the following:
Shave with razor blades
Admire the Beauties of Nature
Crumple a sheet of paper
Have a long talk on the phone
Shoot darts with a popgun
Clean your nails with your teeth
And swallow a lot of saliva.

If he wants to shine at social gatherings
The little bourgeois
Must know how to walk on all fours
How to smile and sneeze at the same time
Waltz on the edge of the abyss
Deify the organs of sex
Undress in front of a mirror
Rape a rose with a pencil
And swallow tons of saliva.

And after all that we might well ask:
Was Jesus Christ a little bourgeois?

As we have seen, if you want to reach
The heaven of the little bourgeois,
You must be an accomplished acrobat:
To be able to get to heaven,
You must be a wonderful acrobat.

And how right the authentic artist is
To amuse himself killing bedbugs!

To escape from the vicious circle
We suggest the *acte gratuit*:

Appear and disappear
Walk in a cateleptic trance
Waltz on a pile of debris
Rock an old man in your arms
With your eyes fixed on his
Ask a dying man what time it is
Spit in the palm of your hand
Go to fires in a morning coat
Break into a funeral procession
Go beyond the female sex
Lift the top from that tomb to see
If they're growing trees in there
And cross from one sidewalk to the other
Without regard for when or why
... For the sake of the word alone ...
... With his movie-star moustache ...
... With the speed of thought ...

Rites

Every time I go back
To my country
    after a long trip
The first thing I do
Is ask about those who have died:
All men are heroes
By the simple act of dying
And the heroes are our teachers.

And second,
    about the wounded.

Only later,
    when the small ritual is complete
Do I claim for myself the right to life:
I drink, I eat, I rest

I close my eyes to see more clearly
And I sing with rancour
A song from the turn of the century

Young poets

Write as you will
In whatever style you like
Too much blood has run under the bridge
To go on believing
That only one road is right.

In poetry everything is permitted.

With only this condition, of course:
You have to improve on the blank page.

LEZ OZEROV

b. 1914

✳

'An oar is lying . . .'

An oar is lying on the coastal sand;
It tells me more about expanse and motion
Than the entire, enormous, brilliant ocean
Which brought it in and tossed it on the land.

DYLAN THOMAS
1914–53

✳

The hand that signed the paper

The hand that signed the paper felled a city;
Five sovereign fingers taxed the breath,
Doubled the globe of dead and halved a country;
These five kings did a king to death.

The mighty hand leads to a sloping shoulder,
The finger joints are cramped with chalk;
A goose's quill has put an end to murder
That put an end to talk.

The hand that signed the treaty bred a fever,
And famine grew, and locusts came;
Great is the hand that holds dominion over
Man by a scribbled name.

The five kings count the dead but do not soften
The crusted wound nor stroke the brow;
A hand rules pity as a hand rules heaven;
Hands have no tears to flow.

LÁSZLÓ BENJÁMIN
b. 1915

❋

Debris

Draggled in spirit, human, we live on.
Yet our *selves* we salvaged, when our senses
fell to false gods, dealt only in offences,
phoney trials, lies.
Deep, deeply hidden, blind, man's natural
endowment stirs and strives in us: a cry
for truth, for love, and for integrity.
For us the true distinction's here:
backbone erect, head high
and conscience clear.

Can truncheons answer searching questions? Dull
thud upon thud, fall leaden arguments,
pulping imagination, feeling, sense,
reeking, and growing ranker till they maul
the flesh, and the bare rack of bones is all
that's left. They set out food and bed as bait
and in their trap the will to act is caught.
The incessant force of fear-corroding words
cancels creation till it falls apart,
and eats away all substance, even thought,
like acids on a corpse.

The tree was insecure, the cave was chill,
we put aside the stone-axe and the bow ...
we turned our faces always towards the new,
and achieved power, and reason, and much skill.

A little farther – and we will lay bare
existence's last secret formula.
Sooner or later, rocket-atom-gunned,
out into space we will have forced our way.
But who will answer for it when we find,
searching the wheels and gears, the crank and crane
of the vast contraption, that we search in vain
for lost humanity?

A castle was your picture? On the heights?
Today you can rejoice if you can dodge
under in any corner there, to crouch
for just the space of the worst winter nights.
But you hauled stone? carved ornaments?
A skilful, willing workman in your prime?
Work with your mind, too, from now on; creation
needs more than muscle, once a man repents.
It's wrecked? You are a man. Start new – this time
at the foundation.

I have no god, religion, destiny;
no dream of miracles dazes me now,
nor am I dogged and tricked now till I bow
to self-appointed fake divinities.
Butting my troubled way somehow, I feel
I'd like to do something so men could toil
away untouched by dread or fright, unbruised,
not hounded down, not crookedly accused,
so that at long last people here might be
at home, and their homeland a true *patrie* –
this little Hungary.

Now it's a trampled anthill, tumbled blocks,
a stellar slag, scrapheap of steel and rocks,
muddle outside, inside perplexity.
No one started or stopped or let it be.
Lunging for balance, for a human stand,
I too see no beginning and no end.

Mark this morass and learn of storms from us –
from me – for you can see that I who was
whole-souled am now a jumble, just
debris.

JOHN CORNFORD
1915–36

❋

*Full moon at Tierz: before the
storming of Huesca*

1

The past, a glacier, gripped the mountain wall,
And time was inches, dark was all.
But here it scales at the end of the range,
The dialectic's point of change,
Crashes in light and minutes to its fall.

Time present is a cataract whose force
Breaks down the banks even at its source
And history forming in our hand's
Not plasticine but roaring sands,
Yet we must swing it to its final course.

The intersecting lines that cross both ways.
Time future, has no image in space,
Crooked as the road that we must tread,
Straight as our bullets fly ahead.
We are the future. The last fight let us face.

2

Where, in the fields by Huesca, the full moon
Throws shadows clear as daylight's, soon
The innocence of this quiet plain
Will fade in sweat and blood, in pain,
As our decisive hold is lost or won.

All round the barren hills of Aragon
Announce our testing has begun.
Here what the Seventh Congress said,
If true, if false, is live or dead,
Speaks in the Oviedo mauser's tone.

Three years ago Dimitrov fought alone[1]
And we stood taller when he won.
But now the Leipzig dragon's teeth
Sprout strong and handsome against death
And here an army fights where there was one.

We studied well how to begin this fight,
Our Maurice Thorez held the light.
But now by Monte Aragon
We plunge into the dark alone,
Earth's newest planet wheeling through the night.

3

Though Communism was my waking time,
Always before the lights of home
Shone clear and steady and full in view –
Here, if you fall, there's help for you –
Now, with my Party, I stand quite alone.

Then let my private battle with my nerves,
The fear of pain whose pain survives,
The love that tears me by the roots,
The loneliness that claws my guts,
Fuse in the welded front our fight preserves.

O be invincible as the strong sun,
Hard as the metal of my gun,
O let the mounting tempo of the train
Sweep where my footsteps slipped in vain,
October in the rhythm of its run.

1. The poem was written in 1936.

4

Now the same night falls over Germany
And the impartial beauty of the stars
Lights from the unfeeling sky
Oranienburg and freedom's crooked scars.
We can do nothing to ease that pain.
But prove the agony was not in vain.

England is silent under the same moon,
From the Clydeside to the gutted pits of Wales.
The innocent mask conceals that soon
Here, too, our freedom's swaying in the scales.
O understand before too late
Freedom was never held without a fight.

Freedom is an easily spoken word
But facts are stubborn things. Here, too, in Spain
Our fight's not won till the workers of all the world
Stand by our guard on Huesca's plain
Swear that our dead fought not in vain,
Raise the red flag triumphantly
For Communism and for liberty.

JOHANNES BOBROWSKI
1917–65

❋

Report

Bajla Gelblung,
escaped in Warsaw
from a transport from the Ghetto,
the girl took to the woods,
armed, was picked up
as partisan
in Brest-Litovsk,
wore a military coat (Polish),
was interrogated by German
officers, there is
a photo, the officers are young
chaps faultlessly uniformed,
with faultless faces,
their bearing
is unexceptionable.

FRANCO FORTINI
b. 1917

✳

Expulsion order

Then nothing new from this eminence
from which one still looks on without a word,
and in the evening the wind drops in the hair.

Then no other path to descend
but the one northwards, where no sun strikes,
and the branches are made of water.

Then one's mouth will soon be mute.
And this evening we shall be deep down at the bottom
   of the vale,
where the feasts have put on all lamps,

and a crowd is silent and friends don't recognize.

TSOU TI-FAN
b. 1918

❋

Ballads

1
THREE SPRING MONTHS

Let trees clap their emerald hands,
Let scarlet flowers raise their bright torches,
Let the prairie wave its green grass,
Let cuckoos sing their spring ballads,
Let our battle songs
Spread to the infinite like the blue sky.

2
BUDS

A peal of youthful laughter,
A thread of unspoken love,
A sealed jar of wine,
An unaccomplished wish,
A flame burning in the heart.

3
DARK NIGHT

It's no crime to light a lamp in the darkness,
For swallows need the blue sky of March
And bees need a flowering orchard.

THOMAS MCGRATH
b. 1918

❋

From '*Letter to an imaginary friend*'

Blessed be the fighters:
The unknown angry man at the end of the idiot-stick
    with his dream of freedom;
Jawsmiths and soap boxers, gandy-dancers setting the
    high iron
Toward the ultimate Medicine Hat: blessed, blessed.
Blessed the agitator; whose touch makes the dead walk;
Blessed the organizer; who discovers the strength of
    wounds;
Blessed all fighters.

JURE KAŠTELAN
b. 1919

✳

Encounters

The dead – they live in us. They grow, they grow.
My young and songful comrades,
the dead – they live in us.
And oft in barracks, workshops, at the break of dawn,
and at the height of day
they come out one by one. And pass.
And without greeting, without jostling, merge in life,
all walk next to each other.
The quick, the dead. Next to each other.

The nameless

If out of breath
the horse returns
from the hill,
give him to drink, mother, trim his bridle
for a horseman new.

If tears have dimmed your eyes
and wounds have marred
your face,
search not, mother, for my grave . . .
The country liberated
is the living image
of your living son.

BORIS SLUTSKY
b. 1919

✳

Physics and poetry

Looks like physics is in honour,
Looks like poetry is not.
It's not dry figures that matter;
Universal law, that's what.

It means that we failed in something,
Something,
        which was ours to do!
It means that our cute iambics
Had weak wings and hardly flew.
Unlike Pegasus, our horses
Do not soar nor even trot . . .
That's why physics is in honour,
That's why poetry is not.

Any argument is pointless,
But even if there is one:
It is nothing so dismaying;
Rather it's amusing fun
To observe the foam-like falling
Away of our rhymes and rhythms
And to watch how greatness
                staidly
Retreats into logarithms.

TO HUU
b. 1920

*

Remember my words

(Nguyen Van Troi, a 24-year-old electrician, was executed in Saigon, 15 October 1964, allegedly for attempting to blow up United States Defence Secretary Robert McNamara.)

There are moments that make History
Deaths that are immortal
Words more beautiful than songs
And men born – one would think – of the womb of Truth.

> NGUYEN VAN TROI
> You're dead
> No, for ever you'll live
> Living or dead: heroic, great.

Death has closed your lips
But your cry – '*Remember my words!*' –
Still rings. And the light from your eyes
On the Party's paper shines.

A thousand years from now, people will still remember
That autumn morn, in the yard at Chi Hoa
You walked between two prison guards
And a priest followed behind.
Your legs throbbed with pain
But your head was proudly high
Your white clothes, the colour of purity
And your thin body, stronger than death.

Hired hangmen, paid propagandists
Two dark rows. Bayoneted rifles
You strolled along, your gaze serene
As if you were the judge.

The grass felt fresh under your feet
Life was renewed in the green of leaves
Yours, the land claiming freedom
Yours, the flesh that yearned for life.
'What crime have I committed?' you cried
They tied you to a stake. Strands of rope,
Ten gun muzzles, a bandage over the eyes.
You shouted: 'The Yankee's the criminal!'

You tore off the black strip of cloth
The fire from your eyes burnt the fiendish ruffians
Face to face, that's the way you met death
Your whole self a never-to-be-extinguished fire.

Trembling with fear, they pulled the ropes tight
Hatred burnt your lips dry:
One must fight like a Communist!
What can guns do to a heart on fire?

'First row, kneel down!' – Barely a second left
Your cry resounded: '*Remember my words!*
Down with American imperialism!
Down with Nguyen Khanh!
Long live Ho Chi Minh!
Long live Ho Chi Minh!
Long live Ho Chi Minh!'
At that sacred moment, you called Uncle thrice.

A volley of shots. Ten U.S. slugs
You fell. But again you rose
Your voice rang: 'Long live Vietnam!'
Blood reddened your earthen bed.

You died. Not a moan from your breast
You died like an angel lying down to rest,
What need for that cross of tinsel
By priestly hands thrown at your side?

You're dead, brother Troi. Know you
Blood for blood, that poignant call!
Caracas partisans for the love of you
Caught an American bandit in that capital.

You're dead, and no longer see
Fire calling for fire in the South ablaze
But no fire can with your heart compare
That meteor glowing with the last breath you breathed.
'*Remember my words!*'
NGUYEN VAN TROI, brother
Your words we shall remember:
One must live and die in glory,
Not cower before the enemy
But give all for the land of one's fathers,
As you did, you, a worker.

Invaded South

If, in the warmth of confidence shared, you ask me
Friend, from the thousands of words the people say,
which one of all makes you most deeply grieve?
Out of my heart's core comes there just but one answer:
The South: my invaded South ...

If, in the warmth of tenderness, you ask me
My beloved, of the thousands of names you know,
which one inspires the greatest faith, most love?
Out of the depths of my heart comes just one answer:
The South: my invaded South ...

You ask me, little one, where's the most beautiful
    country?
There the green coconut-palms in blue water are
    mirrored,
and rice plants flourish their green to the far horizon:
This is the Southland – my invaded South . . .

Dear Southern land, why does my heart still tremble
when a bird flies home at evening, or a plucked note
on the 'dan bao' throbs out on the midnight air,
or the song of a boatman rises from the river?

Why are my days of joy so fraught with terror?
Why am I forever confused, why should I be haunted
by a promise not yet honoured? Why does my throat
constrict, when I try to eat rice? Because you, my
    country,
suffer and struggle alone, our invaded South.

Look, my friend, at the small dark round eyes of the
    children,
those jet-black apples that glitter behind barbed wire,
glitter with tears as they watch the flames around them . .

Who knows, among you, how many heads have fallen
in the past three thousand nights? Who is aware?
Who knows how many rivers are filled with blood,
blood of the South, my country, cut off, and suffering,
for ten years, nearly . . .

Look at those lovely girls, now flushed with youth,
their oval faces glowing with love and hope.
Soon, on a fine spring morning, must they waken
To be turned to ashes by the invaders' bombs!

Listen, my friend; from our invaded South
comes the murderous roaring of their 'flying eagles'!
Hear the howling of those human hunting-hounds,
who come to eat men's livers and drink men's blood . . .

Listen, my friend, to the voices of the living,
mounting like rushing waves of the great oceans,
listen also to the voices of the dead,
persistent, like the wind among coconut palms ...

They all ask for only one thing: liberation!
Save the South – our Southern land! You must save the
   South!
Anger is even stirring the realms of Buddha,
monks rise and give their bodies to the burning,
lighting them up, as torches, for freedom and living.

My country! Mountains and rivers, noble and grand,
country of heroism, flower of the twentieth century,
be proud of your place in the struggle against the last
   empire,
Stand up, good people of the invaded South!

Invaded South, still radiant under the bombing ...

TADEUSZ RÓŻEWICZ
b. 1921

❋

'In a Polish village'

In a Polish village
sleeping under autumn rain
seen only
through years' clear image of fields
rainbow of folklore
in a small Polish village
not heard of
by Morgan Dupont

Krupp Thyssen
not heard of
a village so small
that its name
appears only
on Wehrmacht maps

on an autumn night when wind blows
and black lupines glitter gold in the rain
and puddles are like dead eyes of the sky
on an autumn night they took him
from a room with a floor
hard walked on
by many generations
where the Byzantine face of Mother
dark above dried wreaths of plant
stood silent

Out from the circle of the oil lamp
on an autumn night they took him
a young man
in a linen shirt
from his supper

his wife opened her mouth
and touched her throat
when the three strange men
walked into the room taking him
asking to be shown the way

It happened outside

When he pointing
to show them the
One of the three
shot him between the eyes
through his clear forehead

He fell down in the mud
and stayed there
and those who had killed
walked into the darkness

The sky cleaned its black mouth
with rain
and the dark mother
placed her son's head on her bosom
pierced by swords
In the fields
on the roads
wooden crosses
kneel in the mud
in a small Polish village
where the wind blows
and black lupines glitter gold in the rain

This shot was not heard
this death not seen
by Morgan and Rockefeller
Krupp Cloy and Thyssen

Draft for a contemporary love-poem

For surely whiteness
is best described through greyness
bird through stone
sunflowers
in December

in the past love-poems
described flesh
described this and that
eye-lashes for instance

surely redness
should be described
through greyness sun through rain
poppies in November
lips at night

the most telling
description of bread
is one of hunger
it includes
the damp porous centre
the warm interior
sunflowers at night
breasts belly thighs of Cybele

a spring-like
transparent description
of water
is the description of thirst
of ashes
desert
it conjures up a mirage
clouds and trees enter
the water's mirror

Hunger deprivation
absence
of flesh
is the description of love
the contemporary love-poem

Fear

Your fear is great
metaphysical
mine is small
a clerk with a brief-case

with record cards
questionnaires
when I was born
what is my income
what haven't I done
what don't I believe

what am I doing here
when will I stop pretending
will I pretend
to go elsewhere
later

TADEUSZ RÓŻEWICZ

In the midst of life

After the end of the world
after death
I found myself in the midst of life
creating myself
building life
people animals landscapes

this is a table I said
this is a table
there is bread and a knife on the table
knife serves to cut bread
people are nourished by bread

man must be loved
I learnt by night by day
what must one love
I would reply man

this is a window I said
this is a window
there is a garden beyond the window
I see an apple tree in the garden
the apple tree blossoms
the blossom falls
fruit is formed
ripens
my father picks the apple
the man who picks the apple
is my father

I sat on the threshold

that old woman who
leads a goat on a string
is needed more

is worth more
than the seven wonders of the world
anyone who thinks or feels
she is not needed
is a murderer

this is a man
this is a tree this is bread

people eat to live
I kept saying to myself
human life is important
human life has great importance
the value of life
is greater than the value of all things
which man has created
man is a great treasure
I repeated stubbornly

this is water I said
I stroked the waves with my hand
and talked to the river
water I would say
nice water
this is me

man talked to water
talked to the moon
to the flowers and to rain
talked to the earth
to the birds
to the sky

the sky was silent
the earth was silent
and if a voice was heard
flowing
from earth water and sky
it was a voice of another man

TADEUSZ RÓŻEWICZ

Massacre of the innocents

The children cried: 'Mummy!'
'I have been good!'
'Why is it dark! Dark!'

You can see them
going down
you can see the marks
of small feet here and there
going down

Their pockets full
of string and pebbles
and little horses made of wire

The great plain closed
like a geometric figure
one tree of black smoke
vertical
a dead tree
starless its crown

An address

Not to posterity
that would be senseless
they might all be monsters
the high commission
gives clear warning
the powers rulers military staffs
that monsters will follow
with no brains

therefore not to posterity
but to those who
at this very moment
multiply with their eyes shut

not to posterity
I address these words
I speak to politicians
who won't read me
to bishops
who won't read me
to generals
who won't read me
I speak to the so-called 'ordinary people'
who won't read me

I shall speak to all
who do not read me
nor hear nor know
nor need me

They do not need me
but I need them

ERICH FRIED
b. 1921

❋

Child in Peru

Because his spine is twisted
because he is past shouting
because he stinks
because he is too weak
to go on living
the system
that is to blame
shall also not go on living

Because his spine is twisted
your explanations are twisted
Because he is past shouting
you cannot shout him down
Because he stinks
your whole system stinks
too strongly to go on living
to high heaven
where he won't get

Toy on target[1]

1

Dropping
toys
instead of bombs
for the Festival of the Children

that,
the market researchers said,
will doubtlessly make
an impression

It has made
a great
impression
on the whole world

2

If the aeroplane
had dropped the toys
a fortnight ago
and only now the bombs

my two children
thanks to your kindness
would have had something to play with
for those two weeks

---

1. On the day of the Vietnamese 'Festival of the Children' U.S. bombers dropped toys, even on villages where shortly before children had been killed by their bombs. E.F.

My girlfriends

Slowly in three to four weeks
or suddenly over night
my girls turn into
my aunts and elderly cousins

I see them anxiously
chewing their false teeth
and with arthritic fingers
wipe their spat-at faces

They arrive in Theresienstadt
with suitcases and bundles
They fall out of the window
still groping for their glasses

When they stretch in my bed
they are trying to stand to attention
in order to be spared
when the sick are picked out

I see them discoloured blue
when I kiss them in the morning
stacked in sixes
– the shit and vomited bile

washed off with garden hoses –
ready for transfer
from the gas chamber
to the incinerators

MARCOS ANA
b. 1921

✵

Victim

Knock his wound once in a while;
never leave it free to heal.
His pain must spurt fresh blood
and anguish live on for ever in his entrails.

If he takes to flight, clamour after him
that he is guilty; he must not forget.
Hurl lumps of dark earth in his face.
If flowers begin to grow among his words
tread on their scarlet sap
until they grow as pale as dead men's hands.
Lay waste. Lay waste. His heart must not release
the music locked inside it.

For this is your law, so alien to mine:
if a river rises to converse with the moon,
wall in its water with mountains.
If a star forgetting its distance plunges down
into the unripe lips of a boy,
denounce it to the heavenly bodies.
If a fallow deer drinks freedom and woods,
leash it like a dog.
If a fish should learn to live without water
deprive it of shore and land.
If hands should gently caress the air
dreaming of the thighs of enjoyment,
put them on a chopping-block.

If the dawn breaks passionately bright
drive the green swords of night into its eyes.

If there is a man whose heart
is made out of the wind,
Weight him with stones
and drown him with his knees against his chest.

NANOS VALAORITIS
b. 1921

✳

5 to 7

TO NIKOS STANGOS

Tea at 5 with Miss 7
Cholera in a province of Bengal
The dreadful darkness whitened
With a drop of sun in the night's inkstand

Resurrection with cannonade and fire-crackers
Many happy returns in the morning mirror
Not a word from anyone anywhere
Black stains on silk dresses

The fatigue that made two steps
From here to the corner seem endless
With a television's heart in your mouth
You flicker you speak up you smile and disappear

Image made to nylons and electrons
That I see only with my eyes shut
Cinema that keeps on playing
Within me for years on end

Beyond the definition of non-sense
Your body that doesn't feel
Anything making love
In the arms of nobody

And my burning self
Like a Buddhist in Saigon
Like a student in Washington
A woman in Chicago.

PIER PAOLO PASOLINI
b. 1922

✳

To a Pope

A few days before you died,
death had set eyes on one of the same age as you:
at twenty you were a student and he a labourer,
you rich and noble, and he a poor commoner:
but the same days gilded for you as for him
the sight of old Rome turning new.
Poor Zucchetto, I have seen his remains.
He was wandering drunk at night through the Markets,
and was run over by a tram coming from San Paolo.
The tram dragged him a few yards along the rails among
    the plane trees,
and for a few hours he remained under the wheels:
a few people gathered around looking at him in silence;
it was late and there were few folk around.
One of the men who exist because you exist,
an ill-clothed old policeman looking like a bully,
kept off those who pressed too close, shouting 'Get back,
    you bastards!'
Then a hospital ambulance came and drove him away.
The people dispersed, and all that was left
were a few shreds here and there. The woman
who owned the bar a few yards away,
used to know him and informed a newcomer
that Zucchetto had ended up under a tram and died.
A few days later you also died: Zucchetto
was one of your great Roman and human flock,
a poor drunkard, without family or home,

399

who wandered all night and managed to live who knows
  how.
You knew nothing of him: as you
knew nothing of thousands of wretches like him.
Perhaps it's too hard of me to ask
why people like Zucchetto were not worthy of your love.
There are infamous places where mothers and children
live in an ancient dust, in the mud of other epochs.
Just not very far from where you lived,
within sight of Saint Peter's beautiful dome,
there's one of these places, Gelsomino . . .
A hill quarried into two halves, and below,
between a ditch and a row of new palaces,
a mass of miserable constructions, not houses but pigsties.
A single word from you was enough, a solitary gesture,
and those, your sons, would have each had a house:
but you didn't make that gesture, didn't utter that word.
It wasn't that someone had asked you to forgive Marx!
An immense wave that has kept breaking over
  millenniums of life,
divided you from him, from his religion:
but doesn't one talk of pity in your religion?
Thousands of people during your pontificate,
and under your eyes, have lived in pens and sties.
Sin does not mean doing wrong – and you knew it:
not to do good – that's what sin means.
How much good you could do! And you didn't:
there hasn't been a greater sinner than you.

VASKO POPA
b. 1922

✳

The eyes of Sutyeska[1]

Through flesh and blood the earth is given birth
Clod after clod stone after stone
Certainty after certainty

Through cosmic storms the sky is given birth
Serenity after serenity star after star
Vista after vista

Our strength grows into mountains into
constellations
Hunger into fruit-trees tenderness into flowers
Freedom into infinity

More and more we merge with all
Nothing can despoil us

1. At Sutyeska, partisans, though outnumbered, broke through the Nazi force that surrounded them. Most of the partisans were killed. 1,500 wounded, in a nearby military hospital, were killed by the Nazis.

CHAIRIL ANWAR

1922-49

❋

Me

When my time comes
I want to hear no one's cries,
Nor yours either

Away with all who cry!

Here I am, a wild beast,
Cut off from his companions

Bullets may pierce my skin
But I'll keep on,

Carrying forward my wounds and my pain,
Attacking,
Attacking,
Until suffering disappears

And I won't care anymore

I want to live a thousand years

MIRON BIAŁOSZEWSKI
b. 1922

✸

Secret freedom

They bequeathed their walls
like living plasma.

They bred in families
    great-grand-wardrobes
    great-grand-door-handles.

When the spiral staircase unwound
and the floors caved in,
they still felt the wardrobe in their tiny livers,
they thought: the sideboard exists
    by saying so.
    The mouth creaks –
    A door grins wide ...

Through landscapes broken into syntheses
they went to the promised floor,
promised for each
by himself.

They did not sing Ecclesiastes.

Vanity is for the elect.

The elect are few.

Everybody – in the last resort
Elects only himself.

VIDAL DE NICOLAS
b. 1922

❋

A wish

That son of Cain, let him have no more power
to loose his fury on the unfettered spring
or deal death to the kiss.
Let hatred be restrained from flooding
the pristine margins of the air.
Let knives become
impotent against swallows, and the assassin
powerless to garrotte the dawn.
May war never again
batter the skulls of newborn babes, or sever
the exultant arteries of a man.
Let poisoned fangs and pistols
and slavering jaws be done away,
and nevermore let frenzy lash us
with its insensate waves.

Let nothing remain but a love
as vast as all the oceans,
pouring like a cataract across the pupils
of our eyes, flooding the planets,
filling the songs of poets everywhere.

PÉTER KUCZKA
b. 1923

*

I'd rather go naked

Naked through all the streets I'd rather go,
let them laugh at me if it gives them fun.

Naked through all the streets I'd rather go,
or have them jail me for a crazy one.

Naked through all the streets I'd rather go,
and freeze like trees do, blackness petrified.

Naked through all the streets I'd rather go,
and die as the man who ends with suicide.

Naked through all the streets I'd rather go,
act like a poor dull fool you'd all despise.

Naked through all the streets I'd rather go,
but never dress up in a suit of lies.

LAJOS TAMÁSI
b. 1923

✳

Wayfaring seaman

– From Venus's shrine to Olivet's mountainside,
what ways in my day, how many ways I've tried.
The end of all the roads:
just dust on my boots,
hoar-frost at my temples,
and the bulk of my shadow too black for the sun to
  dissemble.
Out of the alleys I led an army.
The heroes of my imagining shone around me.
I came with an army, and at times I was lonely,
but my ears rang with the city's jubilant night
and I sang, transformed in my own kingly light.
I too blazed up, seized history's avenging sword ...
and over my face jetted the black-red blood,
– my comrades looked to me from prison's degrading pit.
I mounted sullen guard. Back to the bars I stood.
For the forsworn judges I stiffened in salute.
– How long, how many varied roads I've trod.
The end of all the roads:
just dried mud on my boots.
Now a new road is before me, and no
vileness can contrive to slow
my start, or turn my resolve, or keep me from going,
or cripple the wings of the song that is undying.
Though the soul ache, in such keen radiance,
its diamond core grows harder, more intense.
Brother and little sister, we talk it over. I'm ready.

I sleep badly. No matter. See, I am calm and steady.
– All the ways I have wandered to be sorted at last and
surveyed.
The word is what we need, more desperately now than
bread.
Blaze up, blessed hope, rekindle our souls – as you sought
it first in the alleys and every byway and port,
mate,
you who bear the tattoo on your indelibled heart.

MIROSLAV HOLUB
b. 1928

✻

In the microscope

Here too are dreaming landscapes,
lunar, derelict.
Here too are the masses
tillers of the soil.
And cells, fighters
who lay down their lives
for a song.

Here too are cemeteries,
fame and snow.
And I hear murmuring,
the revolt of immense estates.

Ode to joy

You only love
when you love in vain.

Try another radio probe
when ten have failed,
take two hundred rabbits
when a hundred have died:
only this is science.

You ask the secret.
It has just one name:
again.

In the end
a dog carries in his jaws
his image in the water,
people rivet the new moon,
I love you.

Like caryatids
our lifted arms
hold up time's granite load

and defeated
we shall always win.

Harbour

But the sea was measured
and chained to the earth.
And the earth was measured
and chained to the sea.

They launched
cranes, lean angels,
they calculated
the wail of widowed sirens,
they foresaw
the nervous unrest of buoys,
they drafted
the labyrinth of routes around the world.

They constructed
the Minotaurs of ships.

They discovered five continents.

The earth was measured
and chained to the sea.

And the sea was measured
and chained to the earth.

All that is left
is a small house above the canal.
A man who spoke softly,
a woman with tears in her eyes.
All that is left is the evening lamp,
the continent of the table,
the tablecloth, a sea-gull that does not fly away.

All that is left
is a cup of tea,
the deepest ocean in the world.

The forest

Among the primary rocks
where the bird spirits
crack the granite seeds
and the tree statues
with their black arms
threaten the clouds,

suddenly
there comes a rumble,
as if history
were being uprooted,

the grass bristles,
boulders tremble,
the earth's surface cracks

and there grows

a mushroom,

immense as life itself,
filled with billions of cells
immense as life itself,
eternal,
watery,

appearing in this world for the first

and last time.

How to paint a perfect Christmas

Above, you paint the sky
delicate as maidenhair.
Below, pour a little darkness
heated to room temperature
or slightly more.

With a cat's claw in the dark
scratch out a little tree,
the finest tree in the world,
finer than any forester
could ever imagine.

And the tree itself
will light up
and the whole picture purr
with green joy,
with purple hope.

Right. But now you must
put under the tree
the
real big thing,
the thing you most want in the world;
the thing pop-singers
call happiness.

It's easy enough for a cat,
a cat will put a mouse there,
Colonel Blimp will line up
the largest jet-propelled halberd
which shoots and bangs and salutes,
a sparrow will gather
a few stalks for its nest,
mister junior clerk will submit
a stuffed file tied with red tape,
a butterfly will put there
a new rubber peacock's eye,
but what will *you* put there?

You think and think
till the day grows grey,
till the river almost runs out,
till even the bulbs begin to yawn,
you think

and finally

there in the darkness you blot out
a hazy white spot,
a bit like a florin,
a bit like a ship,
a bit like the Moon,
a bit like the beautiful face
of someone (who?) else,

a hazy white spot,
perhaps more like emptiness,
like the negation of something,
like non-pain,
like non-fear,
like non-worry,

a hazy white spot,
and you go to bed

and say to yourself,
yes, now I know how to do it,
yes, now I know
yes,
next time
I shall paint
the most perfect Christmas
that ever was.

The lesson

A tree enters and says with a bow:
  I am a tree.
A black tear falls from the sky and says:
  I am a bird.

Down a spider's web
  something like love
    comes near
      and says:
  I am silence.

But by the blackboard sprawls
  a national democratic
  horse in his waistcoat
  and repeats,
  pricking his ears on every side,
  repeats and repeats
    I am the engine of history
    and
    we all
    love
    progress
    and
    courage
    and
    the fighter's wrath.

Under the classroom door
trickles
a thin stream of blood.

For here begins
the massacre
of the innocents.

Planning

Around the table,
from hand to hand,
from file to file,
from column to column,
march

the refrigerators that are and
the refrigerators that will be,
white and gleaming
like an antarctic flotilla,

the preserves that are and
the preserves that will be,
red and green,
splendid as the pages
of the kings of the glass castle,

the excavators that are and
the excavators that will be,
black and heroic
as a storm in a teacup,

the new-born that are and
the new-born that will be,
with bulging eyes
and a temporary shortage
of dummies,

march
fluorescent lamps,
books of poetry,
telescopes,
overcoats,
moulds,
megawatts
            precise as a surgical needle,
megatons
            certain as next spring,
march
around the table
in the cold dry glow
of cigarettes,
and the gradual welding
of fantasy
            with the steel bars of numbers.

The future
            to three decimal points
            exactly.

But sometimes,
when all's finished and signed,
the excavators,
the new-born,
the apples,
the books,
the refrigerators
pipe up
just for the heck of it,
without a reference number,
in quiet urgent voices –

and what about yourselves, friends,
what about yourselves,
to how many decimal points exactly,

your goodselves today,
your goodselves tomorrow,
to how many points exactly
at home
       and in the street,
and with your wife
          and your friends.
and morning
       and evening,
and on the way up
        and on the way down,
to how many decimal points exactly
you yourselves, friends?

And we should have an answer to that
in this year's plan.

GIOVANNI GIUDICI
b. 1924

❋

You ask me what it means

You ask me what the word
alienation means:
from birth you start dying
in order to live through a master

who sells you out; start consigning
what you have – power, love, hatred –
so that you may obtain
sex, wine, heart-break.

It means you are beside yourself
but you think that you are
just your own self, because
the wind undermines you, and you yield.

You may resist, but a day
seems a century, which consumes you,
what you give away does not return
from where it leaves.

Waiting is another life,
but there isn't another time:
you are time that disappears,
and that which remains is not you.

YEHUDA AMICHAI
b. 1924

✻

Out of three or four in a room

Out of three or four in a room
One is always standing at the window.
Forced to see the injustice amongst the thorns,
The fires on the hill.

And people who left whole
Are brought home in the evening, like small change.

Out of three or four in a room
One is always standing at the window.
Hair dark above his thoughts.
Behind him, the words.
And in front of him the words, wandering, without
    luggage.
Hearts without provision, prophecies without water
And big stones put there
And staying, closed, like letters
With no addresses; and no one to receive them.

The United Nations Command in Jerusalem

The mediators, the peace-makers, the compromisers,
    the pacifiers,
Live in the white house
And receive their nourishment from far away,

Through twisting channels, through dark veins, like a
    foetus.

And their secretaries are lipsticked and laughing,
And their immune chauffeurs wait below, like horses in
    a stable,
And the trees whose shadow shades them, have their
    roots in disputed territory,
And the delusions are children who go out into the fields
    to find cyclamen
And do not come back.

And the thoughts circle above, uneasily, like scout-planes,
And they take photographs, and return, and develop the
    film
In dark, sad rooms.

And I know that they have very heavy chandeliers,
And the boy that I was sits on them and swings
In and out, in and out, and out, and does not come back.

Later on, the night will bring
Rusty and crooked conclusions out of our ancient lives
And above all the houses, the music
Will gather all the scattered things
Like a hand gathering crumbs off the table
After the meal, while the talk continues
And the children are already asleep.

And hopes come to me like daring sailors
Like discoverers of continents
To an island
And they rest for a day or two,
And then they sail away.

A pity. We were such a good invention

They amputated
Your thighs off my hips.
As far as I'm concerned
They are all surgeons. All of them.

They dismantled us
Each from the other.
As far as I'm concerned
They are all engineers. All of them.

A pity. We were such a good
And loving invention.
An aeroplane made from a man and wife.
Wings and everything.
We hovered a little above the earth.

We even flew a little.

ZBIGNIEW HERBERT
b. 1924

✴

Two drops

'No time to grieve for roses, when the forests are burning'
Slowacki

The forests were on fire –
they however
wreathed their necks with their hands
like bouquets of roses

People ran to the shelters –
he said his wife had hair
in whose depths one could hide

Covered by one blanket
they whispered shameless words
the litany of those who love

When it got very bad
they leapt into each other's eyes
and shut them firmly

So firmly they did not feel the flames
when they came up to the eyelashes

To the end they were brave
To the end they were faithful
To the end they were similar
like two drops
stuck at the edge of a face

Report from paradise

In paradise the work week is fixed at thirty hours
salaries are higher prices steadily go down
manual labour is not tiring (because of reduced gravity
chopping wood is no harder than typing
the social system is stable and the rulers are wise
really in paradise one is better off than in whateve
   country

At first it was to have been different
luminous circles choirs and degrees of abstraction
but they were not able to separate exactly
the soul from the flesh and so it would come here
with a drop of fat a thread of muscle
it was necessary to face the consequences
to mix a grain of the absolute with a grain of clay
one more departure from doctrine the last departure
only John foresaw it: you will be resurrected in the fles

not many behold God
he is only for those of 100 per cent pneuma
the rest listen to communiqués about miracles and flood
some day God will be seen by all
when it will happen nobody knows

As it is now every Saturday at noon
sirens sweetly bellow
and from the factories go the heavenly proletarians
awkwardly under their arms they carry their wings lik
   violins

Naked town

On the plain that town flat like an iron sheet
with mutilated hand of its cathedral a pointing claw
with pavements the colour of intestines houses stripped
  of their skin
the town beneath a yellow wave of sun
a chalky wave of moon

o town what a town tell me what's the name of that town
under what star on what road

about people: they work at the slaughter-house in an
  immense building
of raw concrete blocks around them the odour of blood
and the penitential psalm of animals Are there poets
  there (silent poets)
there are troops a big rattle of barracks on the outskirts
on Sunday beyond the bridge in prickly bushes on cold
  sand
on rusty grass girls receive soldiers
there are as well some places dedicated to dreams The
  cinema
with a white wall on which splash the shadows of the
  absent
little halls where alcohol is poured into glass thin and
  thick
there are also dogs at last hungry dogs that howl
and in that fashion indicate the borders of the town Amen

so you still ask what's the name of that town
which deserves biting anger where is that town
on the cords of what winds beneath what column of air
and who lives there people with the same skin as ours
or people with faces or

A halt

We halted in a town the host
ordered the table to be moved to the garden the first star
shone out and faded we were breaking bread
crickets were heard in the twilight loosestrife
a cry but a cry of a child otherwise the bustle
of insects of men a thick scent of earth
those who were sitting with their backs to the wall
saw violet now – the gallows hill
on the wall the dense ivy of executions

we were eating much
as is usual when nobody pays

Episode in a library

A blonde girl is bent over a poem. With a pencil sharp as
a lancet she transfers the words to a blank page and
changes them into strokes, accents, caesuras. The lament
of a fallen poet now looks like a salamander eaten away
by ants.

When we carried him away under machine-gun fire, I
believed that his still warm body would be resurrected in
the word. Now as I watch the death of the words, I know
there is no limit to decay. All that will be left after us in
the black earth will be scattered syllables. Accents over
nothingness and dust.

Emperor

Once upon a time there was an Emperor. He had yellow
eyes and a predatory jaw. He lived in a palace full of
statuary and policemen. Alone. At night he would wake

p and scream. Nobody loved him. Most of all he liked
unting game and terror. But he posed for photographs
with children and flowers. When he died, nobody dared
o remove his portraits. Take a look, perhaps still you
ave his mask at home.

Elegy of Fortinbras

FOR C.M.

Now that we're alone we can talk prince man to man
hough you lie on the stairs and see no more than a dead
   ant
othing but black sun with broken rays
  could never think of your hands without smiling
nd now that they lie on the stone like fallen nests
hey are as defenceless as before The end is exactly this
The hands lie apart The sword lies apart The head apart
nd the knight's feet in soft slippers

You will have a soldier's funeral without having been a
   soldier
he only ritual I am acquainted with a little
There will be no candles no singing only cannon-fuses
   and bursts
repe dragged on the pavement helmets boots artillery
   horses drums drums I know nothing exquisite
hose will be my manoeuvres before I start to rule
ne has to take the city by the neck and shake it a bit

Anyhow you had to perish Hamlet you were not for life
ou believed in crystal notions not in human clay
lways twitching as if asleep you hunted chimeras
wolfishly you crunched the air only to vomit
ou knew no human thing you did not know even how to
   breathe

Now you have peace Hamlet you accomplished what
   you had to
and you have peace The rest is not silence but belongs
   to me
you chose the easier part an elegant thrust
but what is heroic death compared with eternal watching
with a cold apple in one's hand on a narrow chair
with a view of the ant-hill and the clock's dial

Adieu prince I have tasks a sewer project
and a decree on prostitutes and beggars
I must also elaborate a better system of prisons
since as you justly said Denmark is a prison
I go to my affairs This night is born
a star named Hamlet We shall never meet
what I shall leave will not be worth a tragedy

It is not for us to greet each other or bid farewell we live
   on archipelagos
and that water these words what can they do what can
   they do prince

Awakening

When the horror subsided the floodlights went out
we discovered that we were on a rubbish-heap in very
   strange poses
some with outstretched necks
others with open mouths from which still trickled my
   native land
still others with fists pressed to eyes
cramped emphatically pathetically taut
in our hands we held pieces of sheet iron and bones
(the floodlights had transformed them into symbols)
but now they were no more than sheet iron and bones

We had nowhere to go we stayed on the rubbish-heap
we tidied things up
the bones and sheet iron we deposited in an archive

We listened to the chirping of streetcars to a swallow-like
    voice of factories
and a new life was unrolling at our feet

YEVGENY VINOKUROV

b. 1925

*

'Each nation ...'

Each nation
Has given itself
Its own epithet;
To carry its essence,
The aim:
For England – a 'merry old'
For France – a 'beautiful'
And 'holy' was once
Russia's name ...

Conscience

One can have peace of mind by agreeing,
For convenience to call evil good.
But then what should one do,
                              one whose conscience
Unexpectedly unmasks its hood?
What to do when shame comes arriving
In a man, telling him why it came?
Accidentally, eventually, may it happen –
Like the trumpets of angels –
                          that shame!

Human shame,
            the great god,
                      cruel, ancient,

Used to run through the groves with the blade
Of its dagger hid, dressed like mad Furies,
For its victim who trembled, afraid.
And though years flew by, it still pursued him,
Caught him when he expected it least:
Midst a battle,
                    in bed with his woman,
Or while raising a glass at a feast.
I don't know of a miracle greater!
Even now it's an unexplained plan.
I don't know from what place came our conscience,
Where it originated in man.
Choked or not, it will live on forever;
It's Earth's lasting reward for all plights.

One should marvel not at the soul's baseness
But, instead, at its measureless heights.

Birds

What do birds say when they sing? Any sense?
Night's full of sounds that swell, blend and disperse.
Are they paeans to stars' magnificence?
Or hymns to the unbounded universe?

Or maybe they're not songs at all,
                              but, say,
Talks about many things, in different terms.
Like: Morning's coming. The dew's thick today.
Or: Look here, all you birds,
                              I found some worms . . .

'The Goths were being baptized . . .'

The Goths were being baptized.
                              They looked doomed
Going into the stream up to their shoulders . . . .
But up above their heads their own swords loomed;
Their fists were unbaptized to all beholders.
Humility should have its limits too,
Whatever 'meek Commandment' comes along . . .
And I should like to keep my fist in view.
I shall be kind. But let *it* be strong.

CHRISTOPHER LOGUE
b. 1926

❋

Know thy enemy

Know thy enemy:
he does not care what colour you are
provided you work for him
  and yet you do!
he does not care how much you earn
provided you earn more for him
  and yet you do!
he does not care who lives in the room at the top
provided he owns the building
  and yet you strive!
he will let you write against him
provided you do not act against him
  and yet you write!
he sings the praises of humanity
but knows machines cost more than men.
Bargain with him, he laughs, and beats you at it;
challenge him, and he kills.
Sooner than lose the things he owns
he will destroy the world.
SMASH CAPITAL NOW!

> *But as you hasten to be free*
> *And build your commonwealth*
> *Do not forget the enemy*
> *Who lies within yourself.*

ALDO DO ESPIRITO SANTO

b. 1926

❉

Where are the men seized in this wind of madness?

Blood falling in drops to the earth
men dying in the forest
and blood falling, falling . . .
on those cast into the sea . . .
Fernão Dias for ever in the story
of Ilha Verde, red with blood,
of men struck down
in the vast arena of the quay.
Alas the quay, the blood, the men,
the fetters, the lash of beatings
resound, resound, resound
dropping in the silence of prostrated lives
of cries, and howls of pain
from men who are men no more,
in the hands of nameless butchers.
Zé Mulato, in the story of the quay
shooting men in the silence
of bodies falling.
Alas Zé Mulato, Zé Mulato,
The victims cry for vengeance
The sea, the sea of Fernão Dias
devouring human lives
is bloody red.
– We are arisen –
Our eyes are turned to you.

Our lives entombed
in fields of death,
men of the Fifth of February
men fallen in the furnace of death
imploring pity
screaming for life,
dead without air, without water
they all arise
from the common grave
and upright in the chorus of justice
cry for vengeance ...
   The fallen bodies in the forest,
the homes, the homes of men
destroyed in the gulf
of ravening fire,
lives incinerated,
raise the unaccustomed chorus of justice
crying for vengeance.
And all you hangmen
all you torturers
sitting in the dock:
– What have you done with my people? ...
– What do you answer?
– Where is my people? ...
And I answer in the silence
of voices raised
demanding justice ...
One by one, through all the line ...
For you, tormentors,
forgiveness has no name.
Justice shall be heard.
And the blood of lives fallen
in the forests of death,
innocent blood
drenching the earth
in a silence of terrors
shall make the earth fruitful,
crying for justice.

It is the flame of humanity
singing of hope
in a world without bonds
where liberty
is the fatherland of men ...

GÜNTER GRASS
b. 1927

❃

In the egg

We live in the egg.
We have covered the inside wall
of the shell with dirty drawings
and the Christian names of our enemies.
We are being hatched.

Whoever is hatching us
is hatching our pencils as well.
Set free from the egg one day
at once we shall draw a picture
of whoever is hatching us.

We assume that we're being hatched.
We imagine some good-natured fowl
and write school essays
about the colour and breed
of the hen that is hatching us.

When shall we break the shell?
Our prophets inside the egg
for a middling salary argue
about the period of incubation.
They posit a day called X.

Out of boredom and genuine need
we have invented incubators.
We are much concerned about our offspring inside the
    egg.

We should be glad to recommend our patent
to her who looks after us.

But we have a roof over our heads.
Senile chicks,
polyglot embryos
chatter all day
and even discuss their dreams.

And what if we're not being hatched?
If this shell will never break?
If our horizon is only that
of our scribbles, and always will be?
We hope that we're being hatched.

Even if we only talk of hatching
there remains the fear that someone
outside our shell will feel hungry
and crack us into the frying pan with a pinch of salt.
What shall we do then, my brethren inside the egg?

Powerless, with a guitar

We read napalm and imagine napalm.
Since we cannot imagine napalm
we read about napalm until
by napalm we can imagine more.
Now we protest against napalm.
　　After breakfast, silent,
　　we see in photographs what napalm can do.
　　We show each other coarse screen prints
　　and say: there you are, napalm.
　　They do that with napalm.
Soon there'll be cheap picture books
with better photographs
which will show more clearly
what napalm can do.

We bite our nails and write protests.
   But, we read, there are
   worse things than napalm.
   Quickly we protest against worse things.
   Our well-founded protests, which at any time
   we may compose fold stamp, mount up.
Impotence, tried out on rubber façades.
Impotence puts records on: impotent songs.
Powerless, with a guitar. –
But outside, finely meshed
and composed, power has its way.

DAVID DIOP
1927–60

*

Listen comrades

Listen comrades of the struggling centuries
To the keen clamour of the Negro from Africa to the
    Americas
They have killed Mamba
As they killed the seven of Martinsville
Or the Madagascan down there in the pale light on the
    prisons
He held in his look comrades
The warm faith of a heart without anguish
And his smile despite agony
Despite the wounds of his broken body
Kept the bright colours of a bouquet of hope
It is true that they have killed Mamba with his white
    hairs
Who ten times poured forth for us milk and light
I feel his mouth on my dreams
And the peaceful tremor of his breast
And I am lost again
Like a plant torn from the maternal bosom
But no
For there rings out higher than my sorrows
Purer than the morning where the wild beast wakes
The cry of a hundred people smashing their cells
And my blood long held in exile
The blood they hoped to snare in a circle of words
Rediscovers the fervour that scatters the mists
Listen comrades of the struggling centuries

To the keen clamour of the Negro from Africa to the
   Americas
It is the sign of the dawn
The sign of brotherhood which comes to nourish the
   dreams of men.

Africa

Africa my Africa
Africa of proud warriors in ancestral savannahs
Africa of whom my grandmother sings
On the banks of the distant river
I have never known you
But your blood flows in my veins
Your beautiful black blood that irrigates the fields
The blood of your sweat
The sweat of your work
The work of your slavery
The slavery of your children
Africa tell me Africa

Is this you this back that is bent
This back that breaks under the weight of humilation
This back trembling with red scars
And saying yes to the whip under the midday sun
But a grave voice answers me
Impetuous son that tree young and strong
That tree there
In splendid loneliness amidst white and faded flowers
That is Africa your Africa
That grows again patiently obstinately
And its fruit gradually acquire
The bitter taste of liberty.

The vultures

In those days
When civilization kicked us in the face
When holy water slapped our cringing brows
The vultures built in the shadow of their talons
The bloodstained monument of tutelage
In those days
There was painful laughter on the metallic hell of the
    roads
And the monotonous rhythm of the paternoster
Drowned the howling on the plantations
O the bitter memories of extorted kisses
Of promises broken at the point of a gun
Of foreigners who did not seem human
Who knew all the books but did not know love
But we whose hands fertilize the womb of the earth
In spite of your songs of pride
In spite of the desolate villages of torn Africa
Hope was preserved in us as in a fortress
And from the mines of Swaziland to the factories of
    Europe
Spring will be reborn under our bright steps.

GIANCARLO MAJORINO
b. 1928

✳

Industrial landscape

They sit in tram-coaches with napes
under the lamps and knees forward as at Mauthausen,
or stand erect and feel
the nine metres of the intestinal tube
rumble within.
Tomorrow they start all over again,
ride on the trams to get to their workrooms,
where they bend their napes under the vigilant eyes,
as under an axe, of their petty bosses who live on that
    job;
some of them wander around locked up in cars,
colliding, dodging and swearing death to him who
    passes them.
Are you amazed at the youngsters' agitation in Turin?
Amazed that a world with such cracks
in her soles still resists! And yet
fables of love, luxury and joy, either read
or dreamt about keep whirling in their heads.

FERENC JUHÁSZ
b. 1928

❊

Man imposes his pattern upon a dream

The torrid land is suffering,
man's awareness is beginning.
Duckweed shrivels in the fever.
All that was is gone for ever.

Voracious instincts now dwindle.
Only veined cellophanes rustle.
On its ribbed stalk like a green bat
the pumpkin leaf flutters its rag.

Also within into a glassy mess
fused by the fire of consciousness
is that which sprang up once as dense
as weed from depths of existence.

But nurtured hope learns to aspire
as corn grows on the atom's fire.
Sober hormones nurse the hope,
its cause is mine, I'll not give up.

When all's said, man decides alone,
silence gives laws that are its own.
So much more than mere beast is man,
he'll grasp what frees him when he can.

The male locust makes charnel love,
losing life, hands on enough.

Needle-sewn double rowed the jawed
teeth rip at organs, the assured

female is devouring male
her mouth's saws criss-cross and impale,
spiked bow bent in triangle head,
and the heart victim of acid.

Now this is how I stand to you,
giving all, making you fruitful
by consciousness – yet gobbled up
by you, my man-eating epoch!

Hot blood clots by the sun are made
where the tree slops its coolless shade,
the fresh green of tender parsley
casts a russet lacework near me.

The fledgling geese peck in the yard,
fat, shiny, yellow lumps of lard,
skin gritty with feather pimples,
their grease breeding volcanic moles.

A knife glints over them, concern
is poised above me in my turn.
My throat cannot be slit by pain,
I grow, transcend, render it tame.

Shrivelled Evanescence cowers,
mourning for its old psalter serves,
on a wrought brass crucifix its
finger like a green lizard sits.

My small daughter runs to and fro
pleased with her dotted ball, it's blue.
Yet her small soul carries within
outlines of the human pattern.

The strange words, sweet sounds she lets fall
shape desires so clear to all.
She plays, cries, grows, laughs, climbs
under the steel girders of time.

So might our age be remade to
this human pattern – once rescued.
Already, as life's embryo has come
the blind, hermaphrodite atom.

In a deck-chair my mother's sleeping,
on the lawn breathes her pair of wings.
She thinks up for us in her turn
dreams made to a human pattern.

Studded are her gnarled feet with sores
that flowered on stone laundry floors,
dream-roots bearing the tree of sighs
and pain-budded boughs implore the skies.

The slate roof swelters up aloft
and the metal-crested eaves-trough.
Green walnut coolness on my body,
summer's sulphur blaze choking me.

One blood-bellied yellow instant
is the poison-calixed Sabbath.
Wine and sodawater stand upon
my table. I take no absolution.

ERNESTO CHE GUEVARA
1928–67

❋

Song to Fidel

You said the sun would rise.
Let's go
along those unmapped paths
to free the green alligator you love.

And let's go obliterating
insults with our
brows swept with dark insurgent stars.
We shall have victory or shoot past death.

At the first shot the whole jungle
will awake with fresh amazement and
there and then serene company
we'll be at your side.

When your voice quarters the four winds
reforma agraria, justice, bread, freedom,
we'll be there with identical accents
at your side.

And when the clean operation against the tyrant
ends at the end of the day
there and then set for the final battle
we'll be at your side.

And when the wild beast licks his wounded side
where the dart of Cuba hits him
we'll be at your side
with proud hearts.

Don't ever think our integrity can be sapped
by those decorated fleas hopping with gifts
we want their rifles, their bullets and a rock
nothing else.

And if iron stands in our way
we ask for a sheet of Cuban tears
to cover our guerrilla bones
on the journey to American history.
Nothing more.

REMCO CAMPERT
b. 1929

✳

It was in the year of the strike

It was in the year of the strike.
The city lay, a patient stripped of coverings,
in the landscape.
Fever dreams of birds long flown south.
Now the streets exploded with people.
They were hungry, and worse: they'd had enough
of war.
Their leaders waved slogans
and we,
we committed love with each other.

It was in the year of the strike,
the struggle with stones for bread,
that we loved and ran
through the onetime princely park
and sat beneath embarrassed statues,
grey as the winter, a pigeon
escaped from the season's basket
to creep under our clothes,
in search of the spring scent
of love on our flesh.

It was in the year of the strike.
The city fermented like beer.
The hills paid their usual
attention to man and beast.

People ran like tears
through the streets.
The city scowled,
worked its jaw-muscles.
The churches tottered.
The people wanted food and peace on earth.

It was in the year of the strike.
We lived in the coldest room in the city;
I wrote no letters to the reader,
I sold my typewriter
and hungered for the hand of your love,
and full of social sense
it didn't keep me waiting.
We juggled with our ears.
The wallpaper gave torn applause.
The coldest room was a warm theatre.

It was in the year of the strike.
I kissed your eyes into Japanese scallops,
your belly to a rabbit's burrow.
I donned a top hat
– the conjuror, the bride.
The door sighed with amazement
and I bowed gratefully.
At one wave of my hand
your breasts spat fire,
warm, shivering.
The table shut its eyes,
square Calvinist.

It was in the year of the strike.
Restlessly workers trod the streets.
Mothers with children at their knees
slammed shut their cashbooks in despair.
Live bullets were fired.
A son died.
The minister of housing opened up a new bank.

Poets turned into journalists.
In Tunis a bridge was blown up.
The West wavered, true to its office.

It was in the year of the strike.
Love came easy to us.
We were full of surface reality,
I, a doctor with a microscope,
for my work more love than knowledge,
you, the living example in the textbook,
living sinew, tightening,
living mouth, like philosophy,
all living, even the date of birth
in your passport.

It was in the year of the strike
in the coldest room in the city
that we loved
and around us the people
demanding bread and peace, a breeding-ground
for play and love.

It was in the year of the strike,
in the age of the strike.

The consequences still
are with us.

DANE ZAJC

b. 1929

✳

All the birds

We will kill all the birds.
All. All, said the ravens in the dusk.

And in the silence of the night I heard
some in the garden killing my birds.
And I knew
that now there would be in my mornings
no songs,
and I felt
sadness lay hold on my spirit.

All. All the birds, they said.
And I felt
beating around me
dark wings
and glaring at me between them
a raven's yellow eye.
What are you looking for, raven, I asked him.
Under the bark of my skull
I keep no hidden birds.

All. All the birds.
We will kill them all, he said.

And then I felt afraid
that perhaps some night
through dreams of darkness
he would split my skull

and probe with his maniac beak
to see if the nest of my thoughts
sheltered any hidden songbirds.

All. All the birds, he will rasp.

Everywhere now I feel on my neck
A raven's yellow eye.

Something has pierced my soul.
My soul is a slaughtered bird.

All. We will kill them all.
All the birds, croak the ravens
under the sombre sky.

GÁBOR GARAI

b. 1929

❋

A man is beaten up

They are beating up a man in the bar
They are banging and banging his head with their fists
He doesn't cry out or try to protect himself
Even the blood creeps patiently over his face
They beat and beat
   a silent exhibition
broken by one voice:
   – He's probably a gipsy!
They beat and beat
   and the barman comes forward
takes a knee to jerk him outside
into the street
   A man's head smashes
against a block of hard snow
   – Go tumble your mother!
The barman wipes his hands – easy!
The one who beat blood out of a face orders:
– Beer all round for these fellows, with a dash of rum!
The service continues without a break.

A score of other people in the room
They have nothing to do all this while?
They chat and smile together, what is it to them?

Their detachment disguises
   squalid pub-crawls
   racist fantasies

defoliating embraces
genocide volunteers
jerrybuilt residences
wandering H-bombs
curetted foetuses
meat-trusts ordnance-factories
slippery so-help-me gods
prudent no-comment betrayals
specious reasons interests knives
handcuffs stocks keys

like snakes all interlocked
blood-money and forebodings
    frozen hard in the ice

What if this ice should once be thawed?

HANS MAGNUS ENZENSBERGER
b. 1929

✳

middle class blues

we can't complain.
we're not out of work.
we don't go hungry.
we eat.

the grass grows,
the national product,
the fingernail,
the past.

the streets are empty.
the deals have been clinched.
the sirens are silent.
all that will pass.

the dead have made their wills.
the rain's become a drizzle.
the war's not yet been declared.
there's no hurry for that.

we eat the grass.
we eat the national product.
we eat the fingernails.
we eat the past.

we have nothing to conceal.
we have nothing to miss.
we have nothing to say.
we have.

the watch has been wound up.
the bills have been paid.
the washing up has been done.
the last bus is passing by.

it is empty.

we can't complain.

what are we waiting for?

karl heinrich marx

gigantic grandfather
jehovah-bearded
on brown daguerrotypes
i see your face
in the snow-white aura
despotic quarrelsome
and your papers in the linen press:
butcher's bills
inaugural addresses
warrants for your arrest

your massive body
i see in the 'wanted' book
gigantic traitor
displaced person
in tail coat and plastron
consumptive sleepless
your gall-bladder scorched
by heavy cigars
salted gherkins laudanum
and liqueur

i see your house
in the rue d'alliance

dean street grafton terrace
gigantic bourgeois
domestic tyrant
in worn-out slippers:
soot and 'economic shit'[1]
usury 'as usual'[2]
children's coffins
backstair calamities

no machine-gun
in your prophet's hand:
i see it calmly
in the british museum
under the green lamp
break up your own house
with a terrible patience
gigantic founder
for the sake of other houses
in which you never woke up

gigantic zaddik
i see you betrayed
by your disciples:
only your enemies
remained what they were:
I see your face
on the last picture
of april eighty-two:
an iron mask:
the iron mask of freedom

vending machine

he puts four dimes into the slot
he gets himself some cigarettes

1. and 2. Quotations from Marx's letters to Engels in the 1850s
and 1860s. H.M.E.

he gets cancer
he gets apartheid
he gets the king of greece
federal tax state tax sales tax and excise
he gets machine guns and surplus value
free enterprise and positivism
he gets a big lift big business big girls
the big stick the great society the big bang
the big puke
king size extra size super size

he gets more and more
for his four dimes
but for a moment all the things he is getting himself
disappear

even the cigarettes

he looks at the vending machine
but he doesn't see it
he sees himself
for a fleeting moment
and he almost looks like a man

then very soon he is gone again
with a little click
there are his cigarettes

he has disappeared
it was just a fleeting moment
some kind of sudden bliss

he has disappeared
he is gone
buried under all the stuff he has gotten
for his four dimes

PABLO ARMANDO FERNÁNDEZ
b. 1930

❋

From 'Barracks and nets'

4

These are not the chronicles,
he who is writing knows, but we are done
with memory.
The 25th of December of 1956
Mayari Puerto Padre Holguin Jababo Cacocum Banes
Preston Tunas Arroyo Arenas
lands without prophets, without genius,
full of so great a death
while the small lives pass.
The 25th of December of 1956
chosen by chance? Fools!

Death has its ways, they say,
and they lie. Death,
so many times to blame, the innocent,
would not take part in this crime.
This is not a chronicle.
I demand it be said with rage
as a violent tearing apart
white words and fire.
'Redemption of the dead'
no longer far from the truth,
a handsome verse adorned with pages of prophecy,
Man, redeem the living man. Get up and walk
among the living, fight with the living,
earn your bread, and share it.
Man, see that the flowers are for those who live.

See that the oil and the wine of life
are for those with life.
Hector Infante Perez died of this great death,
Alejo Tomas died and Silverio Hernández,
Marcial Perez, José Mendoza and Alcides Aguilera
died of this powerful,
organic, fecund death.
Twenty thousand dead, all with their names,
with their women, some yet to know
    their man;
with their children, some yet to be conceived.
Twenty thousand dead, all with their shoes.
Redemption, useless now as a slogan.
The chronicles will be made in days to come
for every one of these deaths,
and their names will not be forgotten
by those who live.
Dead ones, who freed you from the body of this death?

July 26, 1959

TO FRANK, IN MEMORIAM

He enters the house that has changed streets
where once there were sounds
of a feast.
Till they return things stay as they are.
He comes back to his street
and men on horses sing.
In the multitude that vast silence,
the true voice of the soul is returning home.
Men
and children he always wanted to remember
The exact compass of tenderness,
friends of an exile many nights long
and slow mist, scarcely a murmur.
A thousand, two, three thousand men are singing . . .
Look and it is he who has dropped out to come home.

FAYAD JAMIS
b. 1930

✻

Life

Do you wish this poem to be only
the lilac's shadow the memory of the fountain
pure day drowning in my anguish?
Do you wish this poem only to speak in whispers
in the mid-afternoon
when sleep with its odour of sap enters the nests
and so many live things seem dead?
But now as you listen Spring bursts like a shell
and my poem has no lilacs or sleeping veins
but the sound of reality close at hand.
Myself I move and work and remove
old useless things and hear
my fellow-fighters' breath
and as I smoke this poem is born
and as this poem grows
Spring sings in my land.
You wish that only my silence spoke
and now my bones shout and my voice is not alone
and I tell you that night is beautiful in the window
and more beautiful in the sweat of men who are
    struggling
in workshop and trench
at this moment when a white-winged star
is piercing the world's darkness.
For though you expect a lilac's shadow
to fall on the evening from my poem
you will see only my clenched fist fall and in my verses
life will flower with all its fires.

PAAVO HAAVIKKO
b. 1931

❋

'Statecraft, sagacity . . .'

Statecraft, sagacity
Gone to the mountain council
My lord has planted his banner
We must not go there

And clearly
Alone I am nothing
Come read it now –

Returning to Worms
I take nail and hammer

The hand touches sky
The foot presses down on the ground
Henceforth may nothing divorce
The hand from the sky
The feet from the ground

On the mountains forever
Winds water and fire
Scorched earth
The elements bringing forth bloodshed
Rebellion war
Plague evil sudden death

Statecraft, sagacity
Reappear

And also the men in black
Honour cries out for violence
Sagacity's foresight improves
When the glasses are reddened by flames

We have not come here
To look into wisdom
But into our hearts
We have all of us come here
Not to display sagacity
But the willingness
To make sacrifices.

KAJETAN KOVIČ
b. 1931

*

The hour of conscience

Well, now you know; that's how things are.
No need to throw yourself down on the ground
And bite the stones
No need to roar
For you are not an animal
And what's more, you can't work miracles.

You fought with the machines,
But not in reality.
In fact you love them
They are no worse than horses
Nor are they to be blamed.
They are quite innocent
The others are to blame.

You are yourself to blame
You stood too long upon the lonely brink
You stood too long upon the lonely brink
The old days turn to air
And your pastures are empty for ever more.
Why should you call back
What cannot be recalled?
Scan with your radar,
Change your wavelength.

You are born into this world
You know more about rust than pollen.

The bees will take care of that.
You must see to the rust.
Will you let everything corrode?

You are not a monument;
You are a living ant
And you must carry your small log to the summit of the
    world.
You are of no importance
The important thing is the log.

And perhaps: the ant-hill.

Robots

The robots are on the march.

The first of them is square.
The stone it holds in its hand
Is a cube.
And a cube is forever a cube.
And all that exists is a cube.

The robots are on the march.

The second robot is round.
The stone it holds in its hand
Is a sphere.
And a sphere is forever a sphere
And all that exists is a sphere.

The robots are on the march.

The stone in the sky, the stone on the earth
Has got no choice.
Today is a stone, tomorrow a cube.

Today is a stone, tomorrow a sphere.
Today is a stone, tomorrow a robot.

The robots are on the march.

The cube smashes up the sphere.
The sphere knocks out the cube.
For a cube is forever a cube.
For a sphere is forever a sphere.

The robots are on the march.

As long as a cube is square.
As long as a sphere is round.

ROBERT ROZHDESTVENSKY
b. 1932

*

Before a new jump . . .

We live in one perpetual
waiting room.
Each one of us
                must wait for something always.
A chauffeur
waits for his boss at his home,
and while he waits,
                   plays with the *Volga*'s car-keys . . .
Here is a neat old man who wears pince-nez.
He goes to Vologda for folk-songs;
                      pensive,
he waits.
And muttering about a pension,
an old woman smiles as she sleeps away . . .
A wife
      waits for her meek,
                  submissive mate.
A young girl waits for love –
                afraid.
                    A sergeant
looks at
      the girl.
             And he also must wait
(another hour) till his train's departure.
A helmsman waits the turn:
shoals –
      in an instant!

A teacher waits
                for problems to be solved;
the pupils wait
                for
                    recess to be called.
Collective farms
wait
for the change! ... not distant! ...
All morning in this echo-filled world –
rain.
Now in this echo-filled world
clouds are moving ...
We wait.
We know
it's time for us   .
                to range
from waiting room
to rooms
of deeds and doing ...
We wait for new discoveries.
We call
our friends. We exchange
                        honest words which bite.
We in the waiting room
live! live! But all
during our wait
                we don't sit
                        idly by!
Behind us:
shattered silence in our land!
Our strength –
its steady, vast accumulation.
Our waiting and awakened country, and
the whole wide world,
                        frozen in expectation.

ADRIAN MITCHELL
b. 1932

✳

Order me a transparent coffin and dig
my crazy grave

After the next war . . . and the sky
Heaves with contaminated rain.
End to end our bodies lie
Round the world and back again.

Now from their concrete suites below
Statesmen demurely emanate,
And down the line of millions go
To see the people lie in state.

Nikita Ikes, Franco de Gaulles,
Officiate and dig the holes.
Mao tse-Sheks, Macadenauers,
Toting artificial flowers.

As they pay tribute each one wishes
The rain was less like tears, less hot, less thick.
They mutter, wise as blind white fishes,
Occasionally they are sick.

But I drily grin from my perspex coffin
As they trudge till they melt into the wet,
And I say: 'Keep on walking, keep on walking,
You bastards, you've got a hell of a way to walk yet.'

To whom it may concern

I was run over by the truth one day.
Ever since the accident I've walked this way
  So stick my legs in plaster
  Tell me lies about Vietnam.

Heard the alarm clock screaming with pain,
Couldn't find myself so I went back to sleep again
  So fill my ears with silver
  Stick my legs in plaster
  Tell me lies about Vietnam.

Every time I shut my eyes all I see is flames.
Made a marble phone book and I carved all the names
  So coat my eyes with butter
  Fill my ears with silver
  Stick my legs in plaster
  Tell me lies about Vietnam.

I smell something burning, hope it's just my brains.
They're only dropping peppermints and daisy-chains
  So stuff my nose with garlic
  Coat my eyes with butter
  Fill my ears with silver
  Stick my legs in plaster
  Tell me lies about Vietnam.

Where were you at the time of the crime?
Down by the Cenotaph drinking slime
  So chain my tongue with whisky
  Stuff my nose with garlic
  Coat my eyes with butter
  Fill my ears with silver
  Stick my legs in plaster
  Tell me lies about Vietnam.

You put your bombers in, you put your conscience out,
You take the human being and you twist it all about
   So scrub my skin with women
   Chain my tongue with whisky
   Stuff my nose with garlic
   Coat my eyes with butter
   Fill my ears with silver
   Stick my legs in plaster
   Tell me lies about Vietnam.

IAN CAMPBELL
b. 1933

*

The sun is burning

The sun is burning in the sky
Strands of cloud are gently drifting by
In the park the dreamy bees
are droning in the flowers among the trees
And the sun burns in the sky

Now the sun is in the west
Little kids lie down to take their rest
And the couples in the park
are holding hands and waiting for the dark
And the sun is in the west

Now the sun is sinking low
Children playing know it's time to go
High above a spot appears
a little blossom blooms and then drops near
And the sun is sinking low

Now the sun has come to earth
Shrouded in a mushroom cloud of death
Death comes in a blinding flash
of hellish heat, and leaves a smear of ash
When the sun has come to earth.

Now the sun has disappeared
All is darkness, anger, pain and fear
Twisted sightless wrecks of men
go groping on their knees and cry in pain
And the sun has disappeared.

ANDREI VOZNESENSKY
b. 1933

*

I am Goya

I am Goya
of the bare field, by the enemy's beak gouged
till the craters of my eyes gape
I am grief

I am the tongue
of war, the ember of cities
on the snows of the year 1941
I am hunger

I am the gullet
of a woman hanged whose body like a bell
tolled over a blank square
I am Goya

O grapes of wrath!
I have hurled westward
      the ashes of the uninvited guest!
and hammered stars into the unforgetting sky – like nails
I am Goya

Hunting a hare

TO MY FRIEND YURI

Hunting a hare. Our dogs are raising a racket;
Racing, barking, eager to kill, they go,
And each of us in a yellow jacket
Like oranges against the snow.

One for the road. Then, off to hound a hare,
My cab driver friend who hates a cop, I,
Buggins' brother and his boy, away we tear.
Our jalopy,

That technological marvel, goes bounding,
Scuttling along on its snow chains. Tallyho!
After a hare we go.
Or is it ourselves we're hounding?

I'm all dressed up for the chase
In boots and jacket: the snow is ablaze.
But why, Yuri, why,
Do my gun sights dance? Something is wrong, I know,
When a glassful of living blood has to fly
In terror across the snow.

The urge to kill, like the urge to beget,
Is blind and sinister. Its craving is set
Today on the flesh of a hare: tomorrow it can
Howl the same way for the flesh of a man.

Out in the open the hare
Lay quivering there
Like the grey heart of an immense
Forest or the heart of silence:

Lay there, still breathing,
Its blue flanks heaving,
Its tormented eye a woe,
Blinking there on the cheek of the snow.

Then, suddenly, it got up,
Stood upright: suddenly,
Over the forest, over the dark river,
The air was shivered
By a human cry,

Pure, ultrasonic, wild,
Like the cry of a child.
I knew that hares moan, but not like this:
This was the note of life, the wail
Of a woman in travail,

The cry of leafless copses
And bushes hitherto dumb,
The unearthly cry of a life
Which death was about to succumb,

Nature is all wonder, all silence:
Forest and lake and field and hill
Are permitted to listen and feel,
But denied utterance.

Alpha and Omega, the first and the last
Word of Life as it ebbs away fast,
As, escaping the snare, it flies
Up to the skies.

For a second only, but while
It lasted we were turned to stone
Like actors in a movie-still.

The boot of the running cab driver hung in mid-air,
And four black pellets halted, it seemed,
Just short of their target:
Above the horizontal muscles,
The blood-clotted fur of the neck,
A face flashed out.

With slanting eyes set wide apart, a face
As in frescoes of Dionysus,
Staring at us in astonishment and anger,
It hovered there, made one with its cry,
Suspended in space,
The contorted transfigured face
Of an angel or a singer.

Like a long-legged archangel a golden mist
Swam through the forest.
'Shit!' spat the cab driver. 'The little faking freak!':
A tear rolled down on the boy's cheek.

Late at night we returned,
The wind scouring our faces: they burned
Like traffic lights as, without remark,
We hurtled through the dark.

YEVGENY YEVTUSHENKO
b. 1933

✳

Lies

Telling lies to the young is wrong.
Proving to them that lies are true is wrong.
Telling them that God's in his heaven
and all's well with the world is wrong.
The young know what you mean. The young are people.
Tell them the difficulties can't be counted,
and let them see not only what will be
but see with clarity these present times.
Say obstacles exist they must encounter
sorrow happens, hardship happens.
The hell with it. Who never knew
the price of happiness will not be happy.
Forgive no error you recognize,
it will repeat itself, increase,
and afterwards our pupils
will not forgive in us what we forgave.

Later

Oh what a sobering,
what a talking-to from conscience afterwards:
the short moment of frankness at the party
and the enemy crept up.

But to have learnt nothing is terrible,
and peering earnest eyes are terrible
detecting secret thoughts is terrible
in simple words and immature disturbance.
This diligent suspicion has no merit.
The blinded judges are no public servants.
It would be far more terrible to mistake
a friend than to mistake an enemy.

Babiy Yar

Over Babiy Yar
there are no memorials.
The steep hillside like a rough inscription.
I am frightened.
Today I am as old as the Jewish race.
I seem to myself a Jew at this moment.
I, wandering in Egypt.
I, crucified. I perishing.
Even today the mark of the nails.
I think also of Dreyfus. I am he.
The Philistine my judge and my accuser.
Cut off by bars and cornered,
ringed round, spat at, lied about;
the screaming ladies with the Brussels lace
poke me in the face with parasols.
I am also a boy in Belostok,
the dropping blood spreads across the floor,
the public-bar heroes are rioting
in an equal stench of garlic and of drink.
I have no strength, go spinning from a boot,
shriek useless prayers that they don't listen to;
with a cackle of 'Thrash the kikes and save Russia!'
the corn-chandler is beating up my mother.

I seem to myself like Anna Frank
to be transparent as an April twig
and am in love, I have no need for words,
I need for us to look at one another.
How little we have to see or to smell
separated from foliage and the sky,
how much, how much in the dark room
gently embracing each other.
They're coming. Don't be afraid.
The booming and banging of the spring.
It's coming this way. Come to me.
Quickly, give me your lips.
They're battering in the door. Roar of the ice.

Over Babiy Yar
rustle of the wild grass.
The trees look threatening, look like judges.
And everything is one silent cry.
Taking my hat off
I feel myself slowly going grey.
And I am one silent cry
over the many thousands of the buried;
am every old man killed here,
every child killed here.
O my Russian people, I know you.
Your nature is international.
Foul hands rattle your clean name.
I know the goodness of my country.
How horrible it is that pompous title
the anti-semites calmly call themselves,
Society of the Russian Race.
No part of me can ever forget it.
When the last anti-semite on the earth
is buried for ever
let the International ring out.

No Jewish blood runs among my blood,
but I am as bitterly and hardly hated
by every anti-semite
as if I were a Jew. By this
I am a Russian.

Conversation with an American writer

They tell me:
         you are a courageous man.
That's not correct.
         I've never been courageous,
but crawling – as my fellow-writers can –
for me seemed simply too low and outrageous.
Subversiveness is not one of my fortes.
I saw the blown-up fraud,
         mocked it and fought:
wrote articles,
         did not write police reports;
I simply tried
         to say the things I thought.
Yes,
    I defended those whose talent shone;
I panned the fakes,
         the mediocre writing.
But isn't that what usually is done?
And so my 'bravery' bears much reciting.
O, when our sons make short work of all trash,
they will remember
         with a bitter shame
this strange,
      bizarre time,
           when a simple flash
of honesty
      had 'courage' as its name.

I journeyed through Russia

I am past thirty. I fear the nights.
I hunch the sheet with my knees.
I bury my face in the pillow, shamefully weeping,
that I have squandered my life on little nothings
and in the morning will squander it again.

If only you had known, my critics,
whose goodness is so innocently under question,
how tender thundering condemnations seem
compared with my own scolding,
you would be relieved, if late at night
you found your conscience tormenting you unjustly.
When leafing through all my verse
I find this: by squandering myself so rashly
I have soiled the pages with so much rot ...
but I could not burn it; it is scattered through the world.

My rivals, let us cast away flattery
and the deceptive honour of abuse.
Simply let us consider our own fate.
We have in all of us the one and very same
sickness of soul.
              Superficiality, it is called,
Superficiality, you are worse than blindness.
You can see, but do not care to see.
Maybe it is due to ignorance?
Or maybe, from a fear to tear up by the roots
the trees beneath which we have grown,
not having planted even a fence-post for the future!

And is not that the reason why we always hurry,
skimming the surface, perhaps getting down a few inches,
so that, forgetting courage, we frighten ourselves
with our task to dig down to the heart of things.
We hurry on ... giving half answers,

carrying superficialities like hidden treasures,
and not from cold calculation – no, no! –
but from the instinct of self preservation.
Then strength begins to fail,
and we can neither fight nor fly, –
the pillows of ratbags are already filled
with the feathers of our domestic wings . . .

I was tossed about . . . flung backwards, forwards,
by someone else's sobs or groans,
now into the inflated uselessness of odes,
now into the false usefulness of pamphlets.
All my life I have been elbowing someone out of the way,
and it was I, myself. Caught by blazing passion,
naïvely clattering, I fought with hairpins
where the call was for a sword.
My blaze was feloniously infantile.
I lacked full pitilessness,
and thus, full pity . . .

Like something half-way between wax and metal
I was ruining my youth.
Let everyone who enters on his life
                              make this promise now
to help those who ought to blossom,
and not forget to avenge
all those who ought to be avenged.
Let this avenging be not for the sake of vengeance,
but avenging, incarnated
in the name of righteousness and honour,
in the name of the establishment of goodness.
We won't avenge through fear of vengeance.

The possibility itself of vengeance does decrease,
and our instinct of self-preservation
does not safeguard but kill us.

Superficiality is a murderer, not a friend,
health faking sickness,
entangling in the nets of delusion . . .
By bartering our spirit for trivial things
we run away from the general issues.
The terrestrial globe loses power in a vacuum,
by leaving general issues till later on.
But maybe its unprotectedness
is just the alienation of human destinies
in this enlightened age, so accurate and so plain?

I journeyed through Russia, with Galia beside me,
somewhere towards the sea, hurrying in a Moskvich[1]
from all my sorrows . . .
                            The autumn of Russian vastness
around us was weary of being golden,
from rustling with leaves under the tyres,
and my soul rested at the driver's wheel.
Breathing scents of steppes and birch and pine,
huge tracts of land were hurtling at me
at fifty miles an hour, and with a whistle of wind
Russia was flowing past our Moskvich.
Russia wanted to say something,
and now, having understood some things better than
    anyone,
she thrust our Moskvich into her body
and sucked us in to her innermost being.

And, seemingly, with some kind of premeditation
hiding its essence till the last minute,
Russia prompted me suddenly, past Tula,
to turn in towards Yasnaya Polyana.[2]
And now we entered the faintly breathing homestead,
children of the atomic age . . .
hurrying in our nylon raincoats,
benumbed, we suddenly stood still, hearts failing.

1. A popular Russian car.
2. Tolstoy's home, now a national museum.

Descendants of peasant envoys seeking truth,
we suddenly this very minute became aware
of all the same, the very same knapsacks on the shoulders,
of all the bareness of worn-out feet.
Obeying a silent command
we entered a shady avenue
of leaves transparent with sunset,
named 'Avenue of Silence'.
And this sheer golden transparency,
not retreating from luckless human fate,
lifted vanity like leprosy
while not diminishing its pain.
And meanwhile – the master of this homestead,
invisible, kept us in his view,
and seemed to be present, everywhere around us:

                                       now gliding
like the grey-bearded cloud reflected in the lake,
then his long stride sounding
through the mist of a smouldering hollow,
then showing portions of his face on the coarse bark,
furrowed by cracks and wrinkles.
His brows were shooting upwards, shaggy
in the meadows amongst the tangled weeds,
and the roots exposed along the footpath
were like the veins on his great forehead.
And, not decaying, but regally ageing,
crowning the enchantment with their sound, sound,
all around him rose the enduring trees
like his vast thoughts.
They strained to the clouds and the womb of the earth
roaring more and more fiercely,
and the roots of their tips grew from the sky,
into the depths where the tips of their roots stretched
   down.

Yes, up into the heights and down to the depths,
   together!
Yes, genius – tying the heights and the depths together!

But how many still live ephemeral lives,
in the shadow of great ideas, in vain . . .
Well, then, was it for nothing that the flame of genius
   burned,
for the sake of changing humanity?
Or perhaps the fact that ideas do not age
is evidence of their lack of power?
How many years have passed already, how many,
that our purity, as in a drunken state
throws itself like Natasha Rostova[1]
into false experience – to a rake and a liar?
Again and again, in reproach to Tolstoy –
do we forget, by hiding from the passions,
that Vronsky,[2] in his soft-hearted cowardice,
was more callous than Karenin.[3]
And Tolstoy himself, swayed by his own reasons,
isn't he an example of his own weakness,
raving helplessly, like Levin,
in the blissful effort of making changes?

The labour of geniuses at times frightens
themselves with doubtful results,
but for each of them, broader issues
are won in battle – inch by inch.

The three greatest names of Russia,
let them guard us from our fears.
Through them Russia was born anew
and will be born anew again.

When speechless and unseeing
she tramped through lashes, cudgels,
came Pushkin, simple, translucent,
like her self-realization.

    1. A character in *War and Peace*.
    2 and 3. Characters in *Anna Karenin*.

When she had tasted lack of justice,
seeking for her sorrows' source
like the understanding of a ripened awareness,
came Tolstoy, pityingly harsh,
but with his hands tucked into his belt.

But when the way out was not clear to her,
and anger had ripened irreversibly –
Lenin burst out of the whirlwind, like the end,
and, that he might save her, blew her up!

Such were my thoughts, confused and airy,
on leaving Yasnaya Polyana long ago
and speeding in the Moskvich through Russia
with my beloved sleeping quietly on my shoulder.

The night was thickening, only faintly
                              pink light was spreading
along the rim of the world . . .
                              Lights flew into our faces,
accordions were singing boisterously.
                              A rusty moon
was toppling drunkenly behind the fences.
Turning somewhere off the highway
I stopped the car, laid back the seats,
and with Galia floated into dreams
beyond the delusions of the stars – cheek to cheek . . .

I dreamed of a world
                    without the sick and the fat,
without dollars, francs and pesetas,
where there are no frontiers, no deceit of governments,
rockets and stinking newspapers.
  dreamed of a world where everything is freshly created
as a wild cherry tree stippled with dew,
full of nightingales and thrushes,
where all the nations are related and in brotherhood,
where no one slanders nor abuses anyone,

where air is clean, like morning on the river,
where we live, forever immortal, with Galia,
dreaming this dream – cheek to cheek . . .

But, we did wake up . . .
                                    our Moskvich stood daringly
on ploughed land, its nose into the bushes.
I flung the chilled door wide
and beauty took my breath away.
Above the furious red, coarse, dawn,
a boy with teeth of steel drove a tip truck,
a cigarette pressed fiercely between his lips,
drove furiously, in the violent wind.
And furiously, like a blazing jet thrust,
over the darkness of the ploughed land and the green o
    the meadows
the sun was pushing itself out
from haystack's angry grip.
And the trees were fiercely denuded,
and the stream roared, leaping furiously,
and blueness was reddening and raging
swayed madly by the rooks.

I also would have liked to burst
as in fury, into life, unfolding a fury of wings . . .

The world was beautiful,
                                    We had to fight
for it, so as to make it even better.

Once more I took a deep breath, settled down at th
    steering wheel,
and opened my insatiable eyes to:
Palaces of Culture.
                        Tea rooms.
                                        Barracks.
District Committees.
                        Churches.

Vehicle Inspection Stations.

Factories.

Huts.

Slogans.

Little birch trees.

Jets cracking the sky.

Jolting of little carts.

Jammed broadcasts.
Overgrown statuettes
of milkmaids, pioneers, miners.
Old women's eyes, like those in icons.
Big-bottomed women.

Racketing.

Artificial limbs.

Oil rigs.

Slag heaps
like the breasts of a reclining giantess.
The men drove tractors.

Sawed.

Clocked in, then hurried to the tool bench.
They whizzed down into mines.

Drank beer,

Spreading salt along the rim.
Women cooked.

Laundered.

Mended, managing everything in a moment.
Painted.

Stood in queues.

Dug trenches.

Carried cement.

It was getting dark again.

The Moskvich was all covered with dew
and night was filled with stars to its declivity.
But Galia reached for our transistor,
and thrust its antenna through the window.
The antenna leaned against the universe.
In Galia's hands the transistor hissed.
Shamelessly, in front of the stars,

it boldly broadcast lies in many tongues!
O terrestrial globe, don't lie, don't play!
You have suffered enough, no more lies, no!
I gladly give away my posthumous paradise,
so that on earth there shall be a little less of hell!

The car was plunging into potholes.
(Road builders, what is the matter with you, silly
     buggers!)
It would have seemed that all around was chaos
but in it there were beginnings as well as ends.

There was –
          Russia.
The first love of the future.
And in her, undecaying through the centuries,
Pushkin somewhere began to bubble again,
Tolstoy grew more solid, Lenin took shape.
And, looking into the starry night, ahead,
I thought that great enlightenments
were joining together in that redeeming chain,
that maybe is only short of a link? . . .
Well, what of it, we are alive.
                         It's our turn.

LEROI JONES
b. 1934

✳

Short speech to my friends

1

A political art, let it be
tenderness, low strings the fingers
touch, or the width of autumn
climbing wider avenues, among the virtue
and dignity of knowing what city
you're in, who to talk to, what clothes
– even what buttons – to wear. I address
                    /the society
                    the image, of
                    common utopia.

                    /The perversity
                    of separation, isolation,
After so many years of trying to enter their kingdoms,
now they suffer in tears, these others, saxophones whining
through the wooden doors of their less than gracious
    homes.
The poor have become our creators. The black. The
    thoroughly
ignorant.
            Let the combination of morality
and inhumanity
begin.

2

Is power, the enemy? (Destroyer
of dawns, cool flesh of valentines, among
the radios, pauses, drunks

of the 19th century. I see it,
as any man's single history. All the possible heroes
dead from heat exhaustion
                    at the beach,
                            or hiding for years from cameras
only to die cheaply in the pages
of our daily lie.
                    One hero
has pretensions toward literature
one toward the cultivation of errors, arrogance,
and constantly changing disguises, as trucker, boxer,
valet, barkeep, in the aging taverns of memory. Making
    love
to those speedy heroines of masturbation. Or kicking
    literal evil
continually down filmy public stairs.

A compromise
would be silence. To shut up, even such risk
as the proper placement
of verbs and nouns. To freeze the spit
in mid-air, as it aims itself
at some valiant intellectual's face.

There would be someone
who would understand, for whatever
fancy reason. Dead, lying, Roi, as your children
came up, would also rise. As George Armstrong Custer
these 100 years, has never made
a mistake.

A guerrilla handbook

In the palm
the seed
is burned up
in the wind.

       In their rightness
the tree trunks are socialists
leaves murder the silence and are brown
and old when they blow to the sea.
                       Convinced
of the lyric. Convinced
of the man's image (since
he will not look at substance
other than his ego. Flowers, grapes
the shadows of weeds, as the weather
is colder, and women walk
with their heads down.
                  Silent political rain
against the speech
of friends. (We love them
trapped in life, knowing no way out
except description. Or black soil
floating in the arm.
                We must convince the living
                that the dead
                cannot sing.

Political poem

FOR BASIL

Luxury, then, is a way of
being ignorant, comfortably
An approach to the open market
of least information. Where theories
can thrive, under heavy tarpaulins
without being cracked by ideas.

(I have not seen the earth for years
and think now possibly 'dirt' is
negative, positive, but clearly
social. I cannot plant a seed, cannot

recognize the root with clearer dent
than indifference. Though I eat
and shit as a natural man. (Getting up
from the desk to secure a turkey sandwich
and answer the phone: the poem undone
undone by my station, by my station,
and the bad words of Newark.) Raised up
to the breech, we seek to fill for this
crumbling century. The darkness of love,
in whose sweating memory all error is forced.

Undone by the logic of any specific death. (Old
    gentlemen
who still follow fires, tho are quieter
and less punctual. It is a polite truth
we are left with. Who are you? What are you
saying? Something to be dealt with, as easily.
The noxious game of reason, saying, 'No, No,
you cannot feel,' like my dead lecturer
lamenting thru gipsies his fast suicide.

A poem for speculative hipsters

He had got, finally,
to the forest
of motives. There were no
owls, or hunters. No Connie Chatterleys
resting beautifully
on their backs, having casually
brought socialism
To England.
            Only ideas,
and their opposites.
                Like,
            he was *really*
            nowhere.

DAVID AVIDAN
b. 1934

❋

The desert generation

Let fear break through.

Brave solemn armadillos break through the sated grass
to have a look at the first and last sun in their lives.
Better than you can they realize the meaning of a chance.
This chance is theirs.

Let fear break through.

Let it break through you in short cool volleys, let it
tear you to bits, then cool down.
It will do so long before you break up.
This is its chance – your own, too.

Let fear break through.

You realize only too well you're parts of the desert
    generation.
You can read this sordid discovery in the eyes of children
wandering around those bright streets which your father
    might have built and which
you, with some luck, may someday destroy.
The real thing will happen only when you're gone, only
    when you're gone.

Let fear break through.

You who were made to negate the world,
you whose only vouchsafe may lie in negation,
have caught yourself in flagrante delicto:
you have taken pity.

Let fear break through.

Await it patiently and courageously. Prepare
a cunning ambush. Give it
erroneous chances. Never
trust it. Do not fall asleep. Do not
love sleep lest you fall
into poverty.

Let fear break through.

Let it enjoy slow progress, like a desert army.
Let it march within you, like fear in the desert.
You realize you are part of the desert generation, yet
     very soon
you may hear a voice, a daring voice in the desert,
a voice tearing the sated grass to small burnt shreds.

Let fear break through.

For man is a plant of the field,
and you too are a plant of the field.
Do not assault fear in the field,
for this is the wish of the wind.

Let fear break through.

Soon you'll forget all the words,
all the words you have ever evoked.
Night will walk past you like an orderly,
dark and efficient, efficient and dark,
inside a burning hospital, within
some remote battlefront in which you never
fought nor were given a chance.

Let fear break through.

The morning will resemble all other mornings,
all other mornings and all other deserts.
Fear will break through, even though you won't let it,
and the desert generation will aim
very high.

WOLE SOYINKA

b. 1935

❋

Telephone conversation

The price seemed reasonable, location
Indifferent. The landlady swore she lived
Off premises. Nothing remained
But self-confession. 'Madam', I warned,
'I hate a wasted journey – I am African.'
Silence. Silenced transmission of
Pressurized good-breeding. Voice, when it came,
Lipstick coated, long gold-rolled
Cigarette-holder pipped. Caught I was, foully.
'HOW DARK?' .... I had not misheard .... 'ARE
    YOU LIGHT
OR VERY DARK?' Button B. Button A. Stench
Of rancid breath of public hide-and-speak.
Red booth. Red pillar-box. Red double-tiered
Omnibus squelching tar. It *was* real! Shamed
By ill-mannered silence, surrender
Pushed dumbfoundedment to beg simplification.
Considerate she was, varying the emphasis –
'ARE YOU DARK? OR VERY LIGHT?' Revelation
    came.
'You mean – like plain or milk chocolate?'
Her assent was clinical, crushing in its light
Impersonality. Rapidly, wave-length adjusted,
I chose. 'West African sepia' – and as afterthought,
'Down in my passport.' Silence for spectroscopic
Flight of fancy, till truthfulness clanged her accent
Hard on the mouthpiece. 'WHAT'S THAT?' conceding

'DON'T KNOW WHAT THAT IS.' 'Like brunette.'
'THAT'S DARK, ISN'T IT?' 'Not altogether.
Facially, I am brunette, but madam, you should see
The rest of me. Palm of my hand, soles of my feet
Are a peroxide blonde. Friction, caused –
Foolishly madam – by sitting down, has turned
My bottom raven black – One moment madam!' –
  sensing
Her receiver rearing on the thunderclap
About my ears – 'Madam,' I pleaded, 'wouldn't you
  rather
See for yourself?'

Civilian and soldier

My apparition rose from the fall of lead,
Declared, 'I'm a civilian.' It only served
To aggravate your fright. For how could I
Have risen, a being of this world, in that hour
Of impartial death! And I thought also: nor is
Your quarrel of this world.

                You stood still
For both eternities, and oh I heard the lesson
Of your training sessions, cautioning –
Scorch earth behind you, do not leave
A dubious neutral to the rear. Reiteration
Of my civilian quandary, burrowing earth
From the lead festival of your more eager friends
Worked the worse on your confusion, and when
You brought the gun to bear on me, and death
Twitched me gently in the eye, your plight
And all of you came clear to me.

                I hope some day
Intent upon my trade of living, to be checked
In stride by *your* apparition in a trench,
Signalling, I am a soldier. No hesitation then

But I shall shoot you clean and fair
With meat and bread, a gourd of wine
A bunch of breasts from either arm, and that
Lone question – do you friend, even now, know
What it is all about?

PENTTI SAARIKOSKI
b. 1937

✳

the new suburbs surrounded by woods

the new suburbs surrounded by woods
   beautiful pawmarks
of capitalism

the schools are closing today
   soon it will be Christmas
   they're selling trees for that purpose
      in the market
   the Vicar is masticating the Message
there's not enough silence these days
      except in the churches

   I lose myself in these corridors
      never reaching the heart

when you have lost it all, everything to be said
      has been said
I put my ear against the wall
   and listen to the slow
      erosion of concrete
everybody is building shelters and vaults

and what lies in between

the conditions for life to begin
the conditions for life to cease
and what lies in between

one has to be able to think of it all
get it all into focus
turn fear into knowledge

those who lose their heads
when the changes are slower than predicted
those whose lives seem to pass in vain

in Nuremberg one night I suddenly knew
no one had been executed
all the verdicts were still to be carried out

radicalism and reaction
two sides of one and the same
such as buying and selling

went to the border of two great empires
idols stood leaning against the rocks
skirts and trinkets hung from the branches

not even in these times can gods be overthrown
by simple onslaught
the walls must be fortified first
that they may crumble later

those whose eye sees the near and the far
who make haste
with deliberation and courage
such as their day is their power

'Life was given to man . . .'

Life was given to man
for him to consider
in which position
he wants to be dead:

Grey skies float by,
star-meadows hang

and the earth
comes into your mouth
like bread.

FERNANDO GORDILLO CERVANTES
1940–67

❊

A dead youth

A dead youth. How can he turn the heart of a rifle.
How inflict the shades of nothingness with suffering.
But through his wounds a thing from our lives
escapes, gone over the hill for ever.

The large isolation of the hero is his martyrdom.
Don't walk away from him.

The price of a country

3,000,000 is the pricemark on a country
if somebody wants to sell it.
and someone wanted to
                              and did.
Later they said
                    his sons
were born just to sing it.

Just as if battle is not the most unmistakable
of songs
or death the most grand.

The dead

The dead, the dead
will brace the arms of the revolutionary
sustain the voice of the multitudes
guide the plough of the countryman

the dead ...

who's going to hold the hands of the dead?

Now you know he died

Now you know he died
and you know where your brother's grave is
and you know he had no burial
you know that
because your heart will be
the only earth covering him
and all our days will flower
into new flowers sprung on his grave.

JAVIER HERAUD
1942–63

❋

The new journey

I

Soon I must journey again.
Over there,
towards those white mountains
waiting,
waiting for me.

Towards the same winds
the same orange groves
my feet
must seize the plans
and with my eyes
I want to feel the vines
of the countryside.

A round journey, and alone:
It isn't easy to leave –
everything abandoned!
the difficulty it is to live
in city after city
a street
the streetcar
everything increases the sense
and the endless season
of disenchantment
survives.

2

And you can't go for a walk
along the beaches
if the simple condition
is lethal shells
and submarine spiders.

So, walk on a while
turn to the left
and you reach the mountains
and the rivers.

Look it isn't that I want
to leave life back there –
but I must follow a path
that death is known to stalk.

3

And it isn't that I seek
to protect my step –
at every moment every turn
they set up ambushes for us,
on every occasion they steal
our letters, of course
at every moment they come on
with their tested tricks.

4

But it is better than other ways:
I recommend it –

                    get away for a time
from the bustle
learn what it's all about
in those mountains.

ALAN BOLD
b. 1943

❊

Cause and effect

He thought before the war
Of conflicts, heroism, enemies
Who had to be crushed;
Causes that had to be fought for.

He had no time before the war
For bright skies, fields, the warm
Sun, his woman – only
Causes that had to be fought for.

I see him now after the war
In my lifetime. I notice his love
Of the sun, bright skies, fields, his woman:
Causes that have to be fought for.

From 'The state of the nation'

Let us see the sun through locks of hair
And know the shadows as they fall on flesh
And glorify the sea and its green wash
And elevate the earthly in a prayer
For other people who will come to share
The surplus of this world; and let the ash
That follows battle be deposed in fresh
Feelings that rise to permeate the air.

All the senses can combine in this,
The coalescence of the things on earth
That speak that swim that fly that crawl that hiss
That energize the concept and the birth
Of isolated beings who depend
On others for the way this world will tend.

ANONYMOUS RUSSIAN POET

✳

'*Jews don't plant . . .*'

I

Jews don't plant the grain.
Jews sell things in a store.
Jews get bald when young.
Jews steal more.

Jews are a tricky crew.
They make poor soldiers too.
Ivan fights a battle;
Abie hears money rattle.

Ever since my childhood,
I've heard the same old news.
I'll grow old but I won't escape it:
The shouting, 'Jews!' 'Jews!'

I never sold a thing.
I never stole a thing.
But I carry my pedigree
Like a plague that curses me.

Somehow a bullet missed me,
So they talk (This is not a lie):
'Jews were never killed! See!
All of them come back alive!'

2

But we Jews have a certain luck.
When evil came, it wore no hood,
And used no false flag when it struck,
Made no pretensions to be good.

Throughout this solemn, silent land,
With time not ripe yet for debate,
We found the wall where we must stand,
The point for levering our fate.

(1960)

BIOGRAPHICAL NOTES

These notes are necessarily brief: the activities of some of the poets would require an entire volume (Mao, Ho Chi-minh, Che Guevara) while in other instances the fervour of the poetry does not imply personal involvement in violent social changes. In any case, the most relevant data is in the poems, not in explanatory matter. I have not thought it essential to include detailed bibliographic information here, as the most important poets are generously represented. For further examples of the work of individual poets in translation the reader should consult the books listed under *Acknowledgements*. What follows aims at factual brevity rather than instant opinion.

AI CH'ING (b. 1910) Chinese poet, born the son of a landowner in Chekiang. He studied in France and returned to China in 1932; the experience of the Japanese aggression intensified his political views and he became a communist; he was in Yenan in 1940. He has been professor of literature at the North China People's University since 1950; in 1961 he was branded a rightist.

RAFAEL ALBERTI (b. 1902) Spanish poet, born in Santa Maria; he was educated at a Jesuit college. *Sobro los ángeles* (English translation *Concerning The Angels*, Rapp & Carroll, 1967) is widely recognized as his masterpiece. He became a communist in 1931 and supported the Republicans during the Civil War; he fled to Buenos Aires in 1939 and is now resident there.

MARUF AL-RUSAFI (1875–1945) Iraqi poet, born in Baghdad of Kurdish parents. He taught in Istanbul and Jerusalem; he entered politics advocating Arab unity, and was Iraqi Minister of Education.

YEHUDA AMICHAI (b. 1924) Hebrew poet, born in Würzburg, Germany. He went to Palestine with his parents in 1936, and was educated at the Hebrew University in Jerusalem. He now works as a teacher.

MARCOS ANA (b. 1921) Spanish poet, born in Salamanca. He

joined the Socialist Youth Movement at the beginning of the Civil War, during which his father was killed. He was arrested at the end of the war and sentenced to death, though this sentence was later changed to thirty years imprisonment. For running a clandestine news sheet he was sentenced to death a second time, but again the sentence was altered to a further thirty years imprisonment. Eventually he was released at the age of forty, after spending twenty-two years in prison.

LOUIS ARAGON (b. 1897) French writer, born in Paris. His first collections in the 1920s reflect his involvement with Breton and surrealism. From 1935 to 1939 he ran the communist paper *Ce Soir*. He was in Spain during the Civil War as a supporter of the Popular Front. He published war poetry of resistance in *Le Crève-coeur* (1941). He relates his insight into the totality of man's personality to his love for Elsa Triolet, the subject of many poems.

W. H. AUDEN (b. 1907) English poet, born in York; educated at Oxford. He was the most respected British poet of the thirties, though he has since dismissed some of his political poems. In 1956 he was elected professor of poetry at Oxford. With Chester Kallman he wrote the libretto for Stravinsky's *A Rake's Progress* and Henze's *The Bassarids*. Since 1939 he has lived in the U.S.A. and he now spends some of the year in Austria.

DAVID AVIDAN (b. 1934) Hebrew poet. The linguistic impact of his poetry is mainly responsible for the assimilation of modernism in Hebrew verse.

LÁSZLÓ BENJÁMIN (b. 1915) Hungarian poet, born in Budapest. In 1945 he became politically active and fought for the reform of the Party; 'Debris' appeared in *Irodalmi Ujság* (Literary Gazette) of Budapest on 28 July 1956.

HAYYIM NAHMAN BIALIK (1873–1934) Hebrew poet, born in the Ukraine. After the revolution he moved to Berlin, then to Tel Aviv where he stayed until his death; 'The city of slaughter' (from *Songs of Wrath*) was written after Bialik's visit to Kishinev where a pogrom had taken place in 1903. He is often called the father of Hebrew poetry.

MIRON BIALOSZEWSKI (b. 1922) Polish poet, born in Warsaw Since 1955 he has run the 'Bialoszewski Theatre' with Ludwi

Hering, alternating their own plays with the classics. He published *Whimsy Account* in 1959, and *Mistaken Emotions* in 1961.

ALEXANDER BLOK (1880–1921) Russian poet, born in St Petersburg, the son of the professor of law at Warsaw University. He was brought up by his mother, a botanist and Rector of St Petersburg University; he studied law and philology. He associated with Symbolists and influenced by Solovyov's philosophy he published *Poems About a Beautiful Lady* in 1905; 'The Twelve' and the chauvinistic 'The Scythians' demonstrated his acceptance of the October Revolution; Trotsky, in *Literature and Revolution* (1924), called 'The Twelve' Blok's 'most important work, and the only one which will live for ages . . . it is a cry of despair for the dying past, and yet a cry of despair which rises in a hope for the future'.

JOHANNES BOBROWSKI (1917–65) German poet, born in Tilsit. From 1941 to 1949 he was a prisoner of war in Russia. After the war he worked for a publishing house in the German Democratic Republic.

ALAN BOLD (b. 1943) Scottish poet, born in Edinburgh. His recent poems can be found in *The State of the Nation* (Chatto and Windus, 1969) and in *Penguin Modern Poets 15*.

MATEJ BOR (b. 1931) Slovene poet (real name: Vladimir Pavsič). He fought with partisans during the war. He is now a free-lance writer, and he has translated ten of Shakespeare's plays. His recent poems, *In the Summer Grass*, appeared in 1963.

BERTOLT BRECHT (1898–1956) German poet, dramatist and theatrical innovator. He was born in Augsburg, studied medicine, and was an army orderly in 1918. His expressionist plays include *Baal* (1922) and *Drums in the Night* (1922). He became a Marxist in 1928. He advocated epic theatre in which the now-celebrated technique of 'alienation' was used to provoke the audience's capacity for critical action rather than to promote empathy. Among his best-known plays are the two dealing with the seventeenth century, *The Life of Galileo* (1938) and *Mother Courage* (1939). He worked with the composers Kurt Weill (*The Threepenny Opera*, 1929), Hanns Eisler (*The Mother*, after Gorky, 1932), and Paul Dessau (*The Condemnation of Lucullus*, 1950). In 1947 he was tried before the Committee of Un-American Activities and acquitted; 1949 returned to East Berlin where he developed his Berliner Ensemble. In 1954 he accepted a Stalin Peace Prize though his attitude towards the U.S.S.R. and the G.D.R. is still being clarified with the publication of his papers.

IAN CAMPBELL (b. 1933) Folk-singer and song-writer, born in Aberdeen. He has lived in Birmingham since 1947. The Ian Campbell Group perform 'The Sun is Burning' on Topic Record STOP 102.

REMCO CAMPERT (b. 1929) Dutch poet and novelist, born in the Hague. He was prominent in the post-war 'Experimentalist' movement. His novels *No Holds Barred* and *The Gangster Girl* are available in English translation (Rupert Hart-Davis, 1965 and 1968).

C. P. CAVAFY (1863–1933) Greek poet, born in Alexandria. As a child he lived in England. He returned to Alexandria in 1872 and was a civil servant in Egyptian Ministry of Works there.

FERNANDO GORDILLO CERVANTES (1940–67) Nicaraguan poet and guerrilla. He was a student revolutionary leader, killed in 1967.

AIMÉ CÉSAIRE (b. 1913) West Indian poet and dramatist, born in Basse-Pointe, Martinique. He studied in Paris where he met Senghor. He is credited with coining the word *négritude*. His *Cahier d'un retour au pays natal* was published in 1947 and hailed as a surrealist masterpiece, though in recent years its political content has received more attention. Since the war he has been a *député* representing Martinique in Paris.

CHAIRIL ANWAR (1922–49) Indonesian poet, born in Medan (Sumatra). He worked briefly as an editor but mainly as a fulltime poet. He wrote fewer than seventy-five poems but is consistently named as the one great poet produced by Indonesia. He died in hospital where he was found to be suffering simultaneously from syphilis, typhus and tuberculosis.

RENÉ CHAR (b. 1907) French poet. He had an outstanding record during World War II as the leader of a resistance group in Provence. Albert Camus considered Char the greatest French poet born this century. Four of his surrealistic poems have been set by Boulez in *Le Marteau Sans Maître*. Since the war he has lived mainly in Provence.

JOHN CORNFORD (1915–36) English poet. He was a research student at Cambridge where his father was Laurence Professor of Ancient Philosophy. He was the first Englishman to go to the front in the Spanish Civil War, and was killed in action in Spain, the day after his twenty-first birthday.

JOE CORRIE (1894–1968) Scottish poet and dramatist. Most of his work refers to his life as a miner.

RUBÉN DARÍO (1867–1916) Nicaraguan poet, born in Metapa. He worked as a diplomat in Paris, Madrid, New York, and Buenos Aires. In 1888 he published *Blue* which, as Octavio Paz has said, 'marks the official birth of Modernism' in Spanish poetry. His influence on Spanish poets has been immense.

C. DAY LEWIS (b. 1904) English poet, appointed poet laureate in 1968. He met Auden at Oxford and was associated with him during the thirties. He was professor of poetry at Oxford 1951–5. He writes the 'Nicholas Blake' detective novels.

DAVID DIOP (1927–60) French West African poet, born in Bordeaux. He suffered from poor health throughout his life, and was killed in an air-crash near Dakar.

GUNNAR EKELÖF (1907–68) Swedish poet, born in Stockholm. His first collection *Late Arrival on Earth,* 1932 (English translation Rapp & Carroll) established his reputation as Sweden's most outstanding modern poet. His work draws attention to the immediacy of life rather than to the presence of the past.

PAUL ÉLUARD (1895–1952) French poet (real name: Eugène Grindel) born in Saint-Denis. He was prominent in the surrealist movement as is evident in his *Capitale de la douleur* (1926). He was active in the French resistance to Nazi occupation. He joined the Communist Party in 1942, the year of his *Poésie et vérité.* He was a close friend of Picasso and many other French painters. His later work manifests the delicacy always apparent even in his most political poems of the war years. He died in Paris.

ODYSSEUS ELYTIS (b. 1911) Greek poet, born in Crete. His first books, *Orientations* (1940), and *Sun the First* (1943) are surrealist in style. The 'Heroic and Elegiac Song for the Lost Second Lieutenant of Albania' (1945) draws on the poet's own experiences as a second lieutenant on the Albanian front in the Greek-Italian war. He is now a businessman.

HANS MAGNUS ENZENSBERGER (b. 1929) German poet, born in Bavaria. He studied languages, literature and philosophy. He worked as interpreter and barman with the American occupation forces. From 1955 to 1957 he was a radio producer at Stuttgart. He now edits *Kursbuch*. He has lived as a freelance writer in Norway and Italy. He combines experimental poetic style with intense political commitment; has appeared in the Penguin Modern European Poets series.

ALDO DO ESPIRITO SANTO (b. 1926) African poet, born in Sào Tomé. He works as a teacher.

FAIZ AHMAD FAIZ (b. 1911) Pakistani poet. He studied in Lahore. In 1951 he was arrested and imprisoned in Montgomery jail until 1955. He has worked for Indo-Pakistan friendship and, as the *Observer* of 9 March 1951 noted, was 'a brave enough man to fly from Lahore for Gandhi's funeral at the height of Indo-Pakistan hatred .... The hatred accorded him by members of the Muslim League is due not to his communist sympathies but to his bitter, lively exposure of their deficiencies.' He is editor of the *Pakistan Times* of Lahore and is regarded as the most important poet to write in Urdu since Iqbal.

PABLO ARMANDO FERNÁNDEZ (b. 1930) Cuban poet. He returned from U.S.A. to take part in the Cuban revolution. He was Cuban cultural attaché in London until 1965. His *Libro de los héroes* was published 1964.

FRANCO FORTINI (b. 1917) Italian poet and critic. He was born in Florence, but since 1945 has lived in Milan working for the monthly *Comunità*; has translated Brecht, Éluard, Proust, and others. His Marxist literary criticism is highly prized in Italy.

FERDINAND FREILIGRATH (1810–76) German poet, born in Detmold. He won a reputation early with *Gedichte* (1838). He was acquitted of subversion in Düsseldorf in 1848, and edited *Rheinische Zeitung* in Cologne. He spent 1846 and 1851 in London, and was a close friend of Marx and Engels.

ERICH FRIED (b. 1921) Austrian poet, born in Vienna. He ha

lived in London since 1938; he worked for the B.B.C. but resigned over the political content of broadcasts to eastern Europe. His recent poems can be found in *und Vietnam und* (1966). A collection of his poems in English translation was published by Rapp & Whiting, 1969 (*On Pain of Seeing*).

GÁBOR GARAI (b. 1929) Hungarian poet, now Secretary of the Hungarian Writers' Association. He was awarded the Kossuth prize in 1956; he has translated Blake, Yeats, Brecht, Mayakovsky, and others.

ALEKSEI GASTEV (1882–1941) Russian poet; probably the most gifted of the poets who supported the 'Smithy' group of proletarian writers.

GIOVANNI GIUDICI (b. 1924) Italian poet born in Le Grazie (La Spezia). He lives in Milan and his publications include *La stazione di Pisa* (1955) and *La vita in versi* (1965).

J. BRUCE GLASIER (1859–1920) Scottish poet and journalist. He was born in Glasgow, the son of an Ayrshire farmer. He worked as a designer in ornamental ironwork; was active in the Irish and Highland Land League; was a member of Morris's Socialist League; stood as I.L.P. candidate in 1896 general election; and edited *Socialist Review* and *Labour Leader*. 'We'll turn things upside down' was sung to the tune 'A wet sheet and a flowing sea'.

LEAH GOLDBERG (b. 1911) Hebrew poet, born in Lithuania. She belonged to the left-wing of the Zionist movement; she now holds Chair of Comparative Literature at the Hebrew University of Jerusalem.

GÜNTER GRASS (b. 1927) German novelist and poet, born in Danzig. His novels *The Tin Drum, Cat and Mouse* and *Dog Years* are all available as Penguin Books; he has also been included in the Penguin Modern European Poets Series. He has recently been active in the Social Democratic Party.

ERNESTO CHE GUEVARA (1928–67) Latin American revolutionary, born in Argentina. He studied medicine and used his training during the Cuban revolution. He provided much of the theoretical impetus to the Cuban revolution and after serving in the revolutionary government left to set up guerrilla activities in Bolivia; there he was shot and has become, since his death, probably the figure most admired by revolutionary youth.

PAAVO HAAVIKKO (b. 1931) Finnish poet, born in Helsinki. He spent part of his military service in hospital. He now works with a Helsinki publishing house. 'Statecraft, sagacity' is from a five-part sequence, *The Bowman* (included in *Selected Poems*, Cape Goliard, 1968).

HEINRICH HEINE (1797–1856) German poet, born in Düsseldorf of Jewish parents. He studied law at Bonn but was unable to obtain the state job he wanted in Göttingen. The poems in *Gedichte* (1822), also included in *Buch der lieder* (1827), and the radical essays in *Reisebilder* (1826) made Heine's reputation as a new giant of German literature. He lived in Paris after 1831 as a correspondent for German papers. From 1848 he suffered from spinal paralysis. He was a friend of Marx and Engels, and, in the opinion of Matthew Arnold, Heine was 'a brilliant, a most effective soldier in the war of liberation of humanity'. His lyrics have been set by Schubert, Liszt, Richard Strauss, but perhaps most exquisitely in Schumann's *Dichterliebe*.

JAVIER HERAUD (1942–63) Peruvian poet and revolutionary, born in Miraflores, Lima. He studied cinema in Cuba, joined guerrillas in Peru and was shot to death in 1963.

ZBIGNIEW HERBERT (b. 1924) Polish poet, born in Lwow. He fought against the Nazis in the Polish underground. He has studied law, economics, and philosophy; he has been included in the Penguin Modern European Poets series.

MIGUEL HERNÁNDEZ (1910–42) Spanish poet, born in a village in Alicante; he had little education. A militant supporter of Republic, he was captured and put in prison where he died in squalid conditions. In *The Spanish Civil War* (Penguin, 1965) Hugh Thomas writes: 'The most remarkable poet was, perhaps, Miguel Hernández, a Communist member of the Fifth regiment at the start of the war. He was a shepherd who had been taught to read by a priest in the hills through examples of sixteenth- and seventeenth-century writing.'

GEORG HERWEGH (1817–75) German poet, born in Stuttgart. He studied law and theology. He escaped from conscription to France and Switzerland in 1843; his political group was defeated in the 1848 Baden uprising. He was a socialist of Lassalle's persuasion.

NAZIM HIKMET (1902–63) Turkish poet. He was educated at naval school; he joined the Turkish Communist Party in 1924; and studied French, physics, chemistry, in Moscow; on return to Turkey was imprisoned (in 1928, then again in 1933). In 1938 he was sentenced to a total of thirty-five years in prison for inciting army and navy cadets to embrace communist tactics. He was released during the general amnesty of 1951 and left Turkey to live in the Soviet Union; he died in Moscow.

HO CHI-MINH (1892–1969) President of the Democratic Republic of Vietnam.

MIROSLAV HOLUB (b. 1923) Czech poet, the son of a railway worker and language teacher. As a clinical pathologist he has travelled widely and his scientific training is evident in the precise details of his poetry. He is included in the Penguin Modern European Poets series.

THOMAS HOOD (1799–1845) English poet and humorist born in London. He was editor of *Hood's Magazine* and various other periodicals. In his *Conditions of The Working Class in England in 1844*, Engels noted 'Thomas Hood, the most talented of all the English humorists now living . . . published at the beginning of 1844 a beautiful poem, "The Song of the Shirt", which drew sympathetic but unavailing tears from the eyes of the daughters of the bourgeoisie.'

LANGSTON HUGHES (1902–67) American poet. He worked as a sailor and a cook until Vachel Lindsay encouraged him to devote himself to literature. *The Weary Blues* appeared in 1925; *Fight for Freedom* (1962) is his account of the National Association for the Advancement of Coloured People.

VERA INBER (b. 1890) Russian poet born in Odessa. In 1922 she became a journalist in Moscow, and was associated with the Constructivist group. She was in Leningrad during the siege.

MUHAMMAD IQBAL (1873-1938) Urdu and Persian poet, born at Siaklot in the Punjab. In 1899 he graduated from Government College at Lahore; he studied philosophy (at Cambridge and in Germany) and qualified in law. He lived in Lahore concentrating on writing after his resignation from the educational service. He was sympathetic to Marxist ideas, but believed that Islam held the solution to the problems of humanity.

ISHIKAWA TAKUBOKU (1885–1912) Japanese poet, son of a poor Buddhist priest. His life was one of poverty and ill-health. His collection, *Whistles,* published a year before his death at twenty-seven from tuberculosis, gave real authority to Japanese socialist poetry.

JAROSLAW IWASZKIEWICZ (b. 1894) Polish novelist and poet, born in Kievan Ukraine. He studied law at Kiev university; moved to Warsaw, and was co-founder of the *Skamander* literary group, editor of *Creative Work*, and president of the Polish Association of Writers. He wrote the libretto for Szymanowski's opera *King Roger of Sicily*.

FAYAD JAMIS (b. 1930) Cuban poet. He worked in Paris as a house-painter and metal worker; but returned to Cuba at the time of the revolution. He won the *Casa de las Américas* prize 1962; he now teaches in art school and edits the magazine of the Cuban Writers' Union.

ERNEST JONES (1819–69) English Chartist leader, novelist and poet. In 1848 he was sentenced to two years solitary confinement for sedition. 'The Song of the Low' had wide currency among English workers and was sung to the tune of 'My Old Friend John'. Writing to Marx, 29 January 1869, Engels said Jones was 'the only *educated* Englishman among the politicians who was, at bottom, entirely on our side'.

LEROI JONES (b. 1934) American poet and dramatist, born in Newark, New Jersey. His play *Dutchman*, about the explosive black-white confrontation, was filmed by Anthony Harvey.

ATTILA JÓZSEF (1905–37) Hungarian poet, born in Budapest. His father, a worker in a soap-factory, left his wife and three children destitute; József worked minding geese and pigs while his mother worked as a washer-woman in Budapest. He supported himself through odd jobs and got through provincial school; he studied at the Sorbonne for a year; then returned to Budapest and joined the underground workers' movement. The Communist Party opposed his proposal for a popular front with the social democrats against the Nazis. At the age of thirty-two threw himself under the wheels of a goods train.

FERENC JUHÁSZ (b. 1928) Hungarian poet, born in a small Transdanubian village not far from Budapest. He was closely involved with Laszló Nagy and István Simon. Many of his poems refer to his wife, Erzsébet Szevérenyi, with whom he fell in love at the People's College named after Attila József. Auden has called his poem 'The Boy Changed into a Stag Cries Out at the Gate of Secrets' (included in *The Penguin Book of Modern Verse Translation*) 'one of the greatest poems written in my time'.

JURE KAŠTELAN (b. 1919) Croatian poet. Many of his poems deal with the civil war and the German occupation.

EDVARD KOCBEK (b. 1904) Slovene poet. During the war he was a member of the executive committee of the liberation front; after the war Vice-President of the Presidium of the People's Republic of Slovenia. He is now retired. Some of his best poetry is in *Earth* (1934) and *Horror* (1963).

KAJETAN KOVIČ (b. 1931) Slovene poet. He is an editor in a publishing house. Collections of poetry include *The Roots of the Wind* (1961).

PÉTER KUCZKA (b. 1923) Hungarian poet, born in Székes-fehérvár. In 1953 he was one of the first among communist poets to speak against party bureaucracy and the rigid application of dogma; 'I'd Rather Go Naked' was published in *Irodalmi Ujság* of Budapest, 8 September 1956.

KUO MO-JO (b. 1893) Chinese poet, born in Szechwan and educated in Japan. He founded the Creation Society in opposition to the aesthetically inclined Crescent Society; and translated Japanese versions of western books into Chinese. He is now a prominent cultural leader in China.

HUDDIE LEDBETTER (1889–1949) American blues singer and guitarist, born in Louisiana. He worked as a cotton picker and labourer; and was sent to prison three times, once on charge of assaulting a woman, twice on convictions of murder and assault to kill. Alan Lomax heard 'Leadbelly' sing in 1933 in the Louisiana State Prison and helped to obtain a pardon for him. He died in Bellevue Hospital, New York, of bone infection; 'Leadbelly' sings 'Bourgeois Blues' on the Folkways album *Easy Rider* (FA2034).

CHRISTOPHER LOGUE (b. 1926) English poet and translator;

has issued many of his poems as posters: 'I shall Vote Labour', 'Kiss, Kiss', &c. His recent poems are in *New Numbers* (Jonathan Cape, 1969). He writes the 'True Stories' column in *Private Eye*.

LU HSÜN (1881–1936) Chinese writer (real name: Chou Shujen) born in Shaoh-sing, Chekiang province. He studied medicine in Japan. Though not a communist himself he was sympathetic to the Chinese communist movement in the last ten years of his life. He has often been quoted approvingly by Mao Tse-tung, and his *Selected Works* have been issued in English translation by Foreign Languages Press, Peking.

HUGH MACDIARMID (b. 1892) Scottish poet (real name: Christopher Murray Grieve), born in Langholm near Scottish/English border. He initiated and largely constituted the Scottish Renaissance movement. Once active in the Scottish National Party he helped found, he is now a member of the Communist Party for whom he contested Kinross and W. Perth against Sir Alec Douglas-Home (then P.M.) in the 1964 general election. His lyrics in Scots (*Sangschaw* 1925, *Penny Wheep* 1926) are arguably among the finest written this century; *A Drunk Man Looks at the Thistle* (1926) is the most ambitious modern Scottish poem. His later poems in an erudite English will eventually comprise a huge epic of which *The Kind of Poetry I Want* (1943), *In Memoriam James Joyce* (1955), and parts of *Impavidi Progrediamur* have been published.

ANTONIO MACHADO (1875–1939) Spanish poet, born in Seville. He visited France as a young man, attended courses with Bergson, met Wilde and Rubén Darío. He worked as a teacher of French. He supported the republicans during the Civil War and died in exile in Collioure. He is considered by some the greatest poet produced by Spain this century; Neruda has called Machado 'a classic of the century'.

GIANCARLO MAJORINO (b. 1928) Italian poet, born in Milan where he lives, teaches and edits the periodical *Il corpo*.

OSIP MANDELSTAMM (1891–1938) Russian poet, born in Warsaw (when Poland was part of the Russian empire). He was a member of the Acmeist group. In 1932 he was arrested and deported to Voronezh until 1937; he returned to Moscow but was arrested again and deported to the far east of Russia. Vladimir Markov, introducing *Modern Russian Poetry* (MacGibbon and Kee, 1966) writes: 'After writing an epigram on Stalin, Mandelstamm was sent to a concentration camp where he died. The spectacle of a major poet in rags, half-mad, beaten by his fellow prisoners for stealing bread from them (Mandelstamm suffered from persecution mania and did not eat his own rations for fear of being poisoned) is grisly indeed.'

MAO TSE-TUNG (b. 1893) Chairman of the Central Committee of the Chinese Communist Party.

SAMUEL MARSHAK (1887–1964) Russian poet and translator. Of his Burns translations MacDiarmid said Marshak 'achieved the apparently impossible, capturing not only the sense but the very tone and movement of Burns's works' (*Daily Worker*, 3 July 1964).

VLADIMIR MAYAKOVSKY (1893–1930) Russian poet, born in Bagdadi in Georgia. The son of a forester, Mayakovsky was involved in revolutionary activity even at school. Imprisoned three times for political views, on release from Butyrki prison (1910) he enrolled in art school; he signed the Futurist manifesto *A Slap to Public Taste* (1912). Undoubtedly the poet of the Russian revolution, he put his vast energy into propaganda and designed and wrote slogans for Rosta. His plays *The Bedbug* (1929) – available in English translation in *Three Soviet Plays*, Penguin, 1966 – and *The Bath House* (1930) satirize the bureaucratic tendencies of the Soviet regime; on 14 April 1930, Mayakovsky shot himself; his reasons for doing so have been incessantly discussed ever since and his suicide has been discussed in poems by many Russian poets, including Yevtushenko and Voznesenky.

THOMAS MCGRATH (b. 1918) American poet, born in North Dakota. He has published several collections of poetry, of which *Letter to an Imaginary Friend* (1962) is the most outstanding. His work is little known to the public outside the U.S.A. but he is much admired by American poets.

MIGJENI (1911–38) Albanian poet (real name: Milosh Gjergj Nikolla). His poems are largely about the horrifying conditions he saw in Albania in his lifetime, and so he is approved by the communist government who claim to have eliminated the conditions that so depressed Migjeni.

ADRIAN MITCHELL (b. 1932) English poet, born in London.

He worked as a journalist then as a full-time writer; he wrote the libretto for Richard Rodney Bennett's opera *The Ledge*. His advocacy of public readings of poetry has helped to create a new English audience for poets reading their own work; his poems are in *Poems* (Cape, 1964) and *Out Loud* (Cape Goliard, 1968).

WILLIAM MORRIS (1834–96) English writer, designer, typographer, and political activist. Born at Walthamstow, educated at Oxford, associated with the Pre-Raphaelites, he founded his own firm to manufacture artistically conceived furniture, wallpaper, etc. to combat the vulgarities of contemporary taste. *The Earthly Paradise* was published 1868–70. He joined Social Democratic Federation 1883, but left to found the Socialist League in 1884. His visionary prose work *News From Nowhere* (1891, first serialized in his periodical *The Commonweal*) gave the revolutionary socialist alternative to Bellamy's *Looking Backwards*. Often caricatured as a Utopian dreamer whereas in fact he was a practical and consistent socialist.

NAKANO SHIGEHARU (b. 1902) Japanese poet, critic and novelist. In 1938 the militaristic government banned his work; he was imprisoned during the war.

PABLO NERUDA (b. 1904) Chilean poet (real name: Neftalí Reyes) born in Parral. He was Consul for Chile in Rangoon, Colombo, Batavia, Singapore, Madrid, Paris, and Mexico City. *Residencia en la tierra* (1933) has sustained the large popular audience that first responded to it. As cultural attaché in Madrid he wrote *España en el corazón* (1937) in support of the republicans. He returned to Chile in 1943, joined the Chilean Communist Party 1945 and became a Senator. Because of political persecution he left Chile in 1948. In 1950 *Canto general* appeared and Neruda shared the World Peace Prize with Picasso and Paul Robeson. He returned to Chile in 1952 and won the Stalin Prize in 1953. He now lives at Isla Negra.

VIDAL DE NICOLAS (b. 1922) Spanish poet, born Vizcaya, the son of an industrial worker. He was sent out of Spain during the Civil War and worked in France and Belgium. He returned to Spain after the war and worked in naval construction yard. He was sentenced to six years imprisonment for supporting the strike of Asturian miners in 1962.

OKAMOTO JUN (b. 1901) Japanese poet. A communist, he

founded the journal *Red and Black*. His poems recommend individual resistance to established authority.

WILFRED OWEN (1893–1918) English poet, born in Shropshire. He joined the Artists' Rifles in 1915. After being wounded, he returned to action and was killed on 4 November 1918, trying to get his men across the Sambre Canal. His *Collected Poems*, edited by C. Day Lewis, were published by Chatto and Windus in 1964.

LEZ OZEROV (b. 1914) Russian poet. His poems explore the world from the viewpoint of the post-revolutionary Soviet citizen.

NICANOR PARRA (b. 1914) Chilean poet, born in Chillán. He qualified as a teacher of mathematics and physics in 1938; in 1943 he studied physics in the U.S.A. and returned to Chile as professor at University of Chile. Since 1952 he has been professor of theoretical physics in Santiago. He is the best-known Chilean poet after Neruda.

PIER PAOLO PASOLINI (b. 1922) Italian poet, novelist and film director. His films include *Accatone* and *Il vangelo secondo Matteo*; his books of poetry *Le ceneri di Gramsci* (1957), *La religione del mio tempo* (1961); his combination of religious and left-wing political themes in his work has attracted much controversy in Italy. He lives in Rome.

VASKO POPA (b. 1922) Serbian poet. He took a degree in French and Yugoslav literature at Belgrade university in 1949. He was awarded the Lenau Prize in 1967; his work is included in the Penguin Modern European Poets series.

EUGÈNE POTTIER (1816–87) French poet and communard. His words for *L'Internationale* (set to the march-tune of Pierre Deygeter) have been translated into most languages and the first stanza of the poem is sung by revolutionaries everywhere.

MIKLÓS RADNÓTI (1907–1944) Hungarian poet, born in Budapest. He translated Shelley, Cocteau, and La Fontaine. In 1944 he was sent to a concentration camp in Yugoslavia and then killed by the Nazis retreating west.

ARTHUR RIMBAUD (1854–91) French poet. He ran away from his home in Charleville three times. In 1871 he arrived in Paris and met Verlaine; he wrote precocious poems but revealed disgust with his life in *Une saison en enfer* (1873). He broke with Verlaine (who shot him in a quarrel) in 1873, gave up literature entirely when he was about 19 and lived as a gun-runner and trader in Abyssinia. His right leg amputated because of a tumour, he returned to Marseilles where he died.

YANNIS RITSOS (b. 1909) Greek poet, born in Monembasia. *Tractors* (1934) established him as a leading Greek poet; *Epitaphios*, 1936, some of which has been set to music by Mikis Theodorakis, was written after armed police shot at striking workers in Thessalonika; *Romiosyne* (the Romaic World, 'Romaic-hood') was written during the Greek Civil War. He was arrested after the military putsch of April 1967 and imprisoned.

DAVID ROKEAH (b. 1914) Hebrew poet. A selection of translations of his poems, *Eyes in the Rock*, was published by Rapp and Whiting in 1968.

HENRIETTE ROLAND HOLST (1869–1952) Dutch poet, born in Noordwijk. She married the painter Richard Roland Holst, a professor in the Amsterdam Academy of Art and a friend of William Morris. She developed her poetry under the influence of Herman Gorter (1864–1927). She remained a socialist and opposed Stalin's revision of marxism.

TADEUSZ RÓŻEWICZ (b. 1921) Polish poet, born in Warsaw. During the war he taught in a high school run by the underground. He fought with the Home Army. His first collection *Anxiety* (1945) was seminal in modern Polish poetic style; he founded the 'anti-poetic group'. He received a State Prize for his volume of poetry, *The Plains*, from which 'In a Polish village' is taken. He now lives in Gliwice (western Poland).

ROBERT ROZHDESTVENSKY (b. 1932) Russian poet; one of the young post-Stalin generation of Soviet poets, though his poetry has not become as well known as that of Yevtushenko and Voznesensky outside the U.S.S.R.

PENTTI SAARIKOSKI (b. 1937) Finnish poet and translator of *Ulysses*, *Tropic of Cancer*, and Sappho and Xenephon. He is a Marxist. His poems have been translated by Anselm Hollo (*Helsinki*, Rapp and Carroll, 1967).

NELLY SACHS (b. 1891) Jewish poet. Born in Berlin, she fled to Sweden in 1940; the poems anthologized here are from her first book *In the Habitations of Death* (1946). She was awarded the Nobel Prize in 1966. In his introduction to her *Selected Poems* (Cape, 1968) Enzensberger calls her first book 'the only poetic testimony that can hold its own beside the dumbfounding horror of the documentary reports'.

CARL SANDBURG (1878–1967) American poet; one of the three Illinois poets – Vachel Lindsay and Edgar Lee Masters were the others – who saw Chicago rather than New York as essentially representative of America. He worked as dishwasher, truck-handler, harvest-hand, leader-writer. He defined poetry as 'the synthesis of hyacinths and biscuits'; and published a six-volume biography of Lincoln. *The People, Yes* is widely accepted as one of the greatest achievements in American poetry since Whitman's *Leaves of Grass*.

ILYA SELVINSKY (1899–1968) Russian poet. He fought on the side of the Reds in the Civil War, and was the leader of the Russian Constructivist school of poetry in the 1920s.

LÉOPOLD SÉDAR SENGHOR (b. 1906) Senegalese poet, born at Joal. He studied in Paris where he met Césaire. In 1960 he was installed as first President of the Independent Republic of Senegal. Gerald Moore and Ulli Beier (in *Modern Poetry from Africa*, Penguin, 1966) observe that Senghor is 'the principal African advocate of Négritude and the first African poet to produce a substantial body of work'.

VITTORIO SERENI (b. 1913) Italian poet, born in Luino. During World War II he was a prisoner in North Africa. He is now a director of the publishers Mondadori. Franco Fortini (*Italian Writing Today*, Penguin, 1967) has mentioned that his war-time incarceration deepened his work.

AVRAHAM SHLONSKY (b. 1900) Hebrew poet, born in Russia, but brought up in Tel Aviv. After World War II he returned to Palestine and lived in a *kibbutz* doing manual work in Tel Aviv. He now works for the publishing house of the Israeli Labour Movement. He has translated *Hamlet* and *Eugene Onegin* into Hebrew.

ANTONI SLONIMSKI (b. 1895) Polish poet and dramatist. He was born in Warsaw where he studied painting; in 1935 he fled to Paris, then to London where he edited *New Poland*. He returned to Warsaw 1946. His books of poems include *Window without Bars* (1935).

BORIS SLUTSKY (b. 1919) Russian poet, born in the Ukraine. He volunteered in 1941. He is very much associated with and instrumental in 'the Thaw' in Soviet attitudes.

WILLIAM SOUTAR (1898–1943) Scottish poet. Bedridden for the last thirteen years of his life by 'a form of spondylitis', he lived in his parents' house in Perth. He wrote in both Scots and English and as his friend Hugh MacDiarmid has observed 'showed an increasing preoccupation with Marxism and Left Wing politics towards the end of his life'.

WOLE SOYINKA (b. 1935) Nigerian dramatist and poet, born in Aneokuta in the Yoruba country of Western Nigeria. He was educated at Ibadan and Leeds. In 1960 he returned to Nigeria; he was arrested by the Federal Government in 1967.

LAJOS TAMÁSI (b. 1923) Hungarian poet, born in small Transdanubian village, the son of a casual labourer. Poverty-stricken throughout childhood, he joined the Communist Party in 1945. He is concerned with freeing the writer from party control. 'Wayfaring seaman' appeared in *Irodalmi Ujság* of Budapest 5 May 1956.

DYLAN THOMAS (1914–53) Welsh poet, born in Swansea. He worked as a reporter and broadcaster and attracted a huge public for his work through his dramatic readings of his own poetry. His play *Under Milk Wood* and his *Collected Poems* are published by Dent.

T'IEN CHIEN (b. 1914) Chinese poet, born near Wuhu (Anhui) the son of a landlord. He was hailed as 'the drummer of our time' by Wen I-to. At first influenced by Mayakovsky, after 1949 he turned to folk song styles. He is now a Hopei representative to the National People's Congress.

TO HUU (b. 1920) Vietnamese poet, born in Hue (central Vietnam). He was arrested in 1939 and imprisoned until his escape in 1942; in 1945 he became Chairman of the Hue Insurrectional Committee, and was elected to the Central Committee of the Worker's Party in 1951. He has been called 'the poet of the Vietnamese revolution' (by William Zac in an article in *L'Europe* July/August 1961).

ERNST TOLLER (1893–1939) German poet and dramatist. He was wounded in World War I during which he became a socialist. He committed suicide.

TSANG K'E-CHIA (b. 1910) Chinese poet. He studied at Tsingtao University and taught Chinese in secondary schools. After the revolution he edited the periodical *Poetry* and edited Mao's poems. He is now a representative of Shantung to the National People's Congress.

TSOU TI-FAN (b. 1918) Chinese poet. He works in the Ministry of Culture.

NANOS VALAORITIS (b. 1921) Greek poet, born in Switzerland of Greek parents. He studied at London University and the Sorbonne. In 1963 he edited the avant-garde magazine *Pali* in Greece. He now lives in Athens.

CÉSAR VALLEJO (1892–1938) Peruvian poet, born in Andean village of Santiago de Chuco. He abandoned scientific studies to graduate in literature at Trujillo University. *Heraldos negros* appeared in 1918, *Trilce* in 1922. He spent 1923–30 in Paris; in 1931 he joined the Spanish Communist Party. He was expelled from France for political reasons. *Poemas humanos* was published posthumously in 1939. He was in Spain during the Civil War on the loyalist side; he died in hospital in Paris before the Civil War ended.

ÉMILE VERHAEREN (1855–1916) Belgian poet. He studied law. As a socialist he was particularly concerned with the impact of urban industrial society on the countryside and the social implications of this development. *Les Villes tentaculaires* (1895) and *Les Forces tumultueuses* (1902) are his best-known collections.

YEVGENY VINOKUROV (b. 1925) Russian poet, born in Bryansk. He fought in World War II; and later studied at the Gorky Literary Institute. With Yevtushenko and Voznesensky he is popular among young people in the Soviet Union; his poems are collected in a volume called *Lyric Poetry* (Moscow, 1962).

ANDREI VOZNESENSKY (b. 1933) Russian poet, born in Moscow. He studied architecture but the popular success of his poetry persuaded him to become a full-time poet and as such he visited the U.S.A. with Yevtushenko in 1961. His poems have been widely translated and the Oxford University Press issued *Antiworlds* in 1966.

GEORG WEERTH (1822–56) German poet. He edited *Neue Rheinische Zeitung* in Cologne. He left Germany to live in

England, then in Cuba where he died. Engels called him 'the first and *most important* poet of the German proletariat' (*Der Sozialdemocrat*, Zurich, 7 June 1883).

ERICH WEINERT (1890–1953) German poet, born in Magdeburg. He was an engineer and painter before World War II; and was active as a communist in Berlin from 1921. He left Germany in the thirties, lived in France, and then fought in the Spanish Civil War. He lived in Moscow until 1946 when he took an administrative job in education in East Berlin.

WALT WHITMAN (1819–92) American poet, born on Long Island; he worked as a printer, schoolteacher, and journalist. In 1855 the first *Leaves of Grass* was published; and in 1865 *Drum-Taps*, drawing on his work as an army nurse during the Civil War. He has often been placed as the most authentic literary voice of American democracy; today he is as popular in the communist countries as in the U.S.A.

YEVGENY YEVTUSHENKO (b. 1933) Russian poet, born in Stanzia Zima (Winter Station). He spent his childhood in Siberia, was educated in Moscow; and has toured the West reading his poems with enormous success. His *Precocious Autobiography* (Penguin, 1965) describes how 'Babiy Yar', his famous poem written after a visit to Babiy Yar, outside Kiev, the site of a Nazi massacre of Jews, antagonized the authorities who saw in it accusations of anti-semitism in the U.S.S.R.; Shostakovitch set 'Babiy Yar' in his thirteenth symphony. He is included in the Penguin Modern European Poets series. He has consistently championed Russian artists, for example the sculptor Ernst Niezvestny, against the attacks of Soviet officialdom.

YI KWANG-SU (b. 1892) Korean poet and novelist. He introduced a new declamatory and colloquial style of diction to Korean verse, and has been described as the most important figure in modern Korean poetry.

YI YUK-SA (1904–44) Korean poet. He read sociology at Peking university, was arrested in Peking and tortured to death by Japanese Military Police.

DANE ZAJC (b. 1929) Slovene poet. He works as a librarian; his poems are collected in *Burned Grass* (1958) and *A Tongue from the Earth* (1961)

ZOLTÁN ZELK (b. 1906) Hungarian poet, born to the east of Debreczen, Érmihályfalva. His father was a cantor in the synagogue. Zelk became a grocer's assistant, joined the labour youth, and became a communist in 1945. He denounced his odes to Stalin and Rákosi after observing Soviet interference with Hungary; he was imprisoned and badly treated. 'Nightmare and Dawn' appeared in the *Irodalmi Ujság* of Budapest, 6 August 1956.

INDEXES

INDEX OF POEM TITLES

INDEX OF FIRST LINES

*Some other Poetry books published by Penguins are
described on the following pages.*

SOME RECENT
PENGUIN ANTHOLOGIES

*Not for sale in the U.S.A.

PENGUIN MODERN EUROPEAN POETS

ANNA AKHMATOVA

Anna Akhmatova, who died in 1966, was among this century's greatest Russian poets. Andrei Sinyavsky writes of her: 'From the barest whisper to fiery eloquence, from downcast eyes to lightning and thunderbolts – such is the range of Akhmatova's inspiration and voice.' Richard McKane's moving English translations do justice to a poet whose famous cycle, 'Requiem', was recognized as a fitting memorial to the suffering of millions of Russians under Stalin.

HANS MAGNUS ENZENSBERGER

This selection draws on Hans Magnus Enzensberger's three published volumes and also includes a number of other poems. The poet is a German – though uniquely cosmopolitan in outlook and range of sympathies – who was shaped by the Second World War and who expresses an awareness of the ideology responsible for that war and of the breakdown which followed it. His social and moral criticism owes much to Marxism, yet is free from party allegiance. As direct and accessible as graffiti on a wall, his poems are the most striking to emerge from post-war Germany.

VASKO POPA

This is the first collection of poems by Vasko Popa, the leading Yugoslavian poet, to appear in English translation. A rich poetic imagination and extreme concentration of language lend special fibre to the 'new epic' construction of Popa's poems, which are arranged in cycles. Vasko Popa was recently awarded the Austrian Lenau Prize.

HUGH MACDIARMID: SELECTED POEMS

Compiled by David Craig and John Manson

This book aims to make more readily available a comprehensive selection from the work of a poet who exacts attention on the same level as the accepted masters of modern poetry. For although MacDiarmid was working at the highest level from the early 20s to the later 30s, most of his work has been available in very limited editions, and some not published at all. In his more complex and fluent philosophical poetry, such as *By Wauchopeside* and *Water of Life*, and in such fluent poems as *The Seamless Garment* and *Lo! A Child is Born*, he is at least the equal of Auden and Yeats. For those readers unfamiliar with literary or spoken Scots, a useful glossary of the most difficult words has been added at the foot of each page.

BRITISH POETRY SINCE 1945

Edited with an introduction by Edward Lucie-Smith

British Poetry Since 1945 is the first largely comprehensive anthology of poetry written during this period in England, Scotland, Wales and Northern Ireland. The anthology is arranged to show how the various styles and manners current during the quarter of a century under review relate to one another. Critical notes on as many as 83 poets that are represented, and on their work, as well as bibliographies of each poet's main books make this anthology an ideal introduction to recent British poetry. For those readers already familiar with the field, *British Poetry Since 1945* will prove an invaluable source of reference.

CHILDREN OF ALBION

POETRY OF THE 'UNDERGROUND' IN BRITAIN

Edited by Michael Horovitz

Here at last is the 'secret' generation of British poets whose work could hitherto be discovered only through their own bush telegraph of little magazines and lively readings. These are the energies which have almost completely dispelled the arid critical climate of the 'fifties' and engineered a fresh renaissance of 'the voice of the bard' –

The anthology contains many of the best poems of

Pete Brown	Dave Cuncliffe
Roy Fisher	Lee Harwood
Spike Hawkins	Anselm Hollo
Bernard Kops	Tom McGrath
Adrian Mitchell	Edwin Morgan
Neil Oram	Tom Pickard
Tom Raworth	Chris Torrance
Alex Trocchi	Gael Turnbull

– and *fifty* others – from John Arden to Michael X –

It is edited by Michael Horovitz, with a Blakean cornucopia of 'afterwords' which trace the development of oral and jazz poetry – the Albert Hall Incarnation of 1965 – the influences of the great American and Russian spokesmen – and the diverse lyric, political, visioning and revolutionary orientations of these new poets.

PENGUIN MODERN POETS

1* Lawrence Durrell Elizabeth Jennings R. S. Thomas
2* Kingsley Amis Dom Moraes Peter Porter
3* George Barker Martin Bell Charles Causley
4* David Holbrook Christopher Middleton David Wevill
5† Gregory Corso Lawrence Ferlighetti Allen Ginsberg
6 George Macbeth Edward Lucie-Smith Jack Clemo
7* Richard Murphy Jon Silkin Nathaniel Tarn
8* Edwin Brock Geoffrey Hill Stevie Smith
9† Denise Levertov Kenneth Rexroth William Carlos
Williams
10 Adrian Henri Roger McGough Brian Patten
11 D. M. Black Peter Redgrove D. M. Thomas
12* Alan Jackson Jeff Nuttall William Wantling
13 Charles Bukowski Philip Lamantia Harold Norse
14 Alan Brownjohn Michael Hamburger Charles
Tomlinson
15 Alan Bold Edward Brathwaite Edwin Morgan
16 Jack Beeching Harry Guest Matthew Mead
17 W. S. Graham Kathleen Raine David Gascoyne
18 A. Alvarez Roy Fuller A. Thwaite

*NOT FOR SALE IN THE U.S.A.
†NOT FOR SALE IN THE U.S.A. OR CANADA